BEYOND MASS COMMUNICATION

BOOKS BY THE SAME AUTHOR

1. SATELLITE COMMUNICATION AND FAMILY PLANNING

2. UPROOTED

3. PROBLEMS OF COMMUNICATION IN DEVELOPING COUNTRIES

4. COMMUNICATION GROWTH AND PUBLIC POLICY

5. COMMUNICATION AND VALUES

BEYOND MASS COMMUNICATION

A New Strategy for Planning and Development

KRISHAN LAL SONDHI

1991

B. R. PUBLISHING CORPORATION

[Division of D. K. Publishers Distributors (P.) Ltd.]

Delhi - 110 007

Sales office:
D.K. Publishers Distributors (P) Ltd.
1, Ansari Road, Darya Ganj,
New Delhi - 110002.
Phone: 3261465, 3278368

ISBN 81-7018 - 631-5

Code No. B00553

Published by: B. R. Publishing Corporation [Division of D.K. Publishers Distributors (P) Ltd.] at Regd. Office 29/9, Nangia Park, Shakti Nagar, Delhi - 110007. Phone: 7120113

Laser Set at: Sita Composers Pvt. Ltd., H-135 Ashok Vihar, Phase-I, Delhi - 110052. Phone: 7231789

Printed at : D.K. Fine Art Press, **Delhi.**

PRINTED IN INDIA

DEDICATION

As ever dedicated to my loving
wife Veena, my constant source
of inspiration, love and joy

BEFORE SAWAN BHADON CAME
AND THE EARTH WAS PARCHED
AND LEAVES NOT SPROUTED
VEENA SAID
IF YOU ARE A WRITER,
WHY DON'T YOU WRITE?
AS SIMPLE AS THAT.
AND I DUG AND DUG AND DUG
MY MEMORY INVAIN
BUT THE INK LEFT NO MARKS
AND I WAS DESPONDENT.
WHEN SAWAN BHADON CAME
AND THE CLOUDS DRENCHED
THE WASTELAND
VEENA SAID
WHY DON'T YOU DRENCH THE
WORLD WITH WORDS?
AND I DUG AND DUG AND DUG
AND SLOWLY MEMORY RESPONDED
AND INK BEGAN TO FLOW
AND I FELT SOME HOPE.
WHEN SAWAN BHADON WERE GONE
THE GREENS SPROUTED
AND ALL WAS LUCIOUS
VEENA SAID
WHY DON'T YOU SPROUT
IN WISDOM AND LOVE AND WRITING?
AND SUDDENLY I FOUND
MY BOOK COMPLETE
BUT VEENA SAID :
THE TASK IS NOT YET DONE

ACKNOWLEDGEMENT

There is only one person to whom I am beholden for encouragement for this book: my son Rabindranath. I have named him after the great Poet as every power is in the WORD.

Ravi as we call him, like Abhimanyu, imbibed not the art of warfare but of NATYA. So no power on earth can stifle his art. He has shared this power with me in this literary enterprise.

Case studies conducted by Lady Irwin College are gratefully acknowledged with thanks to Dr. Mrs. Seth and for compilation to Ms. Jyotsna Mathur

Krishan Lal Sondhi

PREFACE

Those who go by the title of the book and think that it is limited to mass communication will be totally in error. In fact, mass communication provides only the take-off point of the book. What is far more significant are the inter- connections and inter-relations of mass communication with other concerns, sectors, areas — which are rarely, if at all, given any thought. It is this area "Beyond Mass Communication" which is the thrust of the book's argument.

Obviously the first concern is with Futorology. With the new Communication technologies emerging, we find that these have characteristics which mass communication does not have. These lead to interactivity, demassification and are not monologous like mass communication. It is argued that these technologies are much more pertinent to the Development task. So the book is relevant to Futuristic studies.

One area which is stressed again and again throughout the book is of Information Economics. The Indian Economist is questioned again and again "Why do you not take any interest in Information-Communication?" For about three decades now Indian Economists have been working on Transport Economics and a body of knowledge has emerged. Latterly Economics of Energy has gained some interest. But in this wide land of ours there is not one single scholar (atleast to this author's knowledge) who has shown any interest in Information Economics. The one solitary case was that of the late Prof. Sukhmoy Chakravarty, my very dear friend and senior colleague (who unfortunately passed away most untimely only a few days back). As a Member of the international Maitland Commission, with his characteristic thoroughness, he very quickly grasped the tremendous tragedy of the situation : the lop-sided Economics of Telecommunications for the Developing World. But Sukhmoy had far too much on his plate to pursue this new discipline in the Indian context. Therefore, the book is specially focussed on students of Economics.

The book is of obvious interest to Media men of all shades because the point is forcefully made that the days of mass media are, or in any case ought to be, over —— we must move on to *class* media: segmentation, specificity, narrow targets.

Organization and management occupy large concerns in the book and therefore, it is hoped that scholars from the disciplines of Organizational Behaviour, Psychology and Management will find something of interest to them and much to react to. With due respects to the protagomists of autonomy and an Indian personality of media, it is shown in analysis that overt, political changes are gimmicks. The outward structure of an organization is a myth and therefore, attempts at autonomy are a myth. Real change of an organization takes place only when the assumptions on which it is built are changed. What the media organizations need is not autonomy and Indianness, but *creativity* and *subjectivity*.

Development Planners are in for a shock. The present cult who want to "go back to Gandhi" are told that they will have to "go *forward* to Gandhi" whom they are more likely to encounter in an Information Society. The concept of "Information Corridor" is introduced. And decentralized manufacturing in batch production mode is suggested as a real possibility through *Microelectronics*. The case study of the Italian Prato- Bennatone experience is illustratively provided. Therefore, it is argued that the Plan frame be altered radically to give centrality to Information- Communication. It is hoped therefore, that Development planners will find something of interest in the book, and something to dilate upon.

There is a great deal of discussion on technology. Distinction is made between three very different aspects of this subject: (a) technology per se (b) technical innovation and (c) change in techno-economic paradigm. It is suggested that our Communication technologists by and large, are pathologicallly fixated to technology per se, particularly cutting-edge technology and largely oblivious of desirable changes in the techno-economic paradigm. Owing to this attitude there is no diffusion of technical innovation in the economic system and therefore, the technocrats' role becomes ineffective and even meaningless. It is high time that our Communication engineers become sensitive to the wider sociological, economic, political, cultural and institutional issues — all of which are examined in detail in the book.

In U.N. bodies like GATT, Information is now being treated not as "services", but as a "commodity." Because the West, and particularly the U.S. want to use Information for international economic *control*. This raises basic issues of Trans-border Flows, Multinationals accessing highly competitive and secret information and the role of international advertising and marketing. The status of the New World Information Order and the role of the South in defending itself from the Information onslaught of the North are analysed in detail. The superior role which India can play is suggested. Therefore, the book would be of interest to those engaged in studies of International Relations, International Law, International Economics and Foreign Trade.

In a word, the burden of the books's thesis can be summed up in three statements:

(a) We know that in any future modern economic system the central role is going to be played by Information — Communication Systems.

(b) We know that India has the wherewithal to be a world leader in this field.

(c) And yet paradoxically *we are in the most wretched state in this field*.

The book is an exhortation, an incitement, a revolutionary call to demolish all existing idols, entrenched vested interests, stultifying controlling systems and free this sector to rise to creativity and leadership.

CONTENTS

CONTENTS

INTRODUCTION

The words "Beyond Mass Communication" have been used advisedly because mass communications, advertising and marketing are the handmaidens and support mechanisms of the mass production assembly line of the First Industrial Revolution. Our thesis is that India can easily go beyond this outmoded and outdated industrial-economic system and we stress Information and Communication in this book simply because the future economic system is going to be Communication-led. It is the Information revolution which is going to lead us to the next industrial and economic revolution and not the other way around as was previously the case.

The THESIS of this book can be summarised as follows:

(1) The myriads of problems facing India can be tackled and possibily solved only if we immediately and urgently make a shift from energy-intensity to information — intensity in our Developmental model.

(2) For a vast variety of reasons India can straight away leapfrog into the Information Society. The Services Sector already contributes 53.3% to the GDP and this is an indicator of the status of economic development. India has the third largest scientific and technical manpower in the world. This manpower is running many of the advanced scientific R&D establishments in the U.S.A. Indians are exceedingly good and therefore, sought after internationally, for their "software" skills. India has already shown that it could leapfrog into the Atomic Energy and Space modes.

(3) The pathway India adopts to become an Information Society will be totally different from what has historically been adopted by the industrial West. Alvin Toffler in "Third Wave" nostalgically talks of Americans returning to rural heartlands in a future Information Society in the United States. Why do we first have to migrate from rural heartlands in a wanton and destructive exercise of industrialism and

then later try to retrace footsteps from ghettos of the megalopolis to the fresh rural air through an Information journey? We can instead jump directly from industrial to information economies and retain the rural heartland. *Information Society does not have to be a post-industrial phenomenon; it* can be reached through other pathways — still retaining the large agrarian scenario. This has to be India's contribution to the discovery of the new Information pathway.

(4) These past 40 years no other sector has been more neglected than the Information-Communication sector in the Indian Planning exercise. We have sunk crores and crores of rupees on wild irrigation projects and dinasyoer public sector heavy engineering projects with infinitely long gestation periods. But the Information-Communication sector, which is what the 21st century is all about is in a shocking state of neglect, disarray and disrepair. A country which boasts of world leadership in science and technology has a shockingly poor telecommunication system, incredibly poor software on the media and disgustingly atrocious organizations to pilot the communications, electronics, broadcasting, film and computer areas to the future of the 21st century.

(5) The Information-Communications is not just another sector like Agriculture or Industries or Transport, it is the *key- sector* the *core sector* of the future. What low-cost energy and oil in particular were to the earlier heavy industry model, Communications and in particular the microchip are going to be for our next Information-based model. The Information-Communication therefore, should be treated as the key-sector of the future and given the highest priority in Planning.

(6) Mahatma Gandhi's India is not going to be reached barefoot, khadi-clad with a bag slung on the shoulders and walking backwards to the village, its Panchayats and the Khadi handlooms. Mahatma Gandhi's village on the contrary, is 180 degrees in the opposite direction. The Information Society is in fact, the true Gandhian Society of the future; just as the Communications Global Village is the true Gandhian Village of the future. Obscurantism will not get us to the Mahatma but the "Information corridor" will.

(7) Our National movement just four decades back was really India's great Renaissance, and not merely a struggle for

political freedom. Dr, Ananda Coomaraswamy has summed it up well; *"For the struggle is much more than a political conflict. It is a struggle for spiritual and mental freedom from the domination of an alien ideal.* In such a conflict, political and economic victory are but half the battle; for an India free in name, but subdued by Europe in her inmost soul would ill justify the price of freedom. It is not so much the material, as the moral and spiritual subjection of Indian civilization that in the end impoverishes humanity."

The Development model we have adopted these past four decades however, has created an India which is a third rate copy of what Europe and the West are desperate in discarding as the hangover of an ugly Industrialism. We are a frightening picture of antequated development thought, corruption, manipulation, wheeling-dealing and utter disregard for duty.

The Information revolution would be a corrective to this naked Industrialism, because it is a revolution which leads to a society marked by healthy ecology, intellectualism and creativity. It will be a spiritual corrective to our present economic debauchry.

(8) Work of Economic modelling at the national level needs to be carried out for the Information-Communication sector. We need to establish the forward and backward linkages of this sector with other vital sectors of the economy and ascertain how the contribution of this sector to the GNP could be vastly increased. This is an economic necessity because we are in a resources crunch, in a balance of payments crunch, in an oil and energy crunch, in a productivity crunch...the list is endless. In sheer desperation we have to enlist the Information based economic paradigm to bale us out.

(9) The whole question of Organisation is extremely important for atleast two reasons. One is that the organization of the institutions which at present look after the Information-Communication sector are so archaic and decadent that these cannot possibly be instruments for the kind of leapfrogging we have in mind.

Secondly, if we are able to get into the Information mode, the whole structure of industrial and ecological organization will change drastically. It will become more batch-production based and akin to a crafts culture in the setting of an extended family. This has vast implications for Indian ecological conditions, as well as for employment.

(10) We are hung up on the latest Information Technology — a case in point is our vain boast that we will soon have an indigenous Fifth generation computer. What is important from the Developmental point is not the technology, but the shift in the overall techno-economic paradigm which needs meshing of the technology with modes of industrial production, economic variables and sociology of institutional mechanisms.

Work along these lines is conspicuous by its total absence.

(11) In the various U.S. forums like the U.N., UNESCO, ITU, IBI, GATT, Information under the ruberic of the Services sector is now being treated by the industrial West as "goods" and not "services". This has vast implications for Trans-border Flows, Multinational's accessing to Information and the whole question of "Free Flow of Information" which has constantly been raised at U.N. forums to the detriment of the Developing world.

How do we cope with these vexing and highly technical and complex questions at international forums? At present the External Affairs Ministry and Foreign Trade attempt the task. But are they qualified? More theoretical work for understanding the complexities need to be done and more appropriate institutions created to handle these internationally.

(12) A huge global market in Information-Communication has come into existence of which we have practically no share. The computer software market alone is of the order of U S Dollars 1000 Billions. At present we are only supplying slave labour abroad. The whole strategy towards competitiveness needs to be developed.

(13) The Information-Communication infrastructure installed in India at present, by any reckoning, is collosal. For example, the advertising world has estimated that the viewership in the nation at any time for the *"Mahabharat"* serial was about 300 million. As against this the biggest showing in the U.S.A. is the Bill Cosby show with a viewership of a mere 50 million. Not only that, the advertising world admits that

the satellite television *information corridor* has opened up rural markets for consumer products on a collosal scale. Soap consumption in rural areas, to take only one example, is going up at the rate of 60% per annum. A detergent NIRMA *has become the largest selling detergent in the world.*

The same remarks could be made about other media channels like radio, the feature film, video viewing etc. In the meantime, telecomunications, databanks, computer systems etc. are all on the way. Yet the state of Communication research is abyssmal. In fact, it would not be an exaggeration to state that there is practically no Communication Research at all. This shows that we have no idea whatsoever as to what and how these technologies are impacting on the social fabric, the economies of the country, values, behavioural change and therefore, we have no formulations for future policy based on enlightening research. The scholastic and research aspects of holistic Communication have to be institutionalised at a high intellectual level, as for example, was done in the case of Atomic Energy and Space development.

(14) At a time when there is an extraordinarily severe resources crunch, when the public sector has huge budgetary deficits, when we are privatising areas like electricity generation and steel, why should Telecommunication, electronics, computer and allied systems be the victims of resource paucity, ineptitude, inefficiency and total incapability of the public and goverment sectors, especially when we are looking to Information-Communication to catapult us into the Information Society. *There is a strong case for all future growth in this sector to be in the private sector.*

(15) Lastly, the question of appropriate institutions to handle this area.

The artificial Ministrial separation of Information, Broadcasting, Telecommunications, Electronics etc. will not hold for future systems in this area. A meshing of technologies is going on and also much greater concern with usage. There is also the question of policy formulation in this sector.

This requires something of an apex Informatics Ministry which would oversea the others as departments under the apex Ministry.

Secondly, there should not be the overwhelming preponderance of career administrators in this area. The manning should be totally by technical and creative people.

A completely new institutional framework is called for — to which we have given no thought at all.

Another important "institutional" point is: why should Policy analysis and policy formulation be the prerogatives of Government and the public sector? With a very healthy and expanding private sector coming up and with such a large number of individual scientists, technologists, thinkers, researchers in the country private Think Tanks dealing with Communication-Information policy analysis must come up in a big, *and these must impact on public policy.* In matters like Communication-Information which are expected to catapult the country to a much larger orbit, the government role ought to be minimal. It is national talent and national thought which ought to determine such crucial issues. In any case India is not what it was 40 years back when Government of necessity had to be the prime mover in everything. We now have tremendous scientific and intellectual talent, very virile entrepreneurs and industrialists, the worlds leading talent in Telecommunications, Software, Creative Arts, Broadcasting. Why should we allow the antequated, archaic, anachronistic rules and regulations and negative attitude of bureaucrats to stifle growth in this sector— which is exactly what has happened. The intellectuals and researchers and academics and entrepreneurs and the private sector must on their own create private think tanks and task forces for *POLICY ANALYSIS* and sharply impinge on Public Policy. *If we leave things to Government and the Public sector we will miss this key opportunity to introduce innovation in Communication-Information.*

The first communication revolution represented the triumph of scientific invention and mechanical engineering; it gave us, typically the telephone, the radio, and the giant printing press.

The second communications revolution is a triumph of scientific *theory* and *human* engineering; and it has given us, typically, cybernetics control systems (whether electro-mechanical or neuro-biological) and mass motivation research.

To put the distinction another way, the first revolution in communications was predominantly a practical and *mechanical* matter; like the first industrial revolution. If in industry there was *mass-production* of goods, in the *mass-media* there was mass production of messages, images and ideas. Both were geared to mass production, mass dissemination, mass mobilization, mass rhetoric and the assembly line concept was common to both.

By contrast, the second communications revolution is as *theoretical* and *"philosophical"* as it is practical. It is revolutionary not only technically but intellectually as well— a thoroughly articulate, self- conscious and sophisticated affair.

Unfortunately, in India, although we have transplanted the "practical" aspects of this second communications revolution by implanting computers, satellites and electronic gadgetary, we have missed out on the theoretical and philosophical aspects. We have so far not treated this second revolution as a foremost intellectual discipline demanding rigorous academic approach, ardous experimentation, imaginative creativity and philosophical enquiry — all these in a manner which address the unique sociological, cultural and politico-economic demands of our present day critical needs in our country.

Time however, waits for nobody and the West certainly are not going to wait for us, limping as we are on the second lap of the communication journey, fumbling with electronics and satellites and computers, but totally innocent indeed, of the vast ramifications of these devices for our social cohesion, cultural renewal and most important of all for the pertinent discipline of Information Economics, than which there could not be a more important area of concern for us. The West are not to be blamed if they march ahead to the Third Communication Revolution around the corner, leaving us fumbling with SKD - CKD imports, heavy external reliance on components, squabbles over electronic switching and our total insensibility to regard Communication not on the debit side as expenditure, but on the credit side as *RESOURCE* (especially in an era when the planned Development effort is being impeded by a resource crunch).

In the West the imminent Third Communication Revolution presents two faces — almost diametrically opposite to each other. One face is that of even more ferocious technologies lasers, optics, fifth generation computers, artificial intelligence, robotics — a frightening array of devices which might very well make Norbert Weiner's prophetic warning come true: cybernetic

devices may come to *control* men and overpower them; instead
of man controlling the machine.

The other face of the Third Communication Revolution is exactly the opposite; it is the somewhat feeble, but nevertheless
very distinct voice of the Western Religious Existentialists who
demand that the next Revolution be a return to the Human
Dialogue, to interpersonal communication, to restoration of
humanity in discourse, to humaneness in conduct. The Existentialists sound this warning note, because these humane elements
of Communication are fast vanishing, if these have already not
totally vanished from the Western hemisphere leaving in their
trail the spectre of a technotronic monster overseaing a desert
of isolated, alienated, painstricken individuals.

The deepest wellspring from which the dialogical philosophy
draws inspiration is the body of writings of a number of contemporary thinkers often classified together as "religious
existentialists": specifically Martin Buber, Gabriel Marcel, Paul
Tillich, Karl Jaspers etc. Although there are indeed, important
difference separating these four philosophers, there are also certain common denominators and chords of agreement — of
which perhaps the most significant is the theory of communication broadly shared among them all. It is not too much to say
that this conceptual framework is the essential premise of each
of their respective philosophies, for it maintains no less that
existence (in its authentic form) is communication — that life
is dialogue. One distinctive service of the religious existentialists
is to have repudiated the technological model; of communication as an inexhaustible monologue addressed to everyone and
no one in the form of "mass communication." *Hence the inspiration of this book "Beyond Mass Communication"*. These writers
have made us aware that human communication, wherever it
is genuine, is always a person-to-person call — never a
transcribed message from an anonymous answering service to
whomever it may concern. The symbolic paradigm of this interpersonal encounter is the relation of I and THOU.

The contemporary religious existentialists speak directly to
our time, and even (where necessary) against our time (as for
example, in their intuitive apprehension of the technotronic
Communication monster that may well be taking shape in the
hazardous advanced and futuristic technologies.) They bespeak

the dawning awareness of an age of alienation and anxiety — awareness cutting across the planes of social science and social action — that the end of human communication is not to command but to commune; and that knowledge of the highest order (whether of the world, of oneself, or of the other) is to be sought and found not through detachment but through connection not by objectivity but by intersubjectivity, not in a state of estranged aloofness but in something resembling an act of love.

The theory of communication upon which these thinkers proceed then, is also a theory of knowledge. It has to do with the manner in which we gain understanding of the world — in particular, the world of other selves. But it has equally to do with the manner in which we gain self- understanding. It is the insight suggested by Dilthey, when he spoke of the "re-discovery of the I in the Thou." More directly, it is the message coveyed by Marcel through his distinctive conception of *intersubjectivity* "My experience, "according to Marcel, "is in a real communication with other experiences. I cannot be cut off from the one without being cut off from the other. The fact is that we can understand ourselves by starting from the other, or from others, and only by starting from them."

Similarly genuine communication, for Jaspers, is not guaranteed by the mere presence of speech in man. Still less does it consist in the unilateral monologue of persuasive rhetoric by which one of us gains power over the other. "The basic philosophical attitude of which I am speaking, "wrote Jaspers in his book *The Way To Wisdom*," is rooted in distress at the absence of communication, in the drive to authentic communication, and in the possibility of the loving contest which profoundly unites self and self. *Communication then is the aim of philosophy, and in communication all its other aims are ultimately rooted: awareness of being, illumination through love, attainment of peace.*"

It is against this broad background that I have taken up the discussion in this book. While some Indians feel that they are technically capable to design and manufacture Fifth generation computers and to work on artificial intelligence I have been more concerned with the Religious Existentialist's call for the Third Communication Revolution as a revival of the human face of communication perceived and experienced in the realisation of the I in the Thou. In our case, as I show in this book, there is no need for revival — because we are inheritors of an ancient civilization which bases its richness on the human face of communication and the *UPANASHIDIC* "Tatvam Asi" (Thou art I). But I am at pains to show that in every area of our national life, the development process, infact, has meant the deliberate disfigurement and distortion of this humane concept of communication. This book is a call to arrest this suicidal tendency and to retain and strengthen the healthy, radiant face of human communication.

I do this by putting forth the thesis forcefully and somewhat obstrusively that it is not enough merely to transplant the engineering and technology of the Second Communication mode — what are even more vital are its socio-economic and even political implications and we have to give this New Information Order *centrality* in our Planning and Development if we are to leapfrog death and decay. We have to go beyond the sentimentality, exotic overtones and archaic degeneracy of Mass Communication to a new order of Communications which is at the heart of the new economic and development order. In the process of doing this, I challenge with impugnity many existing pet notions of economics, development, mass media and planning. I make no apologies for this impugnity, on the contrary I widely disemmenate remonstrance, dismay, impatience and even anger with both Communication technicians and economic development planners who fail to see the writing on the wall, who continue to treat Communications as an exotic and luxury, at best an infrastructure to be encouraged, but fail in the vision that Communication now can provide the centrality to bring us out of the morass we have got into and like the Phoneix help us fly as a new bird from the dying ashes of our present Developmental nemesis.

1

CRISIS IN COMMUNICATION

In the title of my book I have used the words "Beyond Mass Communications" advisedly because my thesis is that India is one of the few developing countries in the world which can immediately leapfrog to the Second Industrial mode — the Information Society by making the resource of Communications *central to a completely new strategy of planning and development.*

It will be readily seen that the application areas I deal with in this book have little to do with Mass Communication and that is why I call them "Beyond Mass Communication."

For example, in Chapter 4 basic questions are raised regarding Information Economic Theory. In Chapter 6, it is suggested that the Plan model instead of being based on the centrality of Energy and therefore, Oil ought to shift to Microelectronics and therefore the Microchip. Chapter 5 challenges existing theories of stages of economic growth and suggests immediate setting up of a Microelectronics and Digital Telecommunication National "corridor" around which a decentralised polity and economy can be built in India. Even Chapter 8 which is about Mass Media puts forth the idea that these media have now to be used not for Mass Communication, but for *Class* Communication, that is for segmented, much smaller audiences for highly specific messages. Chapter 5 also contains the idea of using microelectronics for small-scale manufacturing and thereby attempts to equate a Gandhian economy with the Second Industrial mode in which Communication is central.

In Chapter 7 it is shown that as we move to an Information Society the nature of Organisation of the workplace has to change in a fundamental way and the end setup is not very different from the extended Indian family and workshop conditions of the village craftsman as they exist today. In Chapter 10, I show that merely diffusing innovations on Mass Media as we have been doing with practically negligible results is not at all fruitful. We now need to mesh computers, telecommunications and user networks for very specific objectives. A lot of R&D is required for this. This idea is carried forward in Chapter 11 where it is shown that present Mass Communication Research in India is next to useless. A totally new route to Research is required. In Chapter 12 we deal with international bodies like GATT, which have now come to regard Communication as "goods" and not "services". The Developed world, especially U.S.A. want to control manufacturing processes in the Developing world as well as raw material flow through Information control.

Finally in Chapter 13 I espouse the cause of an institutional set up at the National level which would provide policy leadership for these absolutely new directions to Communication Technologies, which are a far cry from Mass Communication; in fact these are much nearer Class Communication, the emphasis being on microelectronics, digital telecommunications, networking, interactive systems, regularity of feedback management and specificity of message as well as targets — both highly segmented. We have urgently to go "Beyond Mass Communication."

What then are the alternatives we are talking of. A good definition is: "Communication Technology is the hardware equipment, organizational structures and social values by which individuals collect, process and exchange information with other individuals." *All these need to change drastically in the new mode we find ourselves in the 1990s after 40 years of Development effort.*

Mass Communications is the symbol of the First Industrial mode — the mode of mechanical engineering, the assembly line, mass production, massive output based on economies of scale. What mass production is to production of goods, mass communications is to production of symbols, ideas, messages and myths on a gigantic scale of mass consumption.

All this changes dramatically in the Second Industrial mode or if you wish the Information mode. And what brings it about is a device so small in size as to be almost invisible: the microchip. The important technical advances in microelectronics that occurred in the 1970s and the 1980s have spurred the information revolution. Microelectronics is a sub-industry of electronics centred on semi-conductor chips and their applications such as in telecommunications and computers. A semi-conductor is a solid state device which controls the flow of electricity so as to boost, or amplify, an electrical signal. Semiconductors act like valves, and computers are essentially composed of millions of such on-off switches. This miracle has been achieved by further and further miniaturization and Very Large Scale Integration (VSLI).

Basically therefore, what Energy is to the First Industrial mode, Communications is to the Second Industrial mode.

The changes in every way-lifestyle, working conditions, emotional and spiritual attitudes — however, are extraordinarily dramatic as we shift from the Industrial society to what might be called the Information Society. There is a paradigm shift from mass production to batch production, from emphasis on hardware to emphasis on software, from massive production centres to small-scale industry, from centralized control to decentralized processing, from economies of scale to economies of scope, from uniform manufacturing to flexible specialization.

Against this general background let us have a look at the Indian economic development scene. The Mahalnobis two-sector model (extract given in an annexure at the end of this Chapter) with which started our planned development effort in 1950s represents the First Industrial Revolution and we have successfully, although partially, brought about this revolution in India. This was achieved by the Mahalnobis model by government taking the initiative in a Kenysian mode and investing heavily into public sector heavy industry and creation of massive infrastructure and scientific and technical manpower. Mass communication has also developed alongside and occupies massive dimensions in blaring signals of uniformity and centralized control to the homogenised industrial society we have sought to create.

As we have moved into the 1990s a strange thing has happened: not a day passes when we do not read in the press a treatise blaming the present state of India to this very Nehruvian-Mahalnobis model. And equally shrill is the cry that we need to immediately "Go back to Gandhi" (Mahatma Gandhi that is). Blame is being put on the fact that this Nehruvian-Mahalnobis model has resulted in massive investments into capital intensive and energy intensive sectors at the cost of employment generation and equal distribution of the returns of development. Also the model is being blamed for devastating degradation of the ecology, a false search for self-sufficiency, import of high technology instead of "appropriate technology" a staggering crisis in the Energy sector, rural migration, urban depletion, social consequences of development representing a utilitarian calculus of cruelty to the vast unfed, half-naked majority, fiscal bankruptcy and a burgeoning public sector which is a dianasyoer and a drain on the economy.

The air is now filled with slogans of "Back to Gandhi", decentralization, resurrection of Panchayati Raj, human resources development. And also there is a nostalgic resurrection of the Wardha experiment, of the enunciations of J.C. Kumarappa — Gandhiji's ace economic interpretter and a looking back to a romantic rural retreat, which we have somehow lost — not very different from a paradise in the woods of Thoreau or Tolstoy. In a word, an insistence on a shift from the Nehruvian-Mahalnobis model *back* to a neo-Gandhian model.

And this is precisely where these protestors are in error. In life we can never go back; we can only go *forward*. And when we see it in this light we have no difficulty in seeing that all the things mentioned above, which we now so badly need to correct a skewed socio-economic situation- decentralization, small-scale industry, conservation of rural habitats, conservation of energy, ecological preservation, labour intensive production — all these automatically emerge from a Communication-centred model, from an Information Society paradigm. The Second Industrial mode with Communication at its core, therefore, is no different at all from the Gandhian society we now nostolgically yearn for. But the big difference is that we integrate Gandhi not in a *pre- industrial mode*. We don't go back to the village, we go forward to the "Global Village" of the Information Age.

Basically therefore, the shift we need is from an Energy- intensive model to an Information-intensive model.

And this is where we have to go "Beyond Mass Communication" also. We have had enough of blaring on radio and TV on mass propaganda and so-called Developmental Communication. We have had enough of film-making and advertising and sloganeering. We need to get into a new set of

Communication technologies which are characterised by

    (a)   demassification

    (b)   interactivity and

    (c)   asynchronicity

At the heart of these new Communication technologies is microelectronics and digital telecommunications.

Perhaps the matter will be made clearer if we put it in a different way. Central to the First Industrial Revolution was a *"corridor"* of TRANSPORT — a massive railway and highway system. Without this the First Industrial Revolution would have been impossible because implicit in its structure was the long-haul of materials to create massive, centralised production systems. Analogous to this, in the Second Industrial mode is the creation of *a Communication "corridor"* alongside which would spring up natural habitats, decentralised polity, batch production, small-scale industry. The post-Industrial Gandhian economy is just not possible without a highly comprehensive and massive national Communication "corridor" central to which are microelectronics and digital telecommunications. In other words, what Energy and particulary Oil was to the First mode, Communication and particularly the microchip is to the Second.

But our planners, economists and even engineers do not realise the practical urgency of installing such a network post haste. To most of them Communication still is an exotic and a luxury which a Developing country does not have resources for. Nothing could be farther from the truth. Communication in fact, from the 1990s onwards is to be regarded as the most central economic resource around which all other development is to take place. It is a "resource" not an "expenditure" item.

The Economist is still caught up in the web of antiquated thinking: stages of economic growth and cannot see Communication as central to a country in which the economy is still essentially rural and agricultural.

The engineer is more worried about self-sufficiency and designing parts indigenously which have been designed elsewhere several decades back. They do not realise that the task is akin to building a roadway system. In the era gone by we did not have to rediscover Civil Engineering or rediscover bitumen or reinvent the roadroller. We had to rapidly get on with the task of building a massive road and railway system. Similarly we can now take existing designs, existing equipment but must rapidly build an exceedingly vast and efficient national Communication "corridor" which would help us leapfrog to an entirely new mode of existence, lifestyle, attitude, ecology and even spiritual orientation. In fact the real challenge is not in setting up the Communication "corridor", it is learning how to use it for Development, for which a lot of R&D and systems engineering is required.

To recapitulate the thesis of this book therefore: the critical problem in the Third World is that the vast populace in the rural areas is totally unproductive. India is a good case in point. The socially, upwardly mobile number 200 million persons who are highly professional, productive, internationally mobile like any in the industrial West. But the approximately 600 million shortly to become 800 million in the rural areas are very unproductive. This is chiefly because the so-called "village," "cottage" or "small- scale" industries are not central to the Planning model, but really extraneous to it.

Now, with the emergence of Information Technology, the position can dramatically change. Information Technology promises the prospects of a sea-change in both industrial production as well as industrial organization. It makes possible a paradigm shift from "mass production" to "flexible specialization" and, therefore, from factory organization to production in decentralized batch production mode in "cottage industry" setting. This has the promise of vastly upgrading rural life and exponential increase in employment generation.

Microelectronics through its impact of storage, retrieval and access of information has the characteristics of the "key factor" which is generally associated with a technical or organizational breakthrough.

The new techno-economic paradigm will have an important bearing on the concepts of industrialization, import substitution as well as export promotion for a developing economy.

The cheaper information handling potential through *microelectronics and digital telecommunications* indicates a trend towards information intensity rather than energy and material intensity in production. It would introduce flexibility into manufacturing systems, decentralize organizational networks and will represent a quantum jump in potential productivity for small and medium batch production by making plant scale relatively independent of the market size.

It is therefore necessary for India, which is uniquely placed in terms of skills and resources, to plan its future strategy keeping in mind the multi-farious impacts of this new technology that impinges not only on the industrial sector but also on the socio-institutional mechanisms and other behavioral areas.

It is imperative that we must take cognizance of this technology at this juncture and look for a comprehensive plan for the economy *which would model information in the development process.* In outlining the role of the government, the public sector, and the private sector, the model would provide alternatives for an overall growth with reduction in the skewness of the distribution of the fruits of growth.

In the above section I have dealt with the techno- economic aspects of the Communication crisis as I see it developing in India. I now deal with the socio-cultural aspects of this crisis in which I particularly emphasise the new threats to the individual psyche in an increasingly estranged cultural milieau.

In my earlier book ("Communication and Values") the insidious impact of the emerging communication systems in India on our cultural values and social mores has been elaborated. First it was stated that in stark contrast to the emerging technotronic electronic monster, we have had in India intact for centuries, a uniquely humane and holistic traditional communication system. Supreme in this of course, is the oral tradition, which in itself is a vast area for exploration. Mnemonic recitations are repeated as they have been literally for thousands of years. The role of memory in education is incredible and thereby makes our so-called illiterate, extremely wise in conduct and sagacious in judgement.

The Human Dialogue is very much intact, an area of human intercourse, to which the Existential and Religious philosphers of the West: Jaspers, Tillich, Buber and others have drawn our attention in dismay to the aridness that has overtaken this area of humaneness in the industrial West. All in all, what the oral tradition does is to give us the capacity to "hear" ("Shruti — as opposed to Smriti, i.e. written tradition) and it is out of "hearing" that are born all the higher traditions of "Shoonya" (silence), mystic apprehension, intuition and transcendental wisdom all helping to approach what has been perennially the aim of Indian Philosophy and Religion: Self-realization.

Secondly attention had been drawn to the Kinetic arts chief among them: Indian classical dance. It is no coincidence that Lord Shiva mighty and majestic in his primordial stance is atonce Mahayogi (Lord of Yoga) as well as Nataraj (The King of Dance) — thereby suggesting a metaphysical connection between Kinetic stance and the internal meditative processes — an idea not alien to Indian civilization in which posture, stance, style, "mudras", (gestures) movement and its control, play the primary role in Yogic ascendence. All this is absolutely intact — a rare civilisational achievement of India — when compared to the enbalamed mummies of other contemporary civilizations.

Thridly, Indian sound culture — in particular classical Indian music and Bhakti Sangeet (devotional music). This is so mighty and vast an area of exploration that it would fill volumes and take many lifetimes to explore. Suffice to state that Indian music is the surviving repository of primordial consciousness having no beginning and no end and no different in its etiology from say Astrology which Jung calls "archetypal psychology". Indian Ragas are more akin to "archetypal sound" bringing presentiments of other celestial worlds, through a cosmology and planetary system of their own which no Bach or Beethoven or Mozart could compose — but which was structured from the archetypal properties of universal consciousness. These give it powers at once mystical, magical and medical.

The question then is: if all this is true, as indeed it is, then why should we allow some over-zealous engineers, unthinking politicians, and manipulative administrators to put together at the cost of great energy and expense a wired-up electronic-satellite-computer frankenstein with red shot eyes and fierce jaws and gnashing carnivorous teeth to gobble up a rare spiritual legacy of mankind, which has weathered and stood up to so many storms before, and thus amply demonstrated its innate strength and stamina. My question is particularly pertinent, when the West in particular and the whole world in general, right now need the "healing" properties of these old communication modes. Should we not bring in technology and science to reinterpret, refresh, and reinstate these ancient arts, rather than see the last of them. For this purpose, I suggested a challenging role for *planning, policy and organisation.*

It is regretable that since the above mentioned book was published almost three years ago, there is no evidence in any sector of our life - public, private, cooperative, voluntary or any other of taking cudgels with this growing Communication technotronic menace, which has now grown into a gaint and poses a threat to those very values and art forms articulated in the book. In fact, exactly the opposite has happened. Policies in Communication sectors are being pursued which have no clear objective, unless of course this be "harakiri", that is deliberate self-destruction, and annihilation of all those attributes which have made India for centuries what it is: the spiritual master of the world, drawing to its fold all who seek mystery, silence and salvation. Our present communication policies however, make India not the master, but easily the biggest disaster in the world.

The second point I had suggested was that Planning has totally collapsed. The late Dr. D.R. Gadgil talked of *Planning without Policy*: When a sense of direction is totally missing, Planning has merely meant "more of the same, and still more of the same." So with a perverse vengence we are wiring up the country, positioning unimaginably larger satellites, insisting on a personal computer on every conceivable desk and table, having more and more transmitters, broadcasting more and more, louder and louder. When suddenly we have woken up to the realization that without knowing it we have perpetuated one of the biggest disasters: we have transformed communication into noise.

In fact, in communication terms, if there is one word which describes the Indian scene today, it is NOISE. Our streets, our roads, our thousands of feature films, tens of thousands of "filmi songs", thousands and thousands of video parlours, hundreds of TV transmitters, tens of thousands of TV receivers, hundreds of thousands of radios are all creating only one commodity-NOISE. And just as "mass communication" is essentially of the same genre as "mass production"— the only difference being that instead of goods on the assembly line, we mass produce images in the studios — similarly what is NOISE in our sensory function, is CHAOS in our body politic. Deviant behaviour, we know from psychology, is essentially deviant communicative behaviour. Noise therefore, logically leads to chaos.

And this brings me to the subject of this book in which I go beyond the limits, I set in "Communication and Values". In the state of mind in which I was then I could only perceive a causal relationship between our communication systems on the one hand and our social and cultural mores on the other. In other words, the influences were in concentric circles and the circles were still very spacious and their diameters very large so much so that the problem was still peripheral. It is my purpose in this book to demonstrate that since then the problem has become central. The disease has moved from the periphery of social mores to the epicentre of personal psychology. The subject of concern therefore, is the individual and his personal psychology and how the communication process impinges on it.

In the alienation of our personal psychologies, we have begun to move in those directions which constitute the most alarming aspects of Western civilization today. Repressed aggression, compulsive masculinity, shattering insecurity, lack of support from family or society, mental imbalance, fright panic — all leading to the well known paths of sexual perversion, alcoholism, drugs, suicide, violence, terror, murder. All this in large sum can be attributed to this large accumulation of NOISE - which no longer enables soulful communication at any level now.

My basic thesis however, revolves around the aetiology of this noise - not merely its technology, because technology by itself depends upon what use one makes of it. To define my thesis succinctly, four odd decades of *so-called "Development"* *have transformed us from a very" "caring" society to one which is totally "non-caring"*. What our expanded communication system therefore, is doing is to broadcast, enlarge and infinitely expand this property of "non-caring" as an essential behavioural mode in our whole national life at all levels. What is meant by "caring"is described in greater detail in the next chapter, here only a passing reference to its historicity is made.

The Brahmin has always "cared" for learning. He would starve and suffer endless ignominy, but learning he refused to give up. Hence our tradition of learning to this day in India. The Kashatriya always carried his life in the palm of his hand. He "cared" for the integrity of his kingdom so much so that Kshatriyas and Rajputs have laid down their lives without thought of anything else but "honour" as they conceived or perceived it. Hence the continuity of Indian civilization to this day. The Vaishya, being in bounty, has always "cared" for the deprived and given profusely in charity - built reservoirs of water, sheds for animals, godowns for food, the village water tanks, temples, charitable trusts, dispensaries. Hence compassion in our hearts to this day. The Sudra has always "cared" for his craft and stood in awe with folded hands in front of Vishwakarma - the presiding deity of the Crafts. And though eking a meagre living, he has not let his craft suffer, but has carried its subtlety and cunning over centuries. Hence, the nimbleness of fingers and their magical materials to this day.

This "parampara" (tradition) of caring was carried forward under modern and altogether changed circumstances in the Indian Renaissance heralded by the National movement for independence. The seeds of the struggle were nurtured, as has been India's tradition for thousands of years, in "Ashramas" all over India. Ashramas always have been forest-hermitages in which the various scholastic and spiritual disciplines of India have been nurtured and nourished from times immemorial. The word "Ashrama"brings to mind the concept of the Tantrik or the Buddhist Mandala — the geometric circle or pattern which *confines*. This confinement has many purposes: first among these being its property to promote a withdrawal from multiplicity of action to UNITY OF PURPOSE; in a word, it arrests dissipation of valuable psychic forces and gathers it to one point of concentration, one supreme purpose — which is the purpose of the particular Ashrama. Secondly, it brings within the Ashrama's psychic boundaries kindred minds — sharing similar ideals and thereby reinforcing the strength of these ideals, with which we have faced the turbulence of the destructive forces of imperialism, colonialism, barbaric and violent tribes, charltans and adventurers, loafers and hangers on, debauches and upstarts — who exist at all times, but particularly abound at a time when a nation has been in slavery for a long time and is suffering from its after effects, like a patient emaciated after high fever.

At this point let us not forget that even now, India is not free and independent but very much still a slave — in fact a greater slave than she was when the British were here. Let us not forget what the great mystic art historian Ananda Coomaraswamy wrote more than half a century ago: "For this struggle is much more than a political conflict. It is a struggle for spiritual and mental freedom from the domination of an alien ideal. In such a conflict, political and economic victory are but half the battle; for an India free in name, but subdued by Europe in her inmost soul, would ill justify the price of freedom. It is not so much the material as the moral and spiritual subjection of Indian civilization that in the end impoverishes humanity."

As will be apparent to even the most naive observer of the Indian scene, we have not won even "half of battle" because, thanks to the course Development has taken these four decades, our political economy is in shambles with all the signs of this great civilization regressing to some savage, tribal state of anarchy and chaos. As for the "moral and spiritual subjugation" to which Dr. Coomarswamy draws our attention well, there the fight for freedom has not even begun. The Indian mind truly exists today subjugated by the alien and most worthless ideals of industrial Europe — goals and aims, in fact, which the West is trying its best to rid itself of. All those vulgarities are now enshrined in our present day ideals.

But I have gone beyond my limit and left my story behind. Back to the Ashramas in the Indian Renaissance, what strikes one is the fact that every freedom fighter had an Ashrama from within which he mobilised his effort. It can truly be said that just as the cradle of Indian civilization from times immemorial has been the Ashrama, so too the fight against the mighty British was mobilised from these harmless-looking, distant, simple, austere, Ashramas located most of the time in out-of-way rural settings. The setting seemed so simple, pastoral and technologically low that the British never took these seriously, except perhaps for having the C.I.D. keep a distant eye on them. The Bible says "The meek shall inherit the earth." And it is these meek, simple pastoral kinships which gathered the storm which threw out the British in the vortex of the cyclone i.e. powers released by the elemental forces of Nature mobilised in these Ashramas. Literature always captures the truth not generally available and also gives intimations of future trends. The great writer Bankim Chander Chatterjee captured this with mystic premonition in his great novel "Kapal Kundala" which is an Ashrama in the woods where the Guru and his disciples do their sadhana secretly in severe austerity and succeed, through sacrifice and suffering, in overthrowing all vestiges of power, tyranny and oppression. Bankim Chander as a great literary artist was able to envision the course of things to come because it is precisely this role that the Ashramas played in the National Movement.

It is to this category that belonged the Ashramas of the outstanding geniuses of the Indian Renaissance: Gurudev Tagores' Shantiniketan and Sriniketan; Mahatma Gandhi's Sabarmati and Wardha Ashramas in India and earlier Tolstoy Ashrama in South Africa; Lokyamania Bal Gangadhar's Pune establishment with "KESARI" as the newspaper (which is published to this day), Gokhale's Servants of India Society, Swami Vivekanandas' Ramakrishna Mission headquartered at Belur, and branches the world over; Sri Aurobindos Pondicherry Ashrama, Pandit Madan Mohan Malviyaji's Benaras Hindu University; the singer-saint Pandit Vishnu Digamber Paluskar's Gandharva Mahavidyalaya at Lahore and then in other cities; the great work of the Theosophical movement particularly of Dr. Mrs. Annie Besant and Rukmini Arundale at Addyar (Madras); the tremendous work of the Arya Samaj, particularly in the Punjab to which I allude separately in a moment.

I treat the Arya Samaj separately because this wirter's whole family was in the vanguard of this movement in the Punjab with headquarters at Jullundur. The most monumental role was played by the writer's grand-father, Lala Bhagat Ram Sondhi and the author's two grand-uncles, Lala Dev Raj Sondhi and Mahatma Munshi Ram. Lala Bhagat Ramji, in keeping with his name, created an atmosphere of Bhakti or Divine Love in his Ashrama. His Ashrama consisted of his ancestral property at Adda Hoshiarpur and the Arya Samaj Mandir next door. In the home he had installed in his study a simple hand-operated Platten printing press, which he employed to bring out the Hindi paper "SAHAYAK" (Friend) for the "prachaar" or disemmination of the ideals and thoughts and action plans of the Arya Samaj. As prescribed by the Hindu Sanatan Dharma (Eternal religion) he went to the Arya Samaj Mandir Sainkaal (dawn) and Sandhyakaal (dusk) to do "havan" — oblations to fire accompanied by VEDIC recitations, according to the injunctions of the Arya Samaj. He was also Manager of Doaba School and College movement, which had been started by the Sondhi family, and these *institutions* are intact till this day. He was a great scholar and was in the process of translating the Vedas from Sanskrit to simple Hindi for wide dissemination of the Arya

Samaj principles. He owned orchard lands, and gardens in the adjoining city of Hoshiarpur. He utilized the money from these ancestral sources for the work of the Arya Samaj.

The other great Ashrama of the Arya Samaj was of Lala Dev Raj Sondhi who founded the Kanya Mahavidyalaya at Jullundur— one of the most unique institutions for women's education - both school and college level. In this way Lala Dev Raj Sondhi carried forward the great reformist movement of the Arya Samaj which had women's uplift as one of the main planks of nation building and stood for educating women, abolishing child marriage, eradicating the evil of Sati, encouraging widow remarriage. Lala Dev Raj created a wondrous atmosphere in his beautiful Ashrama so much so that the fame of the institution, even in those terrible days of British imperialism, spread far beyond the boundaries of the land and Indians settled in far off lands — Burma, Africa, Thailand, Malayasia and many others sent their daughters to study at the Vidyalaya. They also contributed money to help Lala Dev Raj Ji to meet the expenses. Even music was taught here. Dev Raj Ji specially got a music teacher from Pandit Vishnu Digamber's Gandharva Mahavidyalaya at Lahore. And how did the mighty, learned and sagacious British respond to this great work of Lala Dev Raj. They thought he was a threat to the mighty Empire, his activities were seditious, he was prompting even Indian women to revolt. The British C.I.D. was always harrassing the Vidyalaya's teachers and the Inspector of Schools used all the tyranny at his disposal.

Finally I come to the story of my grand uncle Mahatma Munshi Ram, who in later life took sanyas and became Swami Shraddhanand. He founded the famous Gurukul Kangri at Hardwar about which Dr. Ananda Coomaraswamy has the following to state: "The Gurukula, it has been said very truly, is perhaps the most fascinating educational experiment in India. It is for boys of all castes, from the highest to the lowest, and no distinctions are made. Tuition is free and teachers are unpaid. The first years are devoted entirely to Sanskrit, religion and physical culture and the twelve years following to Western literature, science and laboratory work: at the age of twenty-five the man is ready to go out into the world. The most conspicuous feature of the system is its return to the impersonal and philosphic concepts of culture which have always been characteristic of the East, and the combination of this ancient wisdom with modern and practical knowledge."

These then were the humble Ashramas, which added together, brought to incandescence, as in the spiritual energy of Tantrak Mandala concentration, creation of such inordinately superhuman forces that, as envisioned in the mystic premonitions of Bankims' *Kapala Kundla*, they blew up into smithereens the British despite all power and control and tyranny and technology.

It is something of the same type of spirit an inward-looking life of the Ashrama that could end the alienation of man and make him care for others. *In fact, caring is the crux of Ashrama life.* In Shantiniketan and Sriniketan, Sabarmati Ashram and Belur Math, Bhagat Ashram and Kanya Mahavidyalaya, one finds some characteristics in common: *the scale of infrastrucre and activities is modest, small;* but the stress is on meticulous care manifested in neatness, cleanliness, order, strict discipline, high moral attitude, tremendous sense of responsibility, punctuality, service, spirit of sacrifice and self-abnegation. Above all *the leader himself lives the life he espousses for the followers.*

The beginning of planned Development four decades ago marked a 180 degrees turnabout of this philosophy of our Renaissance. It is symbolised in the very theoretical frame of the Mahalnobis model which like Shiva's trisul has been the presiding deity of our Development effort. If in one word there is an exhortation which this model makes, then that one word is *BIGNESS*. And this indeed, has relentlessly and consistently been the burden of our Development song for four decades. It was justified by Economic Theory in the early fifties as an effort in keeping with Keneysian Theory for the Government to inject larger and larger sums of money into massive public sector projects. So, whether it was the outlay of the Plan or the size of the dam, or the capacity of the public sector plant or the capability of a public body like a Housing Board or Electricity Board — there has consistently been only one criteria to measure its efficacy: how big is it? Bigness has come to be synonymous with greatness.

The Nemesis which has overtaken this pathological fixation to BIGNESS, power mongering and blatant corruption could not be more graphically visible and *symbolic* than in the plight of the city of Delhi, the capital of India in this year of Grace 1990. New Delhi, designed by Sir Lutyen, the great British artist, and one of the most beautiful cities in the world now presents a spectacle more horrifying than the Britain of Charles Dickens.

Symbolising the trishul are the three Authorities dominating the city of Delhi - Delhi Development Authority, Municipal Corporation of Delhi, New Delhi Municipal Committee - each in turn characterised by the same disease BIGNESS. The result: *Death*. Death by cholera, gastroenteritis, hepatitis, epidemics of viral diseases - the list is endless. To this can be added tonnes and tonnes of garbagage, excreta and filth strewn in every nook and corner of Delhi city - stray buffaloes and cows and bulls roaming and obstructing roads, pigs and pigglings running with filth hither and thither. Delhi Development Authority flats developing cracks and sinking below the plinth level in testimony *to the weak foundation* laid by the contractor.

"Weak foundation" in fact, is the basic weakness of all that our Development stands for. After four decades of Development therefore, our achievements can be summed up in five words:

BIGNESS

WEAK FOUNDATION

DELAYS

DISASTER

and DEATH

The burden of my song in this book is, COMMUNICATION which ought to have been a corrective to this disease of BIGNESS, has in fact, been vitiated. It has played exactly the opposite role: the perverse role of dangling before our ears and eyes the seductive charm of BIGNESS. Deviant behaviour as we know from Psychology is basically deviant *communicative* behaviour. The clue to change, to reform, to healing, to normalising, to getting back on the correct course therefore, lies in *correcting the deviant communication*. But the Communication system we have developed over this four decade period, euphemestically called Development Communication has in fact been deviant communication and it has only added fuel to the fire, made a huge conflagration out of what might otherwise have been a small bush fire easy to quell.

The whole book is devoted to the consequences of this perverse communication. It goes beyond the confines of my earlier book "Communication and Values". In that I was satisfied in examination of a macro type of emerging communication system on the one hand and social and cultural system on the other. But now the disease has gone beyond the confines of social and cultural mores to the much more fragile area of personal psychology and personality.

As a result, the very integrity of our personal lives are now at stake and highly vulnerable. We already see developing those cracks in the personality, which were confined to the modern West, and we of the East, although materially deprived, felt spiritually safeguarded. That domain of security for the first time is under attack.

"BIGNESS" in psychological analysis obviously stands for the male syndrome: brute force, ruthless strength — all attributes of masculinity. Alongside or inevitably because of this, it represents repression of the self and suppression of the feminine. This is uniquely a modern Western and in particular, an American phenomenon. Its results are there for all to see in the self-annihilation of Western society. The hallmark of this obsession with bigness and masculine power has brought Western culture to the brink of a spiritual precipice, which no amount of material affluence can assuage. Its pathological symptoms are repressed aggression, compulsive masculinity, awesome insecurity, large scale neuroses, acute disturbances in the psyche, resulting in serious aberrations in personality.

This book therefore, deals with problems of personal psychology and personality which are directly attributable to a deviant communication system through which the "non-caring" media blast daily into our lives causing irreparable damage and destruction.

In the Preface of Communication and Values I had expressed the pious wish: "This provides immense challenges to the creative role of organisation, planning and policy." I cannot and dare not repeat this pious wish any more because it has now been proved beyond doubt that the type of people who wield power and control of our communication system are careless to such exhortations. The warning of Dr. Ananda Coomarswamy, sounded sixty or seventy years ago, is highly relevant now: "What we want is not part of the administration, but control of the Government." The control of the communication system must now change hands. It should come into the hands of its rightful owners; the people of this great land of ours. Our struggles have now to be directed towards that transference of control.

To understand the true nature and pathology of our Development in the last four decades, we can take the aid of two kinds of very different categories of "tools": one the "signal", the other the "symbol". In fact, in any organised system of communication, we have to look for two dominant characteristics: one is signalling, the other symbolling. A sign is a concrete denoter; it signals. "Do this," "Don't do that," etc. A symbol on the other hand, is abstract, connotative, contemplative, knowing, knowledgeable. A sign is external. A symbol is internal. Signs relate mostly to the world of things, symbols to the world of ideas. A sign is a physical thing which is apprehended as standing for something else. A symbol is an abstract meaning of values conferred by those who use it upon anything, tangible or intangible.

A sign thus, is only an outer estimate of things; whereas a symbol catches its true inner reality. When we come to estimate India's Developmental progress in the past four decades from the point of "signs", we are all praise: Agriculture has grown at 3-4 percent, industry 6 to 10 percent, overall growth risen now to 5 percent, scientific manpower is phenonomenal, public sector is bulging at the seams etc. — all harping on that one relentless note - in everything everywhere in our national life we are becoming BIGGER & BIGGER.

But a symbol can be very small, seemingly innocuous and yet like deep X-ray reveal the pathology of the disease deep within, unobservable even to the most trained eye. That "symbol" of our 4 decades of Development is the city of Delhi — not only the capital of today's India, but many past Indias and therefore, rightly its nerve centre and heart throb.

And what do we find in this symbol? Delhi — not only New Delhi but also Old Delhi — together formed indeed, one of the most beautiful cities in the world. New Delhi of course as mentioned earlier, enshrines the imperial vision of the great British artist, Sir Lutyens. This imperialism is not only one of colonial dominance, but much more significant than that: the aristocracy of a creative mind which could envision such grandeur and expansiveness and blend it with India's great indigenous traditions of architecture and town planning. The result — a majestic Rajpath which elevates to the Secretariat and the Presidents House beyond, the concentric circular roads, their expansive, majestic width lined by shady trees. Delhi has more than one hundred gardens and these have been nurtured by each successive empire, not the least by the British.

Old Delhi is no less beautiful. If New Delhi has masculine elegance, old Delhi has feminine charm: the Ridge replete with slopes and greenery and woody undergrowth, the quiet sedateness of the Civil Lines, the Kudsia Gardens with Kashmere Gate on one side and the small temple on the other, which once stood on the banks of the Yamuna. Roshanara Garden, replete with the romance of that name.

In four decades of "Development" we have converted this city into a veritable hell. The cause for this is not to be looked for in any one institution or anyone person responsible for it — for that is the great gift of the "symbol" — it provides you insights into large movements of thought, large changes in perception and visibility, large and cataclysmic phenomenon which typify the mores of an entire age. In that sense therefore, the "slumming" of Delhi is an insight into the pathology of our planned development. The word "slumming" is used advisedly because that in fact is the remarkable feat we have achieved in just four decades; we have converted Delhi — the most beautiful, the most enchanting the most sought after city in the world — into one big sprawling *slum*.

This degradation of the city of Delhi, like the degradation of the process of our development, did not happen in one day. It is the logical process of decay set in over four long decades. At the political level it is observable as first a shift from the gennuinely sincere idealism of Jawaharlal Nehrus' grand vision of a great, strong and self-reliant India to gradual increase of wheeling and dealing upto the present time when manipulation and corruption are standardised and expected procedures. In fact, their avoidance is construed either as infirmity of character or weakness of will.

In the four decades of tortuous history of the city of Delhi, both politically perverse behaviour and financial bungling have played a major role. Amongst the former, the prime factor was the decision to establish East Delhi colonies when expert committees had firmly established that since the level of this area is below that of river Yamuna, there would be no way to drain it of excreta, muck and rubbish which inevitably would find their way into the sub- soil. And this is exactly what has happened. All the diseases in their most virulent form: typhoid, cholera, jaundice, viral infections of the most excruciating nature — all have their genesis in water-borne bacteria which is the contribution munificance of trans-Yamuna colonisation and the perverse political decision which abetted it. *Delhi for all times to come therefore, has been crippled and maimed: it will have a permanent settlement which will constantly produce water-borne diseases.*

In just four decades, Lutyens Delhi has changed beyond recognition. A veritable paradise has been converted into a veritable hell, just as in our development effort, the *genius* of the Indian Renaissance has been snuffed to build a nation of gangsters, smugglers, wheeler-dealers and criminals.

In all this, the role of communication system has been the most significant. It has neither been able to control nor sublimiate these negative tendencies, but has become the handmaiden of these criminal adventures which has brought the nation to the verge of a precipice.

Therefore, if we now wish to find our way back to the springs of pristine virtue of character and culture, we have to revive healthy, holistic, healing Communication.

ANNEXURE

THE STATISTICAL BASIS OF THE PLAN
FORMULATED BY
PROF. MAHALNOBIS

TWO SECTOR MODEL

I used a two-sector model in 1953 which I shall now briefly describe. The total net investment is divided into two portions. One part (a fraction, say,) is used to increase the production of basic capital or investment goods (which may be called the K-sector), and the other part (a fraction say,) is used to increase the production of consumer goods (to be called the C-Sector). It should be noted that and are fractions of the total investment so that + = 1. I should also explain that appropriate fractions of investments in industries manufacturing intermediate (produce) goods should be allocated to in proportion to the value of such intermediate goods used in the capital; goods (K-sector) and the consumer goods (C-sector) industries respectively. The two fractions and can be settled at the choice of the planners. However, once the value of it settled the supply of investment goods produced within the country would become fixed. A change can be brought about only through imports or exports of investment goods. In India I have assumed that, with the progress of planning, the domestic supply of investment goods would become more and more important. That is, although in the beginning India will, no doubt, have to depend on imports of capital goods, the policy would be to make India independent of such imports as soon as possible.[1] In the present model I have, therefore, assumed that there would be no imports or exports of investment goods.

---

1. This does not mean that India would not purchase capital goods from other countries. India would make such purchases but India would also manufacture and export capital goods. Secondly, if for any reason (such as lack of foreign currency, shortage of supply or high prices in the world market, state of blockade or war, etc.) there is difficulty in securing essential investment goods from abroad, India should be able to manufacture such goods within the country.

2

BEYOND OUR RENAISSANCE

I have a little earlier raised the question: what should be the focus, the primary objective, the overriding policy of our Developmental Communication. I suggest that above all it ought to be a regeneration of our spiritual life and not the wheeling — dealing which by and large, is what social and economic programmes and with these our Communication media have precipitated to in the last four decades. And the basic framework of our spiritual enlightenment under changed modern conditions has already been made for us. It is in the Indian Renaissance at the turn of the century of which the National movement for political freedom was a very minor part, and that of urging economic equality with our rulers was of even less consequence.

No body has summed up the situation better that Dr. Ananda Coomaraswamy, who writing at the turn of the century about the "Deeper Meaning of the Struggle" of the National movement wrote: "For this struggle is much more than a political conflict. *It is a struggle for spiritual and mental freedom from the domination of an alien ideal.* In such a conflict, political and economic victory are but half the battle; for an India "Free in name, but subdued by Europe in her inmost soul" would ill justify the price of freedom. It is not so much the material, as the moral and spiritual subjection of Indian civilisation that in the end impoverishes humanity."

And Roger Lipsey who has written Dr. Coomaraswamy's biography under the aegis of the exquisite and highly imaginative Bollingen Series of the Princeton University, U.S.A., when showing how Dr. Coomaraswamy was both conciously and unconciously influenced by William Morris and Ashbee and Ruskin has this to say of the "Arts and Crafts" movement which all these persons including Dr. Coomaraswamy espoused: "The Arts and Crafts movement sprang *more from spiritual discontent than from a critique of social and economic conditions.*"

Our Development process and its attendent Communication rhetoric since the 1950's year of Planning — has been concerned only with "a critique of social and economic conditions" — and that too largely unsuccessfully. Meantime, the spiritual element has slipped entirely out of our hands to this stage of crass materialism and anarchy. The time has therefore, come to go back to the spiritual springs of our Renaissance and seek inspiration afresh for new models of Development and Communication based on that extraordinary resurgence. I have made an attempt to treat this idea in this chapter.

The development process we ushered in the early 1950's after freedom has cast this great Renaissance into complete oblivion. The unique greatness of this Renaissance lay in the fact that whether it was Rabindranath Tagore, or Ananda Coomaraswamy, or Raja Ram Mohan Roy or Swami Vivekananda or Sri Aurobindo or Swami Dayanand Saraswati or any other great luminaries of this period — there is one common thread running through all their ideologies — the reinterpretation of the relevance of India's Perenial Philosophy and thought *in changed modern conditions.*

Our developmental Communication these 40 years has discarded this vision and concentrated only on how to grow cabbaged or nurture kings. The time has come to rediscover who we are, get stamina from our spiritual herritage, get the eternal vision to creatively handle critical modern problems. And this is what now should be the revised role of Developmental Communications.

The Indian Nineteenth Century Renaissance, in a way, was far superior to its European counterpart. The European Renaissance has ultimately resulted only in one thing: the deification of Science. It has resulted in science taking over life and excluding and deliberately denying every thing else from it. But the superstition of science and facts can be infinitely worse than the superstitution of metaphysics and intuition.

Things have come to a pass now where, as a result of science, everything in Western life (because this may happily not yet be true of what are euphemistically called "developing countries") is subject to three basic assumptions.

(a)   The *OBJECTIVIST* assumption — That there is an objective universe out there which can be explored (and hence exploited) by the methods of scientific inquiry, and which can be approximated, progressively more precisely, by quantitative methods.

(b) The *POSITIVIST* assumption, that what is scientifically "real" must take as its basic data only that which is physically observable.

(c) The *REDUCTIONIST* assumption, that scientific explanation consists of explaining complex phenomena in terms of more elemental events (e.g. gas temperature, in terms of the motion of molecules; human behaviour, in terms of stimulus and response).

The tragedy of the situation and the present modern predicament is that none of these approaches can help solve the real problem man is faced with today, namely the crisis of the Spirit.

It is in this respect that the Indian Renaissance was far, far superior. It opened Indian civilization and culture to the fresh and strong breeze of Science from the West — but on India's terms. And these terms consisted of holding fast to her ageless metaphysical tradition. The Indian response to science and modernisation therefore, emerged in the formula represented schematically by an inverted triangle in which Metaphysics looms large on the top in that order of importance— matters of the soul and spiritual realisation being India's uppermost quest. Then came Art and Symbology, which again has been India's eternal way of manifesting and expressing her spiritual energies in the world of creativity. Finally at the lowest rung of the inverted apex came Economics—but a benign Economics — a "Home Economics" enshrined in the concept of "Good Work". This model of the Indian Renaissance which I have described, applies universally to all its leaders be it Rabindranath Tagore or Mahatma Gandhi. Ananda Coomaraswamy or Aurobindo, or the Arya Samaj movement of Punjab or the Brahmo Samaj of Bengal. It is the common spiritual substratum of the National movement.

Notice here how far the modern civilization of Western inspiration has travelled from this Renaissance ideal of India. Metaphysics is not even to be talked about; in fact, it is a matter to be disregarded. Art, on the other hand, has become an exotic — a mere sentiment or at best an "emotion" — but not a "way of knowledge" as India has always understood it, affirming thereby that beauty and wisdom and utility are inseparable and recognising that in Artistic symbolism is manifest the most subtle path to understanding. Instead, Economics — but of a most ruthless type driven hard by what is its fixation; "competition" and abetted by naked power-mongering and aggression all deriving their power from the hidden and all pervasive power of Science has become the dominant force of modern civilization.

It is no wonder then that the major crisis which faces the developed, industrial world is neither search for markets, nor power, nor money, but rather in its ultimate analysis *search for Spirit and of a way which would make possible the reconcilliation of Science and Spirit*. The West is nowhere near the fruition of this enterprise; in fact, in most Western quarters the enterprise has neither been understood nor launched.

In contradistinction, India in its Renaissance emerged as "Jagat-Guru" — the ancient world-teacher because it is she alone in modern times who, in her Renaissance, brought about this raproachment and reconcilliation between Science and Spirit.

India's tragedy these past four decades, has been the perverse direction we gave to Development. Nehru (bless his soul for the searching effort he made) however never did "discover India". And it is for this reason that the whole edifice of planning and progress he designed and erected is in utter shambles and ruins. Everything in India today is on the downward swing, all institutions created in the forties and fifties are in decay, and all the ideals of so-called Development face death and total annihilation.

Nehru's triumvirate of Socialism, Secularism and Democracy, with which he ardently wished to replace the symbolic triumvirate of Brahma-Vishnu-Mahesh, is perverted beyond repair.

Socialism has led to a situation in which 200 million Indians are getting more and more rich every day whereas the 600 million, soon to become 800 million, are below the poverty line. Secularism has led to the emergence of the worst form of religious fundamentalism, in particular, Muslim fanaticism, which makes even the most sober of Indians question: did we not allow Pakistan to be created to take care of this cancerous problem; why is the problem still with us despite the compromise we made? Nehru's great mistake appropos secularism is that the Constitution itself is perverse on this subject. It openly gives licence, nay in fact more, it abets the minorities to not only flourish, but flourish with a vengence— to open schools of their *sectarian* denomination and latterly even exhort for their own sectarian "personal law" and in one State at least, their own *sectarian* flag. Pray, may we ask which other country in the world enshrines wilfully such deliberate treachery and libertinism in its constitution. As for democracy, the word has become synonymous with licence, corruption, opportunism and degredation of the lowest form. Rarely in her history has India touched this nadir of degradation and depth.

All is not lost, however. Following the Hegelian dialectic; if we regard the Nineteenth Century Indian Renaissance as the thesis, the four decades of Development effort as antithesis, then a *CREATIVE* role of Communication, can now present the *SYNTHESIS*.

Let us now examine historically how our great Renaissance ushered in the modernisation process in India. This was done in a unique way which can be called the modernization of tradition and unless we understand this uniqueness we will not know what to communicate in our ever expanding system. For these ideas I am beholden to an excellent piece of Sociological work : Prof. Yogendra Singh's "Modernization of Indian Tradition. Prof. Singh's point is that in its civilizational evolution, India never really has given up her traditions, and never indeed, substituted these with the new invading forces. For example, in the present context of the recent British impact, India unlike some other and weaker cultures has not just become "westernised." Instead she achieves the opposite:

She constantly uses the new forces to renew and modernise her own traditions and give them vital expression. Prof. Singh corroborates his theory with four very crucial and critical examples.

First, despite Western and other influences Indian society continues to retain the "heirarchy" principle as against the modern Western "equality" principle. Heirarchy, in its enlightened sense implies that basic values, what Aldous Huxley alludes to as the "Perrenial Philosophy", define instrumental values and not the other way around as is the case with a materialistic society where economics and politics dominate all other values. Indian civilization therefore, continues to fiercely eschew hedonism and continues to invest tremendous value in non-material aspects of life.

The second characteristic is "continuity" as against "historicity". Indian civilization in fact, has been totally indifferent to history and this also explains why anonymity has prevailed. This has had its negative side, for example, the wily British took advantage of this position to write endless Histories of India in which the British period, obviously the most repressive, occupies more than half the content; Muslim period — by and large outrageous- occupies three-forths of the balance and the Hindu-period — which is what India is really all about- is dismissed as myths and fables.

When we state that Indian civilization holds on to continuity and is not infatuated by history, we are in fact, extending the earlier idea; namely, time is not looked upon as fractured, whatever the cataclysm might be. These are just interregnums, which temporarily interrupt but never, never indeed stop the interminable flow of the Perrenial Philosophy — truths which never change. As a corrolary, unlike the Western concept, there is no fragmentation, which History inevitably implies: British period, Muslim period, Hindu period. It is always "Sanatan Dharma": The Eternal Religious Truth which only takes new forms, by transformation through contact with the new forces. It is clear therefore, why India is indestructible — she alone amongst nations possesses the alchemy to *renew the old through the new — not give up the old for the new*, as feebler civilizations have always done and therefore, perished.

The third characteristic to which Prof. Yogendra Singh draws our attention is that Indian civilisation, in the process of modernisation of tradition, continues to stick to "Holism" as against "Individualism". Nowhere is individualism more rampant than in the U.S.A. "Rugged American individualism" is to Americans a virtue which surpasses all their other virtues — and they are determined in their belief that they are indeed, God's chosen: the most virtuous people on earth today. Little do they realise that there has taken place, during the course of their civilization a complete reversal of values, and what were once virtues are now becoming glaring vices. Individualism, "aggressiveness" (very definitely regarded by Americans as a positive streak in character), marketing, persuasion, strategic management — all these put together only go to make a people the most selfish haughty, introvert and isolated in the world. What will destroy America is not communism or an economic crisis, but unbridled individualism which is summed up in the popular American expression "I don't give a damn". The whole nation does not seem to give a damn to anything except what is perceived as its narrow interest: a far cry from the values bequeathed by their Founding Fathers.

In Indian Society, despite all the upheavals of modernisation, westernisation, materialisation — the essential belief in Holism holds sway. God, Nature, Culture, Man — all are basically regarded as a unity. The main impetus for this belief obviously derives from the philosophy of Vedanta which is pervasive and has penetrated all creeds and cultures and religions in India, and basically regards the Self, the Atman to represent a higher unity which pervades everything. The whole endeavour of spiritual progress in India from times immemorial *has been the effort to regain wholeness*, to regain Paradise Lost through regaining Holism and by going beyond differentiation. "Brahman" according to Vedanta pervades all — and therefore, God, Nature, Culture, Man — all have an underlying unity. It is the endeavour of higher minds to realise this unity and to live this unity.

The fourth and last attribute to which Prof. Yogendra Singh draws our attention is that of "transcendence" in Indian civilization as against "this worldliness" in Western culture. Max Weber diagnosed this as India's primary illness, which has kept her from progress. This of course, is utter nonsense. To begin with, India was under British rule during Max Weber's time and therefore, scientific progress was restricted. Secondly, and more importantly, he overlooked the fact, that despite this predisposition to transcendence, India always renewed and refreshed herself materialistically by absorbing the latest in science and technology and in fact, has been world's ancient leader in Mathematics, Logic, Astronomy, Astrology, Medicine and Sciences.

On the contrary, transcendence in India has always provided the principle of change, the principle of transformation, the principle of creativity. The "tyagi", the "sanyasi" or even the householder who has spiritually "renounced" is "jeewan mukt" and therefore, has conserved the energy at his disposal, *not for wastage by the ego, but for transformation of his own self and that of others,* of his culture and his society. In fact, it is precisely total absorption in "this worldliness" which is exhausting Western civilization and causing many of its myriads of problems.

If we feel that an Indian professor cannot be relied upon, because he is too much seeped in the wooly metaphysics of India, we have the verdict of an American Professor, Dr. Bill Gordon, a man of literature and philosophy, who has been trying to synthesise WESTERN SCIENCE and Eastern wisdom. His work comes very close to his friend and collaborater Dr. Jeremy Hayward (Professor at MIT), whose celebrated book is "Shifting Worlds, Changing Minds — where the Sciences and Buddhism meet." The title itself reflects the concerns.

After years of introspection, Bill Gordon has come out with a paradigm which he feels reflects the substance of Eastern, and particularly the Indian view of life. And this is an inverted triangle in this order:

Metaphysics

Aesthetics

Economics

Here I would like to substitute "Good Work" for Economics. I borrow the words "Good Work" from Schumaker's book of that title.

Bill Gordon is perfectly right. The basis of Eastern life to this day is Metaphysics — the dictionary definition being "Philosophy of *BEING* and *KNOWING*." It is the philosophy of knowing how to live and therefore, is much nearer religion than Western philosophy today which is much nearer logic and science. "Atam-vidya", or knowledge of self, has always been considered in India as the highest form of knowledge.

This knowledge indeed, was not unknown to the West. It was very much the religion of Meister Eckhart, and St. Augustine and the mystics of Medieval Europe.

But after the Renaissance and the Scientific Revolution, Europe parted company with this metaphysical source of power,

Meister Eckhart to whom I have alluded — his Sermons might well be termed the Upanishads of Europe and one is struck by the great energy of will that allows him to concentrate in one consistent demonstration the spiritual being of Europe. There-after, the West diverts its will and attention to Science. Bill Gordon feels the West needs this Metaphysics badly today.

The second step in his ladder, Aesthetics, is again ingrained in the Eastern and particularly Indian cosmology. Nobody has stressed this quite as much as Ananda Coomaraswamy who states repeatedly that Art in India has never been an emotion or a sentiment (as it is indeed in the industrial world today, and therefore, an exotic, a peripheral activity), but rather that "Art is a form of knowledge." And as Joseph Campbell puts it with remarkable perception : "Indian philosophy, therefore, frankly avails itself of the symbols and images of *myth*, and is not finally at variance with the patterns and sense of *mythological* belief." Elaborating on the role of Indian aesthetics, of the symbols and myths the divinities carved in stone, the scripts of the epic tradi-tion, he writes: "In this way a cooperation of the latest and the oldest, the highest and the lowest, a wonderful *friendship of mythology and philosophy, was effected; and this has been sustained with such result that the whole edifice of Indian civilization is imbued with spiritual meaning."

Art in India thus, is not a hobby, an exotic interlude, an eve-ning at the opera or the theatre, it is the very channel for com-municating the knowledge of metaphysical truths. But Gordon laments that this too has been lost to the Western world.

"Good work" is another thing we in the modern, industrial world do not understand. The pernicious influence of the as-sembly line, mass production for economies of scale — the paramount characteristics of the First industrial revolution have created an operating culture and work ethics in our industrial environment that has made the human personality totally ex-troverted and objectified where none of the "subjective" remains. Dr. Ananda Coomaraswamy states that in the Indian, and equally the European Medieval, era, characterised as it is by crafts and guilds, it was an axiom in the prevailing culture that *"Art is the principle of manufacture"*. Meaning thereby that the whole process of "manufacture", that is "work" was the process of *objectifying* that which was deeply felt *subjectivily* within. The union of the subjective and the objective made *work of manufacture akin to Art and the artistic process.*

But with industrialism have come ills, pernicious, cancerous ills in which commerce settles on every branch with profit-making its presiding deity and political manipulation its handmaiden. Then, the whole work environment is vitiated and becomes a factory of robots to carry out mechanical exercises to create limitless wealth and with it power. The great symbol of this evil cancer is the much flaunted capitalism of a country like U.S.A., or for that matter all of Western European countries. Americans do not realise however, that they have come to a point of no return. So excruciating is the work culture of America now that any number of studies show that as far as blue-collar workers in America are concerned, *if they really hate one thing today, it is work.* Give them baseball, give them alcohol and obviously women, but don't mention work — it is a dreaded word which invokes nightmares.

The malady is so severe that Japanese who are trying to put up manufacturing plants in the U.S.A. work on the assumption that American labour just will not work and are increasingly finnicky about choosing locations and communities where American labour will be inclined to do a day's job. What a fall O'Caeser — what a fall from Protestant Ethics, Presbyterian abstemiousness and Jeffersonian rhetoric.

The same is the case with American students — especially undergraduates. *There is nothing they hate more than having to study.* For American Universities with their "functional approach", quizes and readings and term papers and projects and grades, in effect emulate the "factory" system in programming the student to become a robot. The point of diminishing returns has come. With everything objectified and no subjective element left, neither the worker nor the student can identify emotionally and spiritually with the work environment and therefore suffers not only from ennui, but from much worse : from abhorence, rejection, revulsion, revolt.

"Good work" is exactly the opposite of this scenario. In it the motivation to work emanates from the "subjective state", from a sense within, from an idea, from imagination, from a creative impulse and this is realised in an objective form *through work.* This was the basis of the *crafts environment* of the pre-industrial, traditional societies, especially that of India, where the crafts tradition to this-day has been unexcelled and where nimbleness of fingers, imagination of mind and devotion of heart mingle to weave miracles of handiworks. The greatness and uniqueness of this approach, as Dr. Coomaraswamy reminds us again and again, is that the end product is both a piece of art as well as of utility. The tragedy of the Industrial Revolution typified by the assembly line of mass production and mass media is that it has deified utility at the sacrifical altar of art—which has been driven out of our lives.

If we are not impressed even with Prof. Bill Gordon because he represents a soft discipline like English Literature, we have a formidable witness in Scientist-Engineer, Dr. Willis Herman for many years Professor at Stanford University, U.S.A. and now at the Institute of Noetic Sciences in California. He analyses with keen perception: "Conditions for Reconciliation of Science and Spirit." The word *"reconciliation"* is used advisedly because it aptly describes the intention *to undo the deep sense of alienation* that has set in because Science presides over our lives, and Spirit has been banished. Willis tells us that Science is the exclusive master now for the simple reason that its application has led to *outstanding success and power* — yielding both technological and predictive power and hence *tremendous prestige.*

But paradoxically, this very power and success has led to its greatest tragedy. It has resulted in two great tragedies in the modern world. According to Willis, the first is that whereas Science obviously has given great "power" to man, the cosmos described by modern science is *devoid of meaning* and lends no support to the profound insight of thousands of years of human experience. Secondly, and even more grieviously, the adequacy of scientific view is basically questionable because of its systematic neglect of those deep inner experiences from which all societies throughout history have obtained their ultimate sense of meaning and guiding values.

This then was the genius of the Indian Renaissance. On the one hand it uniquely created conditions for the *reconciliation* of Science and Spirit — something even the West has not succeeded in doing and is desparately in need of. Secondly it demonstrated once again India's unique capacity to "modernise her tradition" and renew, revitalise and reinterpret her aims under changed modern conditions.

What then ought to have been communication's role? Is it not obvious? Should it not have been to expand upon, dilate upon the nucleus of this priceless contribution of the Renaissance and disperse it in a manner readily accessible to the lay people? Instead Communication has been a traitor to the great National cause these past forty years. It has been the chief instrument for materialisation of Indian life, the handmaiden of consumerism, cheapness, vulgarity, obscenity, deculturisation, crassness and the great protagonist of crude, narrow material values.

I fall back, as ever upon Ananda Coomaraswamy who stated at the height of our National movement: "It will matter little to humanity whether a few Indians more or less, have held official posts in India, or a few million bales of cloth been manufactured in Bombay or Lancashire factories but it will matter much whether *the great ideals of Indian culture have been carried forward or allowed to die.* It is with these that Indian Nationalism is essentially concerned and upon these that the fate of India as a nation depends."

These past forty years the Indian Communication media — Developmental or other have deliberately allowed the great ideals of Indian culture to die. We are now at a DIVIDE — in terms of Development Planning, Economics, Polity, Communication Technology and every other phase of life. We must call a halt to the fissiparous, debilitating and treacherous tendencies in vogue and bring Communication back to the aid of our spiritual regeneration. This is the primary theme and thesis of this book.

3

BEYOND IMPORTED COMMUNICATION THEORIES

I raise two basic issues in this chapter.

(a) When we are so tremendously strong in the whole area of Communication, Electronics, Solid State Physics etc. why have we made no effort at all in theory building in terms of very advanced and futuristic Communication technologies and their relation to society and change?

(b) Why instead have we hung on to archaic, discarded, irrelevant Communication theory, notions of foreign experts, essentially Americans, basically related to Mass Communications? These may be all right for some jungle tribe, but certainly not for the level of scholastic, research and development potential and sophistication as it avails in India of the 1990s.

Among our strengths I would note:

(i) A Tertiary Sector (Services) which contributes 53% to the GDP.

(ii) Third largest scientific and technical manpower in the world, and especially in the Communication and Electronic areas.

(iii) A unique genius for Computer software development.

(iv) A massive infrastructure.

(v) Tremendous manufacturing capacity.

Why then no attempt at Theory building at all, particularly when we talk all the time of entering "the 21st century" implying thereby, entry into the Information Age.

With the assets I have enumerated above, the conditions appear most favourable for India to leapfrog into the Information Age *and thereby totally transform her society*. One would expect therefore, maximum effort at Theory building in this area. *But there is none at all.*

And the answer is simple to seek. There can be no theory building unless there is research. There is close link between the two. Research refines theory and theory guides research. But how can there be research when Communication (not Engineering, but the social field) is not even an established academic discipline, largely due to the European tradition of Sociology we have inherited.

Further the research we are talking about is not micro attempts of effects of message A on micro audience B. That gets us nowhere. What we desparately need is Policy Research, that is conceptualisation of research in terms of *structure, organization, professionalisation, socialisation and participation.*

Even within macro Policy Research the emphasis we need is on *Information Economics*, because that is the only way we can hope to postulate an *Economic theory which would establish the central role of Information in Development.*

No body is doing this work in the country. The disdain of the Economist for Information research is inexplicable. They have worked for decades on Transport and Energy Economics, but Information does not exist as an area of concern for them. They do not see what Economics has to do with this area. So we do not have the counterpart of scholars like Marc Porat in the U.S.A. who did monumental work in *quantifying* the exact contribution of Information to the economy.

The Social Scientist on the other hand, first considers Communication as a pollution of his discipline (brought up as he is in the European tradition of Sociology) and secondly, is totally innocent of the economic ramifications of this resource.

The Planner is hooked on to "stages of economic growth" and cannot go beyond Agriculture, at most Industry.

When we do not have the academic, scholastic, professional and *THEORETICAL* wherewithal of this discipline how are we going to use it for our betterment.

An apt analogy is: if Homi Bhabha had not established Higher Mathematics and Nuclear Physics as disciplines, how could we have had an Atomic Energy programme? Similarly, Vikram Sarabhai established Cosmic Ray studies, ionospheric studies and space sciences at Physical Research Laboratory, Ahmedabad before we got a Space programme going? Where is the replication of this in the Communication Arts and Sciences? We have Communication Engineering on the one hand and trade schools teaching journalism and audio visual production on the other, but this does not establish the discipline of Communications as we need it for the purpose of conceptualising its growth for social good and sane policy-making.

The entire sector therefore, is going by default, with engineers "wiring" up the country aimlessly and indscriminately, and administrators manning most of the top positions in media and communication organizations. The picture is pathetic beyond words.

1. As the saying goes "There is no practice without theory". Stock-taking of the past 40 years of Development activity points out two things:

(a) No attempt whatsoever has been made by any Indian scholar or institution to come up with a theoretical frame which would conceptualise the role of Communication in Development in the Indian context.

(b) Slavish following of western particularly American theorists — who have concentrated only on Mass Communication's role in Development.

Appropos Communication theory building a number of questions need to be asked:

(1) We have been producing some of the best Economists in the world. Why have they not thought it necessary to do work in the field of *Information Economics and to develop appropriate theories in the Indian context? We talk of leap-frogging to the 21st century - but how can we do that without appropriate theories of Information Economics?*

(2) Why have our Development thinkers not given any thought at all to the burgeoning Tertiary sector and the structural changes which are taking place in the Indian economy as a result of this? The Table 1 succinctly points out this change.

As will be seen, the Services sector now accounts for 53.3% of the GDP. The figure approximates 60% in the U.S., one of the most advanced countries in the world. However, whereas in the U.S.A. out of 60%, Information industry accounts for 40% of the GDP, in India the contribution of Information is probably negligible.

Table I : Structural Changes in the Composition
of India's GDP at Factor Cost

(1950-51 to 1989-90)

Sector	% Share in Total GDP					
	1950-51	1960-61	1970-71	1980-84	1986-87 Terminal Year of Sixth Plan	1989-90
1. Primary	59.61	55.14	48.46	41.62	38.08	29
2. Secondary	14.47	17.28	29.67	21.57	21.60	18
3. Tertiary	25.92	27.58	30.87	36.81	40.32	53
(a) Transport Communication & Trade	11.89	13.80	16.09	18.85	19.73	
(b) Finance and real estate	5.24	5.06	5.76	6.62	7.05	
(c) Community and Personal Services	8.79	8.72	9.02	11.36	13.59	

No systematic work, however, has been done in this crucial area of Developmental Planning and no attempt made at theory building.

(3)   In contrast to the above table, Table II shows the position of the work-force in the U.S.A. It will be seen that in 1980, 46.6% of the total work force was in the Information Sector. In the 1990s the figure will probably be even higher. What work have we done however, to extrapolate rise in employment generation if we give more weightage to Information industry in a decentralised mode.

(4)   We have an American (Prof. Rostow of Harvard University) with his Theory of "Stages of Economic Growth" telling us that predominantly Agricultural communities are not ready for take off to higher levels of economy that is like an Information Society. Why have we not tried to develop a counter theory to assert that the march to an Information society *need not be uniform the world over*. We do not need to suffer all the miseries of the Industrial Revolution before we can hope to enter the Information Age. Countries like India

can leap-frog to the Information Society and transform the traditional village to the post industrial "global village." This in fact, was the very philosophy of visionaries like the late Dr. Homi. Bhabha, who saw in India the potential to become a foremost developed country.

Table II : U.S. Experienced Civilian Labour Force By Four Sector 1800-1980

Year	Sector's per cent of total				Total labour force (in millions)
	Agricul-tural	Indus-trial	Service	Informa-tion	
1800	87.2	1.4	11.3	0.2	1.5
1810	81.2	6.5	12.2	0.3	2.2
1820	73.0	16.0	10.7	0.4	3.0
1830	69.7	17.6	12.2	0.4	3.7
1840	58.8	24.4	12.7	4.1	5.2
1850	49.5	33.8	12.5	4.2	7.4
1860	40.6	37.0	16.6	5.8	8.3
1870	47.0	32.0	16.2	4.8	12.5
1880	43.7	25.2	24..6	6.5	17.4
1890	37.2	28.1	22.3	12.4	22.8
1900	35.3	26.8	25.1	12.8	29.2
1910	31.1	36.3	17.7	14.9	39.8
1920	32.5	32.0	17.8	17.7	45.3
1930	20.4	35.3	19.8	24.5	51.1
1940	15.4	37.2	22.5	24.9	53.6
1950	11.9	38.3	19.0	30.8	57.8
1960	6.0	34.8	17.2	42.0	67.8
1970	3.1	28.6	21.9	46.4	80.1
1980	2.1	22.5	28.8	46.6	95.8

Source : Data for 1800-1850 are estimated from Lebergott
(1964) : with missing data interpolated from Fabricant
(1949) : data for 1860-1970 are taken directly from Porat
(1977) : data for 1980 are based on U.S. Bureau of Labour
Statistics projections (Bell 1979, p. 185).

This is obviously possible in India with a Services sector of 53.3%, a formidable scientific and technical manpower, especially in electronics, telecommunications and computer engineering, formidable talent in software development and some of the finest Economists in the world and a highly developed infrastructure.

(5)   Why have we not been able to draw up a theory which defines Gandhian approach and economy in terms of the Second Industrial Revolution and essentially an Information Society?

(6)   If the "corridor" of microelectronics and digital telecommunications is sagging because of the sluggish functioning of the government bureaucracy why have we not developed a suitable "DEREGULATION" theory which helps us *open up this sector to the private sector* so that we get on with job rapidly?

(7)   Why have we unconciously equated the word Communication with Mass Media and propaganda? Why don't we develop similar theories of development in regard to the emerging and more advanced communication technologies which are interactive, demassified and asynchronous. In these would be included Microelectronics and Telematics ?

(8)   Why have we not developed a suitable economic and planning theory which would encompass the role of meshing telecommunication, computers and user networks ?

In a nutshell why do we assume that the developmental and economic growth patterns through our Communication systems must of necessity be the same as those evolved in the West? Why cannot we develop our own theories and pathways and use Communication-Information in our own unique situation?

The apathy of planners, economists and scholars in this field of Developmental Communication is abyssmal. They have held the subject in utter disdain and not come up with any theory-building on the subject.

Instead of being the active protagonists of such relevant theories which relate to our unique needs and realistic prospects of our emerging as an Information society we have been passive victims of meaningless formulations by Western, especially American Communication experts these past four decades.

The sordid story beings in 1952 when our Planning process started and is roughly the year when Wilbur Schramm (first Professor at University of Illinois, Urban-Champagne and subsequently Stanford University) came out with his book "Mass Media and National Development." None of these expectations however, materialised and a disillusioned Schramm himself withdrew his thesis two decades later.

Another luminary presiding over the so-called "Dominant Paradigm" was Daniel Lerner (from M.I.T) who did most of his field work in the Middle East and his celebrated book is "Passing of the Traditional Society." Lerner was hung up on Modernisation and this according to him was a 4- step process for the Developing world: Urbanisation, Literacy, Media and Modernization (and hence possibly Adoption.)

The Green Revolution in India is one case amongst many others which totally disproves this theory. The Punjabi farmer has shown he does not need to "adopt" alien norms but has shown the sagacity, cunning and will to "ADAPT" the high disequilibrium risk of Indian agriculture.

Another concept Lerner overplayed is "empathy"—the capacity to project one's personality to other situations. His formula was: no modernization-no empathy; high modernization-high empathy. The seven Indian Elections have proved Lerner totally wrong. It is the so- called illiterate Indian peasant (but imbued with robust common sense and wisdom) who has been toppling governments one after another.

The third in this triumvrate is Rogers with his "Difussion of Innovation Theory" with early adopters and late adopters, laggards etc.- all this theory mind you, based on S-curve work done in the city of New York. A large amount of Roger's work was in Indian Family Planning Communication. No comment is necessary. The Government of India has officially announced that this programme has been a failure.

These august oracles met two decades later (in the 1970s) at Honolulu and officially put their stamp on the fact that their theories were misplaced and that Communication at best had a supportive role in Development; certainly not a central one.

In the 1980s, not able to resist their compulsive urge to theoretical rhetoric, they have now come up with a "pluralistic" approach in which–

a) Qualitative data
b) Interpretive theoretical approach; and
c) Critical Theory

will be acceptable along with quantification methodology.

After 40 years, where does it leave the Developing world: at square one-not a clue as to where and how we should proceed. In the interim, atleast in India, the whole area of Social Communication (not just Family Planning) but including Nutrition, Mother and Child Welfare, Health, Immunization, Women's literacy) is grounded- it is an abyssmal failure.

Work therefore, needs to be taken up urgently in-

(a)   Conceptualising a theoretical frame — i.e. Theory building.

(b)   R & D effort in the field.

(c)   Based on the above, a Policy prescription for consideration of Government.

When we examine the dominant communication paradigm which has held sway for over two decades, and which is essentially the handiwork of American sociologists, we find that not only this paradigm is not "caring" of Indian civilizational values, but rather that it quite unabashedly spurns these. In fact, this so-called dominant paradigm is not a well thought out, and carefully put together conceptual framework at all, rather it is a set of loosely related proposals and hypotheses. The tragedy however, is that we in the developing world have taken these notions seriously and even acted upon these. Nothing brings out more patently our present state of intellectual bankruptcy, of an unquestioning mind and above all the total absence of a sense of care of our own heritage and of what we ought to have learnt from the National Movement.

The two pillars of this dominant paradigm are Lerner's views on modernisation based on his study in the Middle East and the "adoption-diffusion" model attributed to Rogers. The models are very deterministic, inasmuch as they correlate modernisation to *Westernisation*. They identify development solely with *economic growth*, and consider urbanisation and industrialisation as the sine quo non of progress. With sages like Mahatma Gandhi, Rabindranath Tagore, Sri Aurobindo and the galaxy of outstanding thinkers behind us, the question is : why did we tolerate such outlandish ideas for so long? We, who are heirs to an aristocracy of thinkers, philosophers and sages, are no longer capable of discrimination or independent thinking?

Lerner of course, takes the cake by making a mesh of the *psychological state of empathy with economic intensity* and this in turn with *media exposure*—all in the cause of modernisation and progress. At this point he introduces the idea of "empathy" which quite unabashedly, according to him, is the "acquiring of attitudes and values similar to those of modern (Western) people." It would have been all right for some primitive, illiterate jungle tribe to have swallowed this, but how could we in India have done this with the force of a unique civilization behind us and the great Renaissance of our National movement? Of course, needless to state, all of Lerner's ideas have proved totally wrong. The Green Revolution is a case in point. Modernisation in agriculture of the most outstanding kind took place, without any of the stages which Lerner espoused.

Roger's "adoption-diffusion" model is a worse case of the lingerning vestiges of Western imperialisam. He uninhibitedly declares that this theory for the developing world is based on *"summary of empirical findings of studies of the adoption diffusion proceses in the United States."* Can anybody in his senses assume that the reality and rationality of a mob say in a metropolitan, highly urbanised, literate and Westernnised, consumption-oriented area like New York city can apply to village India, steeped in culture and values of an ancient civilization. No wonder Rogers model smacks of the marketing-advertising paradigm. No wonder the only clear picture that emerges from his studies is one of urban areas and their consumption- orientation. The upshot of this has been that in the area of Family Planning to which this model has been applied for almost two decades now, shows abyssml failure. During this period, India's population has gone up from 300 million to over 800 million. Where is the adoption-diffusion with its four steps of *knowledge, persuasion, decision, confirmation* and its four stages of *early adopters, early majority, late majority* and *laggards*? The model is an unqualified disaster which has led us up the garden path.

What then is to be learnt from these two models- one, Lerner's Modernisation theory and the other Roger's "adoption-diffusion". The common characteristic, which stands out in bold relief is that both look to the West, both assume a reality and rationality, which neither exists in the East nor at the best of times is desirable. Lerner trumps up the word "empathy" by which he espousess a psychological orientation towards

Western mores, before anything desirable can be attained. How could our intellectuals and scholars have accepted such doctrinaire, imperialistic, deterministic and obscurantist theories? It certainly points to deficient vitality in these so called intellectuals.

Rogers does something even more frightening. He assumes that the reality and rationality of urban America is the same as or perhaps ought to be a model for that of rural India. Naturally his S-curve model of advertising-marketing based on consumerism failed in a society seeped in values and tradition.

Outright villification characterises the obtrusive and uncouth superimposition of these models on our own unique reality. Here is a sample of what Beltram has recorded about Latin American countries and please note the disgust and demigration with which he holds the Latin peasant:

"Most peasants, research has found, presumably by birth and their sovereign will, are not only ignorant but stubbornly bent on tradition. They are also "fatalistic" "not risk- oriented" and "uncreative." Moreover, they have no "future orientation" they lack "entrepreneurship," and suffer from very low "achievement motivation." And superstitious and Catholic as they often are, they have not learnt from the development mystique of *the Protestant ethic and the spirit of capitalism* the virtue of saving and investing."

The only thing one can say about a remark like this is that it is utter nonsense. Moreover, how does such a stand explain the following : that these same illiterate, traditional bound peasants in India atleast:

(a)   brought about a Green Revolution —unique in the whole world.

(b)   Have contributed large-scale growth of the small- scale industry.

(c)   Have shown in the last 6 national elections in India a political acumen which certainly does not exist in the people of the United States, drugged as they are by television in selecting their President and other officials.

(d)   How has Japan come up without Protestant ethics?

What is the solution to this impasse? The solution for the Third World is what might be termed a *Third World Paradigm*, which is truly radical and harbours independence and self-respect and self-assurance. The main pillar of this paradigm is self-reliance. According to Hedebro the concept of self-reliance involves "the use of locally available raw materials, simple production processes, and application of indigenous know-how accummulated over the years". It will be readily seen that this is precisely the basis of Gandhian economics, which we now need very critically in the Third World, and particularly in India, and which I have argued in detail in a subsequent chapter on Development and manufacturing.

Although Nehru did not quite follow this model of self-sufficiency in local habitates using locally available raw materials, and instead went in for an economic policy based on heavy industry with the central place given to the public sector and centralised planning, yet the genius of his leadership lay in stress on complete self-reliance. In all our Five Year Plans in India, the foreign investment in our Plans has not exceeded about 7 per cent; the rest has come out of generation of internal resources. No other developing country has been able to achieve this. The great strength of India is in its self-reliance today, in which through its own scientific and technological manpower, it has been able to create a huge infrastructure and manufacturing base and is well on its way to becoming a Superpower.

The other great lacunae in the Third World Communication is what Patricia Morgan (of the University of Kentucky, USA) dubs as "research weakness." Her ideas are so relevant and hard-hitting that I reproduce these in extensio below.

Attention is drawn in particular to three points she has made. She states, quoting MacLean "As it is now, we seem to act as though there were some magic about analysis of variance which can take the place of exploration, thinking and theory."

Indeed this is true. Communication research effort in the U.S. has become the prey of methodology, positivism and "fallacy of instrumentalism." So preoccupied are these researchers with refining the tools of measurement, that they overlook the fatal fact that the research problem has been left undefined, especially so, in the context of the cultural mileau and the civilizational thrust of countries in the Third World.

Morgan further makes two valuable suggestions. She is all for two specific kinds of research being initiated in the Third World countries. One is "participatory research-"The researcher participates in a local village or region, studying problems from the perspective of the weakest groups." Second, is "action cum research." In this the researcher is not a passive observer, "instead, he or she initiates and takes part in the change process, while following and documenting all relevant events as accurately as possible."

I follow the quotation from her by an extensive quote from one of Prof. Sisirkumar Ghoses' recent pieces in which he shows how the politics of science and science of politics are all but destroying us and calls for "Model of Man" based on the *Vedantic search for humanism and love.* Third world models of communication also ought to be based on such a "Model for Man." The moral of this analysis is that the Third World countries should now take their own initiative for research, and since the human, mystical metaphysical approaches and interests in communication have not to be abandoned, as these have been in the West, *we ought to create our institutions for higher learning and research in communications in the Third World.*

Recaptulating we find that in the dominant Development Communication paradigm there are serious and what might easily be, fatal snags. One is that it continues to traverse the path of so-called "development" we have followed for the past four decades, which has implicit in it strife, conflict and violence and human degradation. We have come to a DIVIDE where we must now change our course. We need a new model of Development and therefore, of Development Communication."

In my book "Communication Growth and Public Policy" I mentioned that Dr. Adam Carle of Peace Studies, U.K. uses the following words as indicative of Development models and in that sequence: *Conflict, Development, Peace. We have now to enter the "Peace" state.* In this state, developing countries will be called upon to evolve *their own unique models of development and growth which will bring peace, creativity and self-fulfilment. We do not need development so much now as PEACE.* So unsettling and traumatic has been the existential experience of the past four decades of development that we have forgotten that there can be be no true development *unless there is first peace and tranquility both in the individual and the nation. A harrassed, disturbed, distressed, diseased person can "develop" nothing.* If the "development" process leads to, as indeed it has done, anarchy, violence, ruthlessness, corruption, manipulation and violence-what development is it"?

So now we have to aim for the Peace state and the sine non quo is that we have to *evolve our own models of growth based on our own uniqueness.*

We give below a brief survey of the outstanding Communication theories and their cultural and spiritual consequences;

(1)   Shannon's Mathematical Model of Communication
(2)   Norbert Weiners' model of Cybernetics
(3)   Lerners "Adoption" model
(4)   Rogers "Diffussion" model
(5)   Critical Theory of the Frankfurt School - especially Habermas' ideas of mass culture and mass communication
(6)   The "Socialist School"of Communication

All these and many more have had the combined effect to "extrovert" the Indian media and Indian psyche and therefore, by implication dilute the capacity for subjectivism and transcendentalism. In other words, the chief characteristic of Indian civilization has suffered and the most salient feature of the Indian psyche has been disturbed.

The only solitary exception to this phenomenon is the school of Existential Philosophers but they stand condemned and uncared for in the Western hemisphere and almost totally unknown and unfelt in the Eastern.

The basic characteristic of Shannon's Mathematical model of Communication is that it is not concerned with meaning at all. It is only concerned with *quantity.* This sounds weird, but this is exactly what it is and we have only to look around in the world to find its validity - in the sense that by and large, governments and individuals are obssessed with enlarging the hardware and infrastructure of Mass Communications and almost totally indifferent to the message being carried.

Shannon's theory is based on the Second Law of Thermodynamics from the world of Physics. This Law postulates that entropy (or disorder tends to infinity). In fact Information in this sense is synonymous with disorder, uncertainity, randomness. "Noise" is the result of disorder, and therefore, technically increase Information, but presents problems of decoding. for this "redundancy" is necessary. This theory is only concerned with the fact that so many "bits" of information are flowing per second, and hence the race for bigger and faster computers, larger telecommunication networks and more sophisticated electronics. "Meaning" is of no concern to this theory.

The subjective personality, let it be noted, works on exactly the opposite principle. The quantum of communication is sought to be low; in "silence" it is sought to be zero. But there is search for richer and deeper "Meaning".

The second model of Communications, which has had a tremendous effect on modern life is Norbert Weiner's concept of CYBERNETICS. Weiner was a Mathematician at M.I.T.,U.S.A., but he also drew on Electrical Engineering and Neuro- Sciences. "Cybernetics" is derived from the Greek word KYBERNETIC which means: "to steer". Earlier all models assumed only one-directional movement: from point A to point B. Wenier for the first time introduced the concept of "feedback"-feedback from point B to point A. *Management of this feedback* lead to the acheivement of"CONTROL"

This seemingly simple and innocuous theory has had the most astonishing and diverse applications in modern life, and in areas as separated as electro-mechanical systems, computation, electronics and most important of all: psycho- neural and behavioural systems.

The theory has also had an impact on other theories. For example, in the Educational field Learning Theory has been completely changed and from the former concept of giving information to the student, has instead become the opposite: managing the "feedback" of the student.

Instruments like thermostats, servomechanisms, autopilots, and all large systems control, like Telemetry control, radar control —all belong to the application of this Theory. In the behavioural and pshychology area, Biofeedback systems are based on this principle.

Even during Weiner's life time, he realised that the negative implications of his Theory could be disastrous:

(1) for one thing, implicit in the concept of Communication as Control, is the implicit *Command system* on which it is based. It is not based on cooperation or collaboration or communion but on *COMMAND*—which perforce has to be carried out and is unalterable and unassailable.

As a corrolary: it is MONOLOGICAL, and therefore, could easily be coercive and mandatory.

But most insiduous of all - Weiner late in the day realised that the command could be not only from man to the machine, but also *from the machine to man*— representing thereby a Frankenstein scenario of the emerging eco-system of Communications in the modern world.

We see therefore, that while the first Theory of Shannon implies stress on *quantity of* Information to the complete indifference to *MEANING*, the second Theory of Weiner is implicit with *Control, Command, monological character* and the Frankenstein probability of *machines controlling men*.

It is not as if there is no idealism in the theory and practice of Communication in the West. The Chicago School of thinkers represented by John Dewey, Margaret Mead and others has always been very sensitive about being careful in preserving and integrating the way Western civilization is brought to primitive and traditional societies. They have always been *CARING and* tried to appreciate the modernising process from the vantage point of those who were being modernised. That is, they were not far from the ideal of "modernisation of tradition" talked about by Prof. Yogendra Singh. Further, they felt that *every culture* had a very special meaning in its own contextual framework, and merely forcing Western civilization on these ancient cultures would do more harm than good-it would create fissures, ruptures, cultural havoc, sociological strain and psychic stress and trauma. As the progress of the so-called Development process shows, their words have turned out to be prophetic. India especially has been a victim. After four decades of Development, these so-called Developing countries find not only their economies destroyed, but what is much more awesome and frightening, total enfeeblement of their moral, cultural, mental and spiritual wealth amassed in a tradition of thousands of years. Science has characteristically, taken only a split second to destroy what the spirit had built up diligently and arduously over centuries. The main culprits in this homicide are the Developed world who in their zeal to push forward the engine of Development have gone roughshod over all that is human and delicate and worthwhile.

The other school of thought which merits our attention is the School of Critical Theory of Frankfurt. Names which immediately come to mind are of Habermas, Adorno, and others who expressed dismay at the development of Western civilization from the turn of the century onwards. Adorno typically in his "The Authoritarian Personality" forewarns the development of Facism and Nazism in Europe and elsewhere in the Western world. The same theme was repeated in books like "Revolutionising Elite", "Power and Society", "Roots of Prejudice." In all these books strong concern is expressed against two normative functions in modern Western society: one, with fixation to power, appropriating power, weilding power over others and the other, to the internationalisation of aggression leading to uniquely sick Western personality typified by "repressed masculine aggression". So with "power" as the main disease syndrome, its use for "suppression" in society is one manifestation of the malady and "repression" in the psyche" the other.

No wonder then that this school sought refuge in neo-Marxist and neo-Freudian ideas. It hoped that an enlightened form of Marxism could releive modern society from "power" suppression and that an equally enlightened Freudianism would help de-repress aggression," which is the most widely prevalent disease of neurosis in the Western world.

Culture and Communication obviously became a primary concern of this School of Frankfurt. And the chief exponent of this cause was Habermas himself, who in turn was to inspire thinkers like Laswell and Levine who eventually became the founding fathers of the discipline of Communications in the U.S.A.

Habermas had no difficulty at all in realising the crucial role of mass culture and its handmaiden, mass communication in fanning the fire of the "power" cult and making it thereby the present day epidemic of the Western world. Conversely, the obsession of the industrial world with "power" was realisable only through "manipulation" and "control" and this brought into limelight the central role of propaganda, brainwashing, marketing, advertising - all of which are attainable only through a mass culture *and mass communication system* which were, as the term suggests "mass" based - proletarian, industrial moboriented- catering to the lowest common denominator in values-and therefore, amenable to avarice, greed, selfishness, materialism and high consumption rating.

The Frankfurt School had the added advantage of being essentially a European and that too a Germanic phenomenon and therefore, much more than the U.S.A. alive to the debauchery of values which a combination inevitably brought in their wake. The European response to this cultural and spiritual threat has been much sharper than in the U.S.A. In fact in the U.S.A., except for the radicalism of the sixties which threw up a solitary Herbert Marcuse, there has hardly been any reaction to the phenomenon we are discussing. It is not surprising therefore, that the Frankfurt School of Critical Theory should establish much stronger roots in Latin America than in the U.S.A., where it never gained ground.

Finally, in the West, we have the verdict of the Religious Existentialists. The names which immediately come to mind are of Karl Jaspers, Paul Tillich, Martin Buber, Erich Fromm, Gabriel Marciel and many others. These philosphers insist that the Third Communication Revolution (First being the mechanical-of the Guttenberg Press, the Second, the Electronic of Satellites, computers etc,) will have to be a return to the Human DIALOGUE - *Dialogical Communication.*

No body has summed up the centrality of such Communication to human existence better than Karl Jaspers. He states: "*Communication* then is the aim of philosophy, and in *communication* all its other aims are ultimately rooted: awareness of being, illumination through love and attainment of PEACE."

The message of these Existentialists is very simple indeed: return (Sanskrit NIVRITTI) to the Human Dialogue, to person to person communication, to honesty and sincerity (in Vedantic terms: to self-realization). They offer this humane theory of Communication that the dialogical veiw-point represents, as an alternative -or a successor - to the technical-strategic syndrome. Their aphoristic message is stupendously simple yet profound:

      (a) Existence is Communication

      (b) Life is dialogue

They firmly believe that genuine communication can only be person to person. They are fully aware of the dawning of an age of alienation and anxiety and therefore, have implicit belief that the end of human communication is not to command but to commune. These Religious Existentialists further believe that knowledge of the highest order is to be found not through detachment but through *communication, not* by objectivity but by *inter*-subjectivity, not in a state of estranged aloofness but in something *resembling an act of love.*

So far we have been discussing only the negative aspects of current Communication theories in terms of the interests of Developing countries. But some attempts have been made to come out with positive statements in the form of a Socialist or Radical theory of Developmental Communication. We make a survey of this literature below. We are beholden to Patricia Morgan of the University of Kentucky, U.S.A. for some of these ideas.

It is quite obvious however, that even this attempt does not fulfill the needs of a country like India. We require original work to meet our unique civilizational requirements and therefore, fundamental work needs to be urgently undertaken in the field of Communication Theory building.

Radical Theory of Development Communication

The field of communication and development was emerging during the same era as communication theorists were acclaiming that mass media have "limited effects." Joseph Klapper (1960) asserted in *The Effects of Mass Communication* that mass media *have little or no direct effects upon thier audiences.* However, communicologists interested in development were proposing the opposite view. They suggested that media is a potent weapon in bringing about social change. They noted that:

> Communication is very much involved in the change process and those who have access to communication facilities are in a position to exert a strong influence on the direction the change will take. From this point of view, it is difficult to understand that communication has not been given considerable attention in nations where socioeconomic improvements are of extreme urgency (Hedebro, p.9).

This concerns the developing countries, but the tendency is the same in the industrialized countries. Change is sought in a number of avenues including economics, politics, culture and psychology. For these reasons, the field of communication and development is quite of an interdisciplinary nature.

Communication messages are manipulated to boost economic growth, establish political stability, bring about socio- cultural integration within a nation, and to create a mental set prompt for modernization. Specifically, communication persons in the field are concerned with questions such as:

How can mass media promote the ideas of rapid economic growth?

How can mass media and interpersonal communication be used to persuade people to adopt new ideas and techniques?

How can mass media be used to persuade people to support governmental policies ?

How can mass media be used to make various cultural groups in a country feel as one and bring about nationalism?

How can mass media be used in education ?

How can mass media be used to bring people information about basic services?

How can media be used effectively in health and nutrition campaigns?

In the mid-1970s, researchers began to criticize the early post-World War II models of development. Staatz and Eicher (1986) grouped these so-called "growth-with-equity" revisionists into two broad categories: the "radical political economist theories" and the "dependency theories." They proposed socialist models of development based on the work of Marxist theorists. Even though these theorists were not Marxist, they used Marxist terminology such as capitalism, class analysis, and accumulation to explain the historical and economic relationship between the industrialized countries and the developing countries. Moreover, they argued that instead of helping Third World countries become economically independent, early models had created increased "dependency."

By dependency we mean a situation in which the economy of certain countries is conditioned by the development and expansion of another economy to which the former is subjected (dos Santos 1970, p. 231).

Conditions of gross social and economic inequities began to surface in the 1960s (Rogers 1976a). Earlier notions regarding development came under criticism because Western models were not succeeding. In most instances, wealth was being concentrated in the elitist social sector. Very little, if any, wealth was trickling down to lower economic groups. In the developing countries, a growing underclass was emerging composed of what Mc-Namara (1973) referred to as "the poorest of the poor." Also, rapid economic growth resulted in a wide range of unintended negative "side effects" in countries such as Nigeria, Pakistan, and Iran. Hirschman (1981, p. 20) describes the "side effects" as "ranging from civil wars to the establishment of murderous authoritarian regimes...."

Hence, the widely voiced need to find an alternative model for communication in international development was not simply due to pessimism within the arena of communication. Rather, it stemmed from the failure of the total Western development philosophy.

Generally, in a socialist model, aspects other than economic growth are to be emphasized. Basically, countries are to focus on providing basic services and educational programs. Special attention is given to assuring that there is equality in the distribution of goods and services. In addition, emphasis is placed on national development for self-reliance and economic independence.

This critical theory of development assumes that there are direct relationships between socio-economic and socio-phychological processes (Grossberg 1984). Critical theory focuses on the "quality of life" of the citizenry of developing countries. *Inyatullah (1967, p.101) thought of development as "a process through which a society achieves increased control over the environment, increased control over its own political destiny, and enables its component individuals to gain increased control over themselves."* Similarly, Teharanian's (1980) summary of the "quality of life" indicator affirms that development must be perceived as *the "development of man" to attain his potential, spiritually as well as economically. This concept states that the aim of development is to integrate the best traditional features with modern features.* Its goal should be to provide for human needs without destroying the environment. Communication scientists have contributed to the socialist model by devising approaches which focus on: self-reliance, rural and traditional media, popular participation in the decision- making process, and development journalism.

The concept of self-reliance involves "the use of locally available raw materials, simple production processes, and application of indigenous know-how accumulated over the years (Hedebro, p. 105). This micro-level approach proposes that greater socio-economic changes will occur if the media and the messages were adapted to the cultural realities of the targeted audience. Also, self-reliance requires use of what is referred to as "appropriate technology." This is proposed in the English economist E.F. Schumacher's (1973) book *Small Is Beautiful* in which he advocates deemphasizing high technology which may be inappropriate because of environmental agricultural, or social situations of developing countries. For example, a man-made plow or something similar may be more appropriate for a particular soil type than a heavy tractor. Similarly, the Maoist philosophy in this regard is to "insist that technology serve and be controlled by the people" (Rifkin 1975).

The second appraoch in the new paradigm proposes that media be modified to serve developmental aims by means of indigenous communication systems. Several factors determine the use of communication technology for local purposes. They include whether the government allows access to media; and whether facilities are designed for local productions and located near rural areas. Also, utilization depends on financial constraints and whether personnel can be trained to operate the technology (Hudson 1983).

The concept of using traditional media in development projects has proven to be successful. Lambert (1982) reports that popular theatre provides two-way interpersonal communication among rural residents. His study of SISTREN, a women's theatre group in Jamaica, concludes that this kind of media aims to free the oppressed audience in artistic form by dramatically drawing it into role play. Likewise, Lent (1982) stressed the use of folk media in policy. He found that folk media can popularise developmental policies among the populace especially in rural areas. In a study of indigenous communication systems, Wang and Dissanayake (1982) discovered that use of such systems, ensures that more people will participate in projects. Specifically, Awa (1982) suggests printing newspapers in the vernacular of the audience, while Teharanian (1979) states that the emphasis should be placed on informal (interpersonal) channels of communication. He mentioned that this channel sends immediate feedback, thereby enhancing evaluation of projects.

Some socialist philosophies believe that citizens can best communicate their wants; so they should be incorporated as an essential component of the decision-making process of national policy. Participation"....increases motivation and people's interest in their own communities and their nation. Participation means dialogue" (Hedebro, p. 107). There must be vertical communication initiated from the level of the masses and horizontal communication among various levels in society. In an examination of empirical and qualitative approaches to development, O'Sullivan and Contreras (1980) concluded that decision makers should place less emphasis on expertise and more on understanding the broad issues of projects.

Grunig (1978) devised a "general systems theory" of communication and development based on the assumption that if individuals are given decisions to make, then, they will actively seek information so that they can make the best decisions. Unlike most other communication scientists, Grunig (p. 75) contends that "Communication does not cause change. Change creates the need for communication." Thus, the role of communication is to help individuals adjust to changes and make decisions.

In his research, Grunig documented a relationship between communication behaviour and decision situations of Colombia landowners and peasants. Decision concepts were used to predict information seeking. The "decision-situation model" (as it was referred to) accurately predicted two occurrences. First, the model predicted that individuals will seek information when they are confronted with a situation in which their decisions will be reflected in projects. Secondly, it predicted that individuals seek information only about feasible alternatives. In addition, he implied that structural changes must be implemented before media exposure can have any effect.

Lastly, socialist models have advocated the concept of "development journalism." "Development journalism" is a concept which refers to the use of journalists in presenting and promoting development policies. In their selection of news items and programs and through a certain mode of presentation, the media can stimulate interest in societal matters. The media

give individuals knowledge that will increase their understanding of the community. In an essay on the concept, Ogan
(1982) defines development journalism based on its perception
and practice in several countries. The essay notes that the concept can be thought of as a sort of communication support structure for policy in service of the existing political system. On the
other hand, development journalism can be critical and independently interpret policy if the media are separate from the
government. However, the essence of the concept is (in accord
with the social responsibility theory of the press) to evaluate
the significance of policy and its relevance to the members of
the society.

One of the criticism of development journalism is that it lacks
much of the flare of regular news reports. Chalkley (1980)
provides five suggestions for spicing the news of development.
They include: simplifying technical terms, humanizing development stories; illustrating articles with pictures and charts; em-
phasizing local personalities; and expanding news content to
include national and international events.

Yet, inspite of criticism of earlier capitalist models, some of
the perspectives of the new socialist model, as well, had serious
inadequacies which made them unsuitable for developing
countries. These inadequacies occurred mainly because of two
reasons. First, they were inappropriately applied into anti-
socialist systems. Next, countries did not correctly implement
certain perspectives of the model. Socialist models were viewed
as having problems because the researchers were not evaluating
the models properly. However, there have been some successful
implementations of socialist approaches.

One situation which has hindered the success of socialist
models is that some nations did not change their overall
development orientation, rather they attempted to implement a
few socialist policies into existing non-socialist politico-
economic systems. Their overall politico-economic systems had
been either capitalist or Marxist. Both are European ideaologies
which are unsuitable for situations in the Third world.

Each nation or region had its own historical and cultural forces which shaped its past, and each responded to intervention
from external forces in a particular manner; therefore, each nation must implement policies for development which are in

harmony with its historical societal needs. To paraphrase Mao Tse-tung, "Every nation must ultimately find its own way and its specific design of society on the basis of its own economic, political, and cultural preconditions" (Hedebro, p. 88).

Second, socialist leaders did not get the co-operation of the large numbers across various socio-economic classes. In some countries, corruption was rampant among some governmental personnel; wealth was being consolidated in the hands of a few; and political stability was often being threatened by military takeovers. These new so-called socialist strategies were quite similar to early Western developmental strategies. "Both call for political and economic centralization, industrialization, and urbanization as major factors of development" (DeWalt 1983, p. 17).

Lastly, socialist theorists were too utopian in their views and gave little attention to technical know-how. Staatz and Eicher 1986, p. 52) noted that shortcomings especially in the area of agriculture included:

> Abstract theorizing, inadequate attention to the need for technical change in agriculture, lack of attention to the biological and location-specific nature of agricultural production processes, and lack of a solid micro foundation based on empirical research at the farm and village level.

Determining how to actually carry out the various idealistic aspects of a socialist approach can be frustrating to some nations. Many nations have inappropriately applied socialistic perspectives. For example, Uganda, under Idi Amin, felt that self-reliance should mean the dissolution of all ties with former exploiters of their nations. On the contrary, nations should apply a selective approach in deciding which socio-economic bonds will remain and which need to be broken. In addition, a country should not focus entirely on appropriate technology, instead as Hedebro (p. 109) explained, "In many cases, large-scale technology is necessary to produce the goods and infrastructures needed to make production with appropriate technology effective."

Participation is necessary if developmental projects are to be successful. Nations claim that they desire participation and exchange of information, but they do not often provide the channels by which this type of communication can easily move through. The channels do not have to always be mass media. In media-poor countries, alternative channels could be local forums or mass letter writing campaigns. Moreover, in some countries as the Philippines under President Marcos, some mass media systems work to the detriment of positive developmental goals. The mass media do not offer opportunities for the sharing of ideas and seek to discourage increase in participation. In order to bring about a society in which everyone can contribute, governments should allow for greater discussion of ideas; media should serve as a forum and a mediator of ideas between the people and the government; and most of all, the media should seek to provide knowledge, so that people can make the best possible decisions.

The final weakness I see with socialist models is in rural communication policies. While media technology may be reaching the rural areas under new socialist policies, the media content may not be relevant to the people in those areas. Socialist models must allow rural people the opportunity to help design media infrastructures in rural areas or at least provide the opportunity for program production by rural citizens.

Socialist models show the greatest potential for success. Yet many countries appear to be holding back with full implementation of such models. Perhaps, this is because of the apparent weaknesses of communication research in the area of development. Halloran (1980) commented that the reason why rate of accomplishment is often higher than in the case of top-down development by government; the cost to government, which often lacks sufficient resources in most poor countries, is much less and more likely to be affordable; and the nature of development activities is more flexible and more appropriate to changing local needs because of the decentralization of planning, decision- making, and execution.

Tanzania was formed in 1964 as a union between the mainland country of Tanzanyika and the island of Zanzibar. Tanzania's socialist philosophy is one of African socialism which is based on cooperative efforts and rural development, social change by means of mobilization of the people for self-reliance, and political democratic processes. Former President Julius K. Nyerere stated, "If development is to benefit the people, the people must participate in considering, planning, and implementing their development plans" (In Tanganyika African National Union, 1971).

The nation's communication strategy has been to combine mass media messages, by means of radio, with local radio group forums. The most famous media campaign in Tanzania was the 1973 "Man Is Health" campaign. The object of the campaign was to increase health and hygiene awareness. The campaign involved about 2 million people. Surveys were made in certain villages before and after the campaign. The results showed that on the average each household in the entire sample improved their health environment (Hall and Dodds 1974). The campaign resulted in a gain in knowledge about vital health practices among the participants. When compared to the knowledge of control groups, their increase was about 20 per cent higher.

The media campaign was successful for a number of reasons. First, there was cooperation among various governmental bodies. Since independence the government has compiled information on how to implement successful media campaign. Second, the campaign was able to create enthusiasm and support on the part of the participants. Third, the government was instrumental in creating and sustaining local-level support. Lastly, the campaign approach had a clearly stated theme and time period for the mobilization.

These countries have had successes in implementing their respective socialist philosophies. Hedebro pointed out that these represented alternatives to the Western views of development and that the differences lie in several areas.

1.   The media themselves are not seen as independent factors for social change. Instead, they are used, where appropriate, to contribute to the fulfillment of development objectives that are formulated for the society as a whole.

2.   China and Tanzania coordinate their various development efforts more than countries following a Western model.

3.   Channels of information are to a much greater extent built up in such a way that messages may flow in both direction, vertically between leaders and population and horizontally between individuals and groups at similar levels in the social stratification system.

In summary Teharanian (1980) pointed out that modernization models have had two sets of consequences for international and intercultural communication. First, communication has promoted values and systems which are bureaucratic and technologically oriented. Secondly, these orientations have created international dependency and domestic civil strifes. In other words, early perspectives of the dominant (Western) paradigm have caused media to become dysfunctional. But, if implemented into the development scheme properly by means of verified socialist approaches media can play a positive role in bringing about economic, political and social changes.

4

BEYOND OUTMODED
PLANNING

As I write these lines there is before me a cutting of this day's letter to the Editor in the Times of India titled: "Nehru Irrelevant" and in part, the question is asked "as to why all Nehru gifts' are no longer relevant in the 44th year our independence?" The answer is very simple which I expound in Chapter 5 on "Beyond Stagnant Development". Nobody has anything against Nehru. It is just that like all business or economic cycles the Nehru-Mahalnobis Planning and Developmental paradigm has run its course, and all institutions and formulations of this paradigm *are on a downswing. The situation is crying out loud for injection of a new "techno-economic" paradigm.* And the burden of this book is that this injection has to be of the new communication systems which would make *the Information Resource central to the deveolpment process.*

In a nutshell, the 40 years old Plan frame itself must now change. Central to the First Industrial Nehruvian-Mahalnobis model has been Energy and the long haul of materials. This has to be replaced by centrality of Information. The microchip has to replace oil.

The past 40 years of Development model itself could not have been possible without just one single resource, namely the "Transport Corridor". Thanks to the British we had a vast system of railways and highways, which we rightly expanded in the last 40 years. But we now urgently neeed a new *pathway:* an "Information Corridor" along which a decentralised, spatially dispersed, rurally preserved politico-economy can be developed. The Planning process has to be completely revamped to be sensitive to these new and urgent demands.

The situation also demands a shift from mass communication to class communication. By class we do not mean restoration of caste, or eliteism or high brow culture, but for want of a better word it means that the mass communication era of blaring to everyone and therefore to no one, or blaring to "whomever it may concern" or addressing to an unseen anonymous mob, is most certainly over. Its continance will get us neither communication nor development. "Class" communication means small, segmented, specific, homogenous targets.

And it so happens that the advances in technology are on our side. The Communication technology revolution with the ushering in of the microchip, semiconductors, computers, digital telecommunication, optics, lasers etc make possible:

> distributed information
> feedback and interactivity
> demassification

I treat this in detail in Chapter 8 "Beyond Appropriate Technology."

All these changes in the techno-economic situation, the socio-cultural disposition, the upward mobility of millions and the downward movement of even more millions, the end of the Energy era and *the urgent need to mobilise the Information era* require an altogether new approach to Planning, a totally different Plan frame and an altogether new tribe of Planners. Where are the Planners to be found?

The very planning for the Communication-Information sector shows up the tremendous inadequacies of our approach to planning and of our tools of planning. These are over four decades old and totally irrelevant to emergent problems.

First of all, the Nehru-Mahalnobis approach is the opposite of what we need now. Mahalnobis' two sector model basically desired to catapult India into the heavy industrial mode of the First Industrial revolution and it admirably succeeded in it. Now, at the present point of growth, the very input which was nectar, is veritable poison. Heavy industry or even concentrated industry is now a kind of diyanasor which will only lead to destruction—to unemployment, adverse balance of payments, high ICOR, low productivity, high use of scarce energy and unnecessary waste of transport potential. What we need now on the contrary is decentralised industry in batch-production mode to exponentially increase employment, drastically lower ICOR, use of much less energy, transport and capital and need to optimise use of local materials.

Secondly, Nehru's era was all right for recourse to Keynesian economics great reliance on government spending. Now the private sector has come very much into its own, so we should not stifle the market economy, but rather give it support and direction to multiply assets fast.

Thirdly, the models used like Leontiff are self-defeating. They neither allow *innovation* nor *leap-frogging*, but only result in mechanical, historical projections of the depressed, chaotic and stifled growth of the past. We, therefore, end up doing more of the same, and are not able to get out of the rut so as to *get into a higher orbit of economic functioning*. We must use new forms of econometric tools and methods which have built-in use of latest scientific knowledge, technological upgradation, innovation and leapfrogging. Planning for Communication- Information demands this approach as a must; otherwise we simply cannot get into the rhythm of telecommunication, computers, electronics and networks—which indeed we are not doing, because *we are bogged down by the traditional sectors* and traditional approaches.

Technological upgradation is possible only with knowledge and this in turn needs not only information, but assimilation of information. We are exporting all our scientific and technological skills and are left only with technological backwardness, though we shed tears for the brain drain.

Finally, the call of the present is "Think globally, act locally." We are doing neither. We are certainly not part of the global information culture because we have shut ourselves out from these influences and possibilities. And we are certainly *not* acting locally, because institution-building is conspicuous by its absence.

Communication-Information sector forces us to think and plan differently-radically-different-from what we have been doing these past 3 or 4 decades.

If we desire growth in the Communication-Information sector, we have to be conscious of paradigm shifts in the concept of this sector's relevance to Indian needs. Upto the 1960's, the dominant paradigm treated this sector essentially as publicity, diffusing information and providing public relations. The 1970's and 1980's have seen it emerge as a basic *infrastructure* almost on par with Transport and Energy. Form the 1990's it is imperative that we move forward and recognise Communication-Information as a major *economic resource* and the core of national planning and development.

This concept will become clear from a number of illustrations. Firstly, any production can be considered to consist of three inputs: (a) Materials (including Transportation); (b) Energy; and (c) Information. What is being suggested here is that on the long wave Kondratiev curve we (developed as well as developing countries) are at the end of the Energy-intensive paradigm. To save Energy, Materials and Transport, therefore, we need a shift in techno-economic paradigm to Information intensity.

The second illustration is that the Services sector in India is as high as 53% (of the GNP). However, it is probably not as productive as it could be because it represents largely (a) Wealth of urban 150 million upwardly mobile; (b) Government and public sector salaries and cost.

If a shift in services could be made to (a) Communication-Information, (b) Rural areas, it would become a tremendous growth sector for allieviating poverty and unemployment.

A good model to keep in front of us is the U.S.A.,where 40% of GNP and 50% of the workforce relate to Information sector and the projection is that in a decade 70% of total workforce in U.S. will be engaged in Information industry. Major exports, almost 30%, are in this sector, India is at a stage of economic growth where it could leapfrog into the Information Age.

Another vital economic factor to bear in mind is that it is only through Information that we can make a shift to decentralised manufacturing. In India, we must immediately leapfrog from the First Industrial mode to the Second. That is from (a) Mechanical Engineering to Information Systems; (b) Mass Production to Flexible Specialisation; and (c) economics of scale to economics of scope.

Microelectronics through its impact of storage, retrieval and access of information has the characteristics of the "key factor" which is generally associated with a technical or organizational breakthrough.

This new techno-economic paradigm will have an important impact on the concepts of industrialization, import substitution as well as export promotion for a developing economy.

The cheaper information handling potential through microelectronics and digital telecommunications indicates a trend towards information intensity rather than energy and material intensity in production. It would introduce flexibility into manufacturing systems, decentralize organizational networks and will represent a quantum jump in potential productivity for small and medium batch production by making plant scale relatively independent of the market size.

It is therefore necessary for India, which is uniquely placed in terms of skills and resources, to plan its future strategy keeping in mind the multifarious impacts of this new technology that impinges not only on the industrial sector but also on the socio-institutional mechnisms and other behavioral areas.

It is imperative that we must take congnizance of this Information technology at this juncture and look for a comprehensive plan for the economy *which would model Information in the development process.* In outlining the role of the government, the public sector, and the private sector, the model would provide alternatives for an over-all growth with reduction in the skewness of the distribution of the fruits of growth.

For this reason, the development of Information Economics as a discipline and of Information Economic Modelling as a major Project are necessities of the future. At this point, it will be relevant to provide a conceptual framework before proceeding with this discussion.

Theoretical Frame

Two Professors, Peore & Sable at MIT in their book "Second Industrial Divide," suggest that we are now at a divide when a shift will have to be made from the assembly line and mass production mode to decentralised, batch-production mode using Information Technology. A shift that is, from mass production to flexible specialisation. They are talking essentially, or rather solely, for the developed world. However, an Argentinian lady, Carlota Perez, who is Economic Adviser to her Government and extremely capable, in several papers on "Microelectronics, Long waves and World Structural change" argues that this paradigm shift applies even more to the developing world. We are at the end of the Kondratieve curve and Developing countries must now shift investments from energy-materials intensity programmes to Information intensive programmes. Prof A.S. Bhalla, an Indian Economist working at I.L.O. writing on "Microelectronics and small scale industry" argues that

developing countries have wrongly ignored rural and small
scale industries, which are treated peripherally and as an exotic
and not central to the Development model. He would like to
see this happen. Finally, Prof. Christopher Freeman at Sussex
University, England in his extensive work on "The Diffusion of
Technical Innovation and changes of Techno- economic
paradigm" supports all the above points.

Nearer home, late Dr. Homi Bhabha, late Dr. Vikram Sarabhai
and Dr. M.S. Swaminathan have been of the view that Mahatma
Gandhi's village India can be achieved, albeit in a high- tech-
electronic-satellite mode. They conceived of a plan to set up
Agro-neuclear complexes all over India—particularly rural
India. Waste from the nuclear reactor was to be cycled through
fertilizer production and side by side there was to be agriculture
and small scale industry. Electronics was to be a special ancilliary industry. These complexes were to be connected via satellite communication. Information Technology is central to this
Bhabha-Sarabhai Rural India Plan.

Unfortunately the modalities of all these theoretical ideas
have not been worked out, because in the past seven plans we
have stuck closely to high Energy-Capital Materials intensity
model. It is for consideration, that whereas many developing
countries might not be at an appropriate "stage of economic
growth", but India for a variety of reasons is at a point where
a shift can be made now from Materials- Capital- Energy intensity to Information intensity for decentralised industry, agriculture and services development. How this is to be actually
achieved is what the Steering Committees and Working Groups
should consider in our Planning process and mechanisms.

Definitions

A word needs to said about definitions. The word Communication in this book does not stand for telecommunications
alone. Telecommunications undoubtedly is the crucial link. But
we now know from developmental experience that no single
Communication technology can achieve any worthwhile results.
What is needed for any developmental objective, is a "package"
of technology channels. Therefore, the crucial requirement now
is the adquate meshing of Communication technologies as for
exmple, Telecommunications, Sound Broadcasting, Television,

Computer systems and data banks, satellite communication, Electronic industry (as support), marketing and advertising channels, Film, Extension services—the list is extremely large. All these channels taken in holistic term can be called Information Technology, (with Telecommunications of course, as something which links all of them).

Emerging out of the above conceptual framework a totally different approach to Communication-Information sector is suggested for the future in India. In the past seven plans it has been sector-based. It is suggested that from the 8th Plan it should be *Problem-based*.

And first of all we should address ourselves to those problems which have emerged as *chronic syndromes* from the experience of the last seven Plans. For example, it will be grossly wrong to assume that the endemic problem of poverty and unemployment of the 600 million (soon to become 8000 million) will be solved simply by having a free market economy. Therefore, the first challenge to the Communication-Information sector from the 8th Plan onward is eradication of poverty and unemployment.

Here the first consideration obviously is to be given to Agriculture, which sector presents an alarming picture; (a) Agriculture in all ways is on a down-swing; (b) Supporting infrastructure of Irrigation, soil fertilisers has serious problems; (c) 70% of our Agriculture is dry farming which badly needs some literacy skills in the farmer; and (d) Actual percentage of rural literacy is doing down.

One whole large area of concern therefore, is how can the Communication-Information sector from the 8th Plan onwards take up some of the burdens of the Agriculture sector?

As we enter the 8th Plan, the economic scene presents a picture in which the close relationship which has existed between Industry and Agriculture in the last 7 Plans, is no longer tenable. That is, Industry seems to be coming into own and now will not be so much dependent on Agriculture. However, it cannot be said that we are attaining Industrial output which actually we are capable of. Here some of the questions which rightfully can be approached by Communication-Information are the following:

(1) One of the very serious drawbacks of the present industrial scene is the pathetic state of the capital goods industry and that despite the fact that we started off our Planning process, three decades ago with a remarkable manufacturing capacity. The debacle has been largely due to the fact that we have not built up any design-capacity. It is for consideration whether our policy of industrial liberalisation will not further reduce our R&D capability land in turn nullify whatever little design capability we have.

It is for consideration therefore, that instead of indiscriminately going in for capital goods imports, we make a basic change in industrial policy and shift to decentralised batch production using Information Technology to help decentralisation. The concepts of khadi, Village Industries, District level industries, small scale industries are no longer tenable in their present archaic and essentially peripheral role to the main industrial thrust. They have to get a new incarnation in a high-technology mode and a new industrial thrust ought to make these small, decentralised units the basic thrust areas, just as the large centralised public sector ones have been in the 7 Plans so far. *Information Technology is central to this paradigm shift in industrial production as well as manufacturing.*

Obviously, the above suggested secnario has vast implications for employment which will grow expoentially. Information Technology can play a key role in technology upgradation of existing capacities. An extremely serious problem in the industrial sector is the skewed manpower. While in the last 7 Plans the growth rate at best has averaged 4%, the skilled (i.e. high trained technology manpower) has grown at 14 to 15%. *The result has been exodus abroad of about 10% of the best high-tech manpower* (who in fact, paradoxically are more or less running the R&D establishment of a highly advanced country like U. S. A. albeit financed in training by us). *Indian industry on the other hand, is on the verge of almost total technological collapse because all that we are left with, is a maintenance skilled culture and a complete absence of design-skilled culture.* Here Information Technology could come to the rescue in a number of ways, which will be spelt out in the chapter on "Technology".

All the above factors are adding upto and contributing to an ever-rising ICOR and here also Information Technology can play a major role in raising productivity.

The decentralised-distributed manufacturing method through use of Information Technology, is really the only true and *durable* path to poverty alleviation. IRDP NREP etc. are non-durable paths.

Summing up, it is for consideration that a new investment plan be considered whereby some of what at present is going largely to (a) Capital goods imports (b) Poverty alleviation programmes, goes in larger meassure to a more durable invest-ment in *decentralised batch production manufacturing through Information Technology support.*

The one most important lesson we have learnt from the past 7 Five Year Plan, is that major investment has been in Capital, Materials and Energy-intensive sectors. The creation of in-frastructure is all right, but after a certain point this investment has been disastrous in creating huge industrial digansours, over-capitalisation in antiquated Technology and machinery, immen-sely long gestation periods, with consequent low returns and low rate of growth.

We are absolutely and certainly at a *DIVIDE* in our nations' development history, and therefore, in future Plans the macro economic aggregate must reflect a *paradigm- shift* from Capital-Materials-Energy intensity to *Information-intensity.* Because only Information- intensity can provide for *decentralised mode of production* in *batch-production mode-* realising Mahatma Gandhi's Village India, albeit in a Communication- Electronic-Computer-Satellite mode.

This new *pathway* apart from stopping migration from rural areas and arresting ecological destruction can create almost *full-employment.*

If we regard any production activity to have three major in-puts i.e. (a) Materials (which inculdes Transport) (b) Energy; and (c) Information then what we are stating is that from the 8th Plan, Materials capitalisation and Energy must be severely con-strained (in the public sector-these could be left to the private sector) and *the bulk of the investment should go into Information* to achieve decentralised, small-scale, batch production.

As it is, we know that small-scale industry is providing 40% of the growth in the industrial sector, not because of but in spite of, government policies. One can imagine therefore, the fillip to entrepreneurship, small-scale manufacturing and decentralised mode of batch production if Government comes up with this new policy from the 8th Plan and invests heavily in Information Technology in order to make it the handmaiden of decentralised, small-scale, batch production. The stress is on Information Technology because it is only this which will take care of problems of materials, prices, marketing, costs, export opportunities which the decentralised, small-scale industrial sector will require.

It is this *paradigm shift* in *public expenditure* to Information-intensive decentralised manufacturing which really could take care of the endemic problem of 600 million deprived in this country and not supply-side economics of which we are crying ourselves hoarse. This is because another clear message from the last 7 Plans is that there never has been any trickle-down effect. On the contrary, there is every evidence to show that there has throughout been a *trickle-up effect* in the sense that black money has found its way to Banks abroad. An IMF report has informed us that in one *overseas bank alone* the amount standing to the credit of businessmen is Rs. 1332 crores. There must be similar amounts in several banks.

Related very closely to the mode of industrial production is the *organisation of industrial production*. The past 7 Plans tell the story of abysmal administrative hurdles, horrifying shop-floor management and callous indifference to workmanship and quality.

The way to meet this challenge is not by trying to bring Management to the Administrator (That is not his job in the first place) but rather to *realign the structure of organisation*. This means changing vertical communication and reporting system to horizontal ones to create a sense of "peer" and "group" relationship and to diagonal communication flow for project-management mode. It is obvious that this can only be done by Information Technology to restructure organisations.

Recapitulating then, high ICOR is a very serious problem in the Indian economy. It is somewhat lower in Agriculture Sector, but is likely to get worse because of increasing cost of inputs. Information Technology can play a very vital role in lowering ICOR by raising productivity.

One of the lessons of the last 7 Plans is that Government has burdened itself with sectors which it must shed immediately to the market sector. Good examples are: Tourism, Hotel business, Airlines. Information Technology is definitely one of these very important sectors. There is no earthly reason why public expenditure should provide budgetary support for the Telecommunications, Electronics, Computer Systems, Data Banks, Educational Software and a great deal of broadcasting material.

One lesson from the last 7 Plans is that we have been mainly concerned with material resources to the neglect of utilising human resources, in which we are very rich. Information Technology has a crucial role in this usage.

We have been under the illusion in the last 7 Plans that the savings rate has been about 26%. Suddenly we find it is an error and it is considerably lower. In meeting this challenge of productivity Information Technology has to play the foremost role.

One lesson we have learn from the last 7 Plans is that resources are too thinly spread and become infructuous expenditure. In the 8th Plan there should be least or absolutely no expenditure on capital-intensive sectors, and maximum on labour-intensive and decentralised sectors like Information Technology.

Contribution from Direct taxes to national income has come down from 6% in 1975 to 1% in 1988. Information Technology could play a tremendous role in monitoring collection.

Foreign exchange situation has emerged as a major critical area after 7 plans. A global Information System for scanning and monitoring and information dissemination like MITI, Japan could be very helpful to foreign trade.

We have concentrated so far on Information Technology for agricultural and industrial purposes. But the *BEHAVIOURAL* role is equally important. The question which has not found a solution is; why has *diffusion of innovation* succeeded in the Agriculture Sector but not in the Social sector (which in a holistic way may be regarded to include Health, Family Welfare, Nutrition, Childcare, Women's literacy etc.). This is another lesson from the past 7 Plans which provides a challenge to Information Technology.

Finally, an institutional frame for Communication and Information Policy Analysis is required. At present Engineers control technology decisions, Economists do not quite appreciate the futuristic role of Information Technology and many areas of this sector are under general Administration. A totally new and innovative institutional arrangement is needed for scenario building, perspective planning and leap-frogging.

Why is Information Technology Uniquely and Specially Relevant for Economic take off in India?

There are several significant reasons: first and foremost is the nature of the *Technology* itself. It is highly labour-intensive, employs highly skilled labour as well as unskilled labour, both to our advantage. It can employ women, as well as partly, partially or superficially employed persons. Secondly the mix of capital investment is most suited to our economic conditions: (a) Value-added- Capital-less than 5%; (b) Value-added-Labour-90 to 95%. By changing the nature and organisation of industrial production, *Materials* demand is reduced. Less use of steel etc.

Information Technology is not only for information, motivation etc.; it is also an *Economic Resource*. It is the *Quartenary Sector*. (Capital cost of projects therefore, would go down with less demand on (a) Government budgtary support, (b) Financial institutions-IDBI etc. (c) Stock Market-capital bonds etc. It is a technology particularly lending itself to *entrepreneurship*. Many persons technically qualified could become entrepreneurs. This means less pressure on jobs and employment.

Information Technology with attendant electronifiction and less moving parts than mechanical engineering drastically reduces *energy*—which is now consuming one-third of Plan resources.

Pressure on Transportation will get drastically reduced-both air and trains. (As an example six full Air-buses Bombay- Delhi-Bombay would not be needed if speech and data communication between these cities were excellent). One decade of I.T.U. Geneva studies conclusively prove the inverse relationship of *Communication to Transportation*.

Information Technology can lead to *spatial spread* of activities. Now every activity whether industrial or commercial tends to get concentrated in the metropolitan and larger towns. Instead, these activities could be diversified in all areas of the country leading to more equitable income distribution.

Technology upgradation and technology education on a massive and continental scale can only be done through Communication Information System.

There is no reason why we should not have export *competitiveness* if we go in for this technology in a big way, because: (a) our technologists and scientists are excellent; (b) skilled manpower is amongst the best in the world, and (c) wages are the lowest; and (d) there is high value added in this technology. In fact, we should have an edge over China, because our industrial pattern is more diverse.

The ideal model for India to leapfrog is to have a mix of traditional and very advanced technologies. Amongst the very advanced would be Biotechnology, Information Technology and Material Sciences. We are on the wrong path in importing huge plants as we are doing now.

Huge opening up of the *private sector* is possible through ancilliary, components and subsystem manufacture. This however, requires massive entrepreneural planning.

In this Technology Hardware is 10%, Software is 90% of the operation. We are very strong in Software and in fact, could capture world Software market which is of the tune of US Dollars 1000 Billion per year. Our present share of this is practically negligible.

Poverty alleviation and Rural Development can be truly brought about by Information Technology. Our Agriculture can not sustain the growing rural population, because, as it is there is overcrowding and overcapitalisation in the Agricultural Sector. Information Technology can provide an escape route by creating avenues in the secondary and tertiary sectors.

The Growth Power in India's Tertiary Sector -- A New Factor in Developmental Planning

Finally, taking the figures of the year 1986-87 for the sake of example, we give below some arithematic to show the exponential rate at which the Tertiary sector is expanding in India. No systematic economic analysis has been made of this recent phenomenon, especially regarding its implications for the underprivileged. But in keeping with the thesis of this book, the question we raise is:

(a) What percentage of this expansion constitutes the Information-Communication sector. (In the US. for example out of the 60% contribution of services to GDP, 40% comes from the Information Sector).

(b) What steps need to be taken to increase exponentially the contribution of Information-Communication to this sector, and in turn to Rural Development. An exercise of that kind would constitute a true attempt at Communication Policy Planning.

Structural Changes in the Composition of India's GDP at Factor Cost

(1950-51 to 1984-85)

Sector	% Share in Total GDP				
	1950-51	1960-61	1970-71	1980-84	1984-85 Terminal Yr. of 6th Plan
1. Primary	59.61	55.14	48.46	41.62	38.08
2. Secondary	14.47	17.28	20.67	21.57	21.60
3. Tertiary	25.92	27.58	30.87	36.81	40.32
(a) Transport, Communication & Trade	11.89	13.80	16.09	18.83	19.73
(b) Finance & Real Estate	5.24	5.06	5.76	6.62	7.05
(c) Community & Personal Services	8.79	8.72	9.02	11.36	13.54

In 1986-87, there has been a spurt in the tertiary sector, arising particularly from the *high rate of qrowth of Govt. expenditure.*

It is agreed that except for very exceptional years, agricultural contribution to GDP will continue to decline, since in any case, the rate of growth is less than 3%, whereas Sixth Plan claimed for rate of Growth of agriculture and allied activities of about

4%. In the period of Seventh Plan, the overall rate of growth indicated (5.0%), can be achieved only by the high performance of the Tertiary Sector, reaching a rate of growth of contribution to GDP higher than that of agriculture and industry combined.

This inequality raises a major distribution problem. As agriculture and allied occuptions affect 3/4th of our population and industry contributes only 1/5 of GDP, *the fruit of the much higher growth in the Tertiary Sector will increasingly become the deciding factor as to what contributes to the welfare of the under-privileged.*

Another important price is more concerned with the distribution of income than employment and shows the spectacular growth of India's Tertiary Sector while agriculture has declined in its contribution of GDP, it is Tertiary Sector which has captured the whole of the agricultural loss.

At current prices, the share of primary sector has dropped to about a third from a figure nearly 55.14% in 1960-61 and 48.41% in 1970-71. The rise in current contribution is about 45%. It is pointed out that the contribution to growth at the current rates to each of the sectors are just 1% from agriculture and allied activities, 1% from industry, but well over 3% from Tertiary Occupations

Components of Growth Contribution to GDP 1986-87

Simple arithematic can be applied to the existing contribution of the primary, secondary & Tertiary Sectors to show the dominance of the Tertiary Sector, now and over the last ten years in particular.

If agriculture is advancing at 3% per year and accounts for about 1/3 of GDP, as its contribution to growth might be reckoned at 1% (1/3 X 3% = 1%).

By the same token, the Secondary sector which currently holds about (20% or) 1/5 as to contribution to GDP and whose average growth over the decade has been about 5%, too, will also be contributing only 1% (1/5 X 5 = 1%).

On the other hand with a current distribution of 45% (1986-87) if the Tertiary Sector rises at 8.5%, its contribution to GDP, Growth would be 3.8% (45/100 X 8.5).

In other words, if the growth in the current year should be 5.8% overall, about 65% of that growth would be coming from

Tertiary activity i.e. 2/3 of all growth. Estimates for the poor were introduced in the Fourth Five Year Plan. However, when it was realised that "the poor" did not form a homogeneous group and that the different sections of the poor faced different constraints, specific programmes for various sections of the poor were formulated.

Since industry's share has been nearly stationary over the last 15 years and agriculture is sharply declining, the higher growth of tertiary sector is analysed indicating that it constitutes perhaps 45% of GDP in 1986-87. It was over 40% in 1984-85, which was the terminal year of the Sixth Plan.

Planning and the Status of Women

Before closing our discussion on the role of Communication- Information in Planning we must take a look on how this impinges on the status of women in India. The approach of the Government to women's development is one of adhocism leading to marginal benefits. A chapter on women was included in the Sixth Plan which was followed by attempts to cover women under poverty alleviation programmes and the starting of a few new schemes. However, Government programmes designed for women have not been proportionate either to their needs or their numbers. As far as labouring women are concerned there has been no thrust to improve their lot by concerted efforts. This is in spite of the fact that the Seventh Five Year Plan document recognizes the plight of working women.

The strategy of direct attack on poverty was formulated in the early seventies and special programmes. There is a sharp decline in the share of Indian primary production in GDP from 1950-51 to 1984-85. This factor was known theoretically because of the lower rate of growth of agriculture as against industrial and tertiary occupation from 1950-51 onwards.

The major anti-proverty programmes included the IRDP (the Integrated Rural Development Programme), the DWCRA the Wage Employment Programmes, Special Area Development Programmes etc. All these programmes though well intentioned have not resulted in substantial benefits for women as is evident from their analysis.

IRDP : Data shows that the target of 30% of women beneficiaries has not been reached in the past few years. The percentage of female beneficiaries was 9.89 in 1985-86 and 15.13 in 1986- 87. The data shows that the overall impact of this programme was only marginal on rural women. Mere 3.03 lakh women beneficiaries in 1985-86 and 5.6 lakh in 1986-87 hardly touch the periphery of the unemployment problem of women. The studies on IRDP also show that the access of the poorest strata of women and of female headed households to IRDP was poor. A study in Kerala shows net decline in the income of 18% female beneficiaries, no change in the income of 13% beneficiaries and more than 30% increase in the case of only 4% beneficiaries. It is interesting to observe that men tend to dominate the decision making in IRDP schemes taken in the name of women.

The DWCRA has also had limited success. It has not resulted in the growth of women's organizing capabilties and leadership qualities.

The planning of the programme does not take adequate care of the different components of self-employment for example the programme does not provide for adequate training, for skill formation and for adequate qualitative and quantitative training in the areas of management including financial, marketing and overall management. It is observed by most of the DWCRA studies that the poorest women are usually left out from DWCRA groups and thus the programme was to serve the better off among the poorer or sometimes non-poor groups of women.

One major problem of planning for anti-poverty programmes for women is that there is an over emphasis on self- employment even for the women from the poorest families. These women are observed to be unwilling or incapable of taking up self-employment because

- They have low level of literacy and have meagre income of their own.
- They have poor risk-bearing capacity and a low level of enterprise.
- They have poor credit worthiness.
- They suffer from various socio-psychological constraints which come in the way of their taking up self-employment.

The second major problem with the designing of these programmes is regarding the inadequacy of these programmes to reach women. It is difficult to reach women because:

- The incidence of illiteracy is higher among women and they are less exposed to the outside world.
- They have a lower status in the family and in the society.
- Social norms prevent them from freely meeting male functionaries and because of these socio-psychological constraints, they are inhibited from taking up self-employment.

Unfortunately, the extension of the self-employment programmes, does not take care of all these aspects. No special attempts are made to remove these constraints in order to reach women. The general strategy of extension and implementation has a male bias which neglects the needs of women with the result that not many women come forward to take up self-employment. Unless the extension strategy is modified radically, poor women will not be helped much by anti-poverty programmes.

In addition, women also suffer because of the household approach of most self-employment programmes. The household approach identifies the head of the household—the man in most cases—as the main beneficiary. As the approach does not see the women of the household as an independent person or as a separate entity, it tends to ignore her claims as a beneficiary and consequently neglects her needs also. The male orientation of these programmes is reflected in the identification of the scheme, in the extension strategy and in the designing of the scheme.

The predominantly male ownership of family assets further restricts the access of women to self-employment, since they cannot take advantage of credit/loan schemes. Though it has been recommended that women should be provided bank loans upto a limit without any security. in reality banks ask for security. As women are not normally able to provide this, they find it difficult to get loans for self-employment.

There are also problems regarding the planning component of these programmes. These relate mainly to the identification of schemes for women providing support in the areas of technology and training and planning for purchase of inputs and marketing of goods. Some of the studies in this area show that weak planning and adhocism in the approach considerably limit the success of the programmes.

Lastly there are problems arising from the indifference of the concerned authorities towards women's needs. This indifference is reflected in the low priority given to women's programmes and in the lack of involvement of the machinery in carrying out these programmes. The planning and implementation of these programmes therefore, lack the required commitment. The programmes are also scattered and spread thinly with the result that they do not make much impact on the economy. The absence of a separate place for women in most programmes, poor monitoring and almost total absence of official evaluation studies of the impact of these programmes on women will indicate the indifference as well as the weak planning and monitoring of these programmes.

All these problems of Planning for women present a challenge to Communication media and Information Technology which we have hardly paid any attention to.

5

BEYOND STAGNANT
DEVELOPMENT

After four decades of planned development effort, when in every way, our country is at a *DIVIDE*, two major trends are discernible. One are of those persuasion, you might call them neo-Gandhians, who see everything vicious, degarding, exploitive and destructive in the Nehruvian- Mahalnobis model which heralded massive industrial strength, centralisation and maximum use of materials and energy. The neo-Gandhians want to revert to a simpler way of life, in fact, to a romantic pastoral quality with overtones of Thoreau's Walden Pond, Tolstoy's baking bread with his own hands, and Rousseau's Noble Savage. We read it every day in the press: they want decentralisation, small-scale industry, Panchayati Raj — in fact, a complete dismantling of the superstructure.

Those of the other persuasion, largely from Leftist philosophies — want to protect Nehru's dream of a mighty Public Sector and self-reliance.

Both views are purely idological and idiosyncratic and miss what is the essential quality of any philosophical postulation: *a central concept* which encompasses, explains and justifies the myriads of ramifications.

And it is this argument which brings us to the main thesis of the book: the proposed centrality of Information in Development.

As has been stressed again and again in this book: the paramount characteristic of the techno-economic paradigm based on *MICROELECTRONICS* is that in the development process it enables a shift from Energy and Materials intensity to *INFORMATION INTENSITY*. This stems mainly from the very visible change in the general relative cost structure towards ever cheaper information handling potential through *microelectronics* and *digital communications*.

The decreasing cost and growing potential of microelectronics results in an increasing relative jump into the future.

That is why it can provide a *radical shift* in engineering and managerial "common sense" for most profitable production. For example, whereas the assembly line was based on the constant repetition of the same sequence of movements, Information Technology is based on a system of feedback loops for the *optimization of the most diverse and changing activities*. This is a modern way of putting what the back-to-the-village wallahs are stating, albiet in archaic, discarded, impractical language.

At this point the question which some Economic pundits, particularly Western, might raise is: but are developing countries ready for the injection of these new technologies? Are they at the appropriate stage of economic growth? Can they integrate such a techno-economic shift in their development process?

I do not know about other developing countries, but on all counts, the answer for India is an emphatic "YES". Since the overreaching is now at its relatively early stage, it is possible to attempt *a direct entry* without going through the technological stages it leaves behind. Meaning thereby: we need not replicate the whole Industrial Revolution of Europe, destroy our villages, create unliveable megalopolisis and surrender to a lifestyle which encourages debilitation, defilement, nervous wreckage and suicide.

The above technoeconomic innovation is being advocated because the new technologies allow "leapfrogging" for some of the countries which do not carry the inertia of the previous industrial structure. And in any case we have already proved our national capacity for leapfrogging in such difficult areas as Atomic Energy and Space technologies.

Finally, a word of warning: the risk for a country like India of "missing the boat." The changes projected above will not fall from the heavens. They require deliberate action at the political, planning technological and administrative levels in order to alter the course of direction at this DIVIDE— and start points of new organization and skills for the future.

It is here where typical developing country governments might miss the opportunity's opened by the transition, *under the weight of inertia resulting from past economic, industrial and political deadweight* and also of course, from a complete failure to understand the tremendous "change and growth" possibilities of the new paradigm. In a word, to close on a political note, we need a new incarnation of Nehru and a new incarnation of Mahalnobis for India at this point of time in the 1990s— can we scan the horizon for these? Are they visible?

I now deal with the substantive discussion on the proposed new developmental paradigm in two parts:

(a) First I present a fairly extensive theoretical critique of the postulation.

(b) and then by way of illustrating the theory in practice I give details of the PRATO experience in Italy.

Prato consists of thousands of textile looms in Italy, as traditional and as primitive as in India. The Italians could have dismantled these, and put up massive textile mills. Instead, the Italian public sector intervened, retained the traditional looms, but by networking through Information Technology both internally and globally have succeeded in making Italy the largest exporters of garments in the world. Nothing could be more pertinent or illustrative to the Indian situation.

As we have entered the 1990s — precisely after four decades of planned development effort in India, there could not be greater disillusionment, bitterness, disenchantment and revulsion against the Development process we have followed these 40 years. Although India has emerged strong in many ways, there is the undeniable feeling of distress and dismay, of development having highjacked the common man, highjacked everything that is human—human resources, human want human needs, humanity itself. And there is a widespread demand that the approach to development and planning and our concern for the common man be changed drastically and immediately.

Similarly, the story of Developmental Communication in particular and of Mass Communication in general is no different. It is being asked: what has Mass Communication achieved these past 40 years in India? Unfortunately, because we have followed the British tradition, the Sociology of Communication has not got established as a discipline and therefore, there is no body of higher learning in this field. There is no systematic research, no data, no insights, no ideas and no projections into the future nurtured by thought and wisdom as to what are the societal effects of Communication in India.

The stray Communication research here and there is of no avail. We want to treat Communication as the fourth pillar, which along with the Legislature, Executive and Judiciary upholds society. And what we desperately need is macro Policy research, that is conceptualisation of research in terms of structure of society, social and industrial organisation, professionalisation, the whole area of mass motivation leading to socialisation.

Although as we noted above, systematic work at this level of high scholastic learning is not established in these areas, yet by putting together patches and fragments of knowledge which we have, the picture that emerges is one of utter dismay and despair.

In my earlier book "Communication, Growth and Public Policy" based on chapter and verse, fact and figures, I showed that in the past decades of development the role of Communication in the areas of Education and Rural Development has been minimal if not zero.

Since then, as a result of the findings of voluntary agencies and some surveys of the Programme Evaluation Organisation of the Planning Commission the picture that emerges is that the whole area of Social Communication is one big Zero — in this can be included women's literacy, mother and child care, health, family planning, nutrition, adult literacy etc — to the extent that the Government of India have now felt it necessary to declare officially that the Family Planning programme has been an unqualified disaster.

This is the time and place to point out that success in the Green Revolution in Agriculture *has nothing whatsoever to do with Mass Communication*. First and foremost the crucial factor in this agricultural miracle is the tremendous infrastructure created by Government: canals, tubewells, fertilizer plants, tractorisation, arrangements for direct loans to the farmer, pesticides, availability of know-how from Agricultural Universities patterned after the Land-grant Universities of U.S.A. The second factor is the tremendous role of the farmer — even if illiterate, his wisdom, cunning and courage to take big risks in the high disequilibrium economics of agriculture — by willing to invest in new techniques and technologies. Economists therefore, have termed this as a case of "adaptive" behaviour — as distinct from "adoption" of new values — it is only adaptation to the high uncertainity and risk of agricultural disequilibrium. There is no credit to Communications here and certainly none whatsoever to mass communication, nor any mumbo-jumbo of diffusion of innovations theory, nor "adoption" of new values and attitudes. *It is purely an economic act of a risk-taking farmer "adapting" himself to the high disequilibrium economics of agriculture.*

The true development of India starts with the National movement—with the models thrown up by Mahatma Gandhi, Gurudev Tagore and the galaxy of stars on India's renaissance firmament.

Let us go to the fresh waters of Gandhian Economics and read what J.C. Kumarappa after a lifetime spent at the Wardha Ashram, has to tell us. Let us go back to the Indian village with him and not Washington D.C. to get money from the I.M.F. Let us also go to the clear waters of Gurudev Tagore's thoughts and visit Shantiniketan and Sriniketan, where Gurudev started work in Rural Reconstruction long before Gandhiji came on the scene. Let us also not forget the great mystic, scholar and art—historian, Ananda Coomaraswamy, and his visionary insights into the ancient arts and crafts of India.

Actually all these great mystic-leaders of the Indian Renaissance were saying one and the same thing.

(1) They rejected modern industrialism—ruthless as it is in its exploitativeness, aggressiveness, bigotry, violence and utter destructiveness.

(2) The "machine" they were prepared to accept but only in terms of the great spiritual, metaphysical and artistic tradition of India.

(3) The most important task was the revival of India's self-respect through rehabilitation of her great philosophies and religions and experiments in sociology and creations of art.

(4) For this purpose they had to build institutions— basically ASHRAMS, forest, hermitages— embodying the principle of Tantric Mandalas which arrested dissipation of spiritual energy by keeping it within the confines of the bounded circle.

These great sages and savants of India threw up models for every aspect of life and thought-economic development, education, health, medicine, art—and the one strain common to all was the blending of ancient metaphysics and modern thought.

So virile and powerful was the influence of their thought that discerning Europeans and Americans fell at their feet in support and service. An American, Elmherst gave his money, property, life-service to Gurudev's SRINIKETAN. C.F. Andrews, the Jesuit priest who was Principal of St. Stephen's College, Delhi, renounced his job, thereafter to act constantly as an emissary between the Mahatma and Gurudev. Annie Besant truly had her nine lives and amongst the other incredible things she achieved, she helped Pandit Madan Mohan Malaviyaji to create the Benares Hindu University at Benares. Mr. Arundale, the Englishman, gave all he had to help the talented dancer, his wife Rukmini to found the KALAKSHETRA at Madras.

The list is endless. The one prominent thread in these efforts is that they sought to create a new modern India, but on her deepest roots and grassroots. Naturally the village was the centre of the creative effort, because the continuity of India's village integrity in its arts and crafts, living and achieving, social structure and religious belief, ecological integrity and economic self-sufficiency traced back to centuries of unbroken and unprecedented historicity. This was the true base of India's economic development.

Although these leaders had great hopes that they would be able to synthesise successfully the thoughts of the East and the science of the West, in the end, their dreams were shattered. Gandhiji wrote in HIND SWARAJ that industrialism was unalloyed exploitation, misery and deprivation. And although Gurudev had been much more optimistic, towards the end of his years, as World War II broke out and Hitler marched all over Europe with his mass killings, he wrote CRISIS IN CIVILIZATION and openly confessed that his faith in Western civilization was gone; *if there were to be any renewal in the future its winds would blow from the East.*

It must be recorded that the Indian renaissance was superior in spirit and thought to any other in that era. The best that Mao could come up with was Marx, and here he was back to the neurosis of industrial Europe. In Europe on the other hand, idealism expressed itself in the form of the Frankfurt School of

Critical Theory with Habermas, Erich Fromm and others. But the neo-Fruedian and neo-Marxist view was that psychological repression in modern man was in fact, the outcome of suppression in the social order, which was what Marxian thought was all about. But nothing earth-shaking has come out of this view; capitalism at any rate is wholly unscathed by it. As far as the Far Eastern countries are concerned: Korea, Taiwan, Japan, Hongkong, Singapore, which the World Bank holds up as ideals to the Third World, these do not even merit comment. Just to be able to manufacture a motor car cheaper than what the Americans are able to do, is not even meritorious, far from being inspiring. The role of the East is not to be able to compete with the West in cheapness and inanity. Its primary mission must needs be a civilizing one—one which is an education to the West. No such prophecy of wisdom has come from these so-called NIC's Newly Industrialised Countries — theirs is only a celebration of vulgar imitation and corroding cheapness. India's mission can never be on these lines of frenzy and extrovert consciousness bent on competitiveness for illusiory ends.

And then came along Jawaharlal Nehru. In a recent issue, the *Times of India* reproduced copies of two letters which Mahatma Gandhi had written to Nehru a little before Gandhiji's death. It stated that Gandhiji first sent the letters in Hindi and later copies in English, presuming that Nehru might take them more seriously if these were written in English.

The sum and substance of the letters were: Gandhiji urged Nehru that, now that India had gained independence, the Government's policies ought to be such *that they focus on Village India*. The *Times of India* article comments that Nehru was infuriated and just could not understand the Mahatma's obsession with Village India.

Nehru's conception of developing India was totally different. He was in a hurry to transform it into a modern, powerful, prosperous state. The seeds of his inspiration went back to the days of Fabian Socialism in England, when Laski was at the London School of Economics, George Bernard Shaw was very much alive and kicking and the Webbs-Sydney and Beatrice-were around. This was also the period when Keynes was coming into his own. The post World War I period relied heavily on Keynesian economics, because there was no alternative to revive shattered European economies except by heavy doses of investment by the State.

This was precisely the model Nehru followed and the person who was responsible in bringing it to fruition was the genius Mahalnobis who was Physicist turned Statistician turned Planner and Economist. It is really Mahalnobis' two- sector model, which we implemented from the Second Five Year Plan onward, which has made India the very "powerful" country it has become today. Basically the model consisted of heavy investments of technology and money into Public Sector Heavy Industry. But also associated with this were large investments in Science and Technology, Research and Development and not least of all heavy investments in technical educational establishments like Medical Colleges and Institutes of Technology, which have been instrumental in making India produce the third largest manpower of scientists and technologists in the world after the U.S.A. and U.S.S.R.

This is also understandable on the long wave Kondratiev curve. In 1947, India could hardly produce anything either in industry or agriculture. As is required in this model, heavy investment into technological innovation was made in 1948 and in four decades it has made India a power to reckon with in the world.

The spin-offs of the Nehru-Mahalnobis model are staggering. From a country of no consequence in 1947, India today is an industrial power to reckon with. This achievement is the direct result of this model. To begin with: India is an industrial giant.

The model emphasised an incredibly large public sector industry. Out of this has emerged an exceedingly large private industrial sector. Built into the model was a component of Science and Technology and another of Technical manpower training, the Indian Institutes of Technology and Engineering Colleges and CSIR Laboratories and Agricultural Universities. Our R&D establishments have put India on the world map of Atomic Energy, Space and other frontier sciences. India is amongst the first ten industrialised nations; it has the fourth largest armed forces in the world; it has the second largest manpower of Agricultural Scientists incidentally next to U.S.S.R; U.S.A. is number three in order. Its savings rate is one of the highest in the world: 26% and upward social mobility has led to the emergence of a middle class of 150 to 200 million people.

The above is the positive side of the model, but there is also the negative side. The model is totally skewed; it puts everything upside down. India is still one of the poorest countries of the world; more than half of its population is below the poverty line—wtih people going hungry. This is sin against man. Village life—its arts and crafts and economy, which were sacred to the Mahatma and Gurudev and Dr. Coomaraswamy, are in advanced stages of destruction. The country has lost its sense of heritage, vision and civilizing mission. Voilence is rampant everywhere. Development has in fact, meant the destruction of all values and the letting loose of unbriddled corruption and manipulation. The model is skewed against the rural areas, against the poor and common man, against grass roots economy and against the roots of culture. The culture and the arts which have their roots in the soil are also languishing. The India of the National movement, of the great Renaissance which the Indian struggle heralded, is totally dead. It is a country without vision, caught in internecine warfare, corruption, manipulation, militarism, bureaucratic ineptness and evil-mindedness and finally political fiendishness. All of it certainly a far far cry from what Mahatma Gandhi, Gurudev Tagore, Lokmanya Tilak and all the great Nationalists gave their life for.

In more conceptual terms the present Indian dilemma can be stated as follows: Models of capitalism can be applied to India, because what we have in India is State capitalism. Business cycles are common in capitalist economics and Schumpeter suggests long wave trade cycles of 40 to 60 years. Typically therefore, what has happened in India is that on the Kondratiev curve, with the passage of four decades, the innovation injected by the Nehru- Mahalnobis model in the form of heavy dosage of heavy industry in the public sector, *has petered out and all the institutions created to implement that model, whether scientific, economic, policy-level or administrative, are in advanced stages of decline and decay*. Nobody at policy planning or political level is willing to face up to this essential reality either out of utter ignorance or utter deceit. Instead, homilies are constantly made regarding the need for efficiency, hard work and productivity.

This is simply a lot of nonsense, because there is nothing wrong with the hard work and productivity of the Indian people. *In fact, they are the most intelligent, the most resourceful and most hardworking of any in the world and this is porved when Indians are given a chance outside their own land.*

What is critically needed at this point of time are not useless homilies but, as Jawaharlal Nehru did; fresh injections of innovations into the politico-socio-economic system. An innovation invariably implies a shift in the techno-economic paradigm. And what we argue here is that there ought to be an immediate paradigm shift from the heavy industry public sector techno-economic model *to one in which Information Technology with attendant decentralised modes of production has the central place.*

Here we take note of four scholarly references.

The first reference I wish to give is of the work of two Professors— Peore and Sabel-Political Scientists at MIT. They have written a book "Second Industrial Divide." As the title suggests: what the authors are stating is that we are at a divide—the divide which brings to an end the First Industrial Revolution of the West and now the Second era starts which takes us into the decentralised, Informatics mode in which we are back into more or less a cottage industry mode, except that it is a high-tech mode. Peore and Sabel then go on to describe various countries as case studies and the role of Numerical Control Machines in the new "Second" era economy. The critical difference is a paradigm shift from "mass production" of the First Revolution to "flexible specialisation" of the Second.

This process also implies another fundamental change from the First Industrial mode—the hardware is not changed; only the computer software is changed. Which means that the same machine can perform many functions and can be utilised for several totally different tasks.

This is where the second reference comes in, and it is very pertinent. An Indian Economist, Prof. A.S. Bhalla has been working on this theme at the ILO, Geneva. An article of his appeared in the issue of the *Political and Economic Weekly*. It was titled: "Micro-electronics and small scale industries" Bhalla makes the poignant point that in their grandiose plans, developing countries typically ignore small-scale industries. This is certainly true of our planning in India. The macro-economic aggregate modelling which has the imprint of Nehru-Mahalnobis genius, has throughout concentrated on heavy investments in the heavy public sector industry. Small scale industries are avante- gard, at the fringe of the model; frankly quite outside the model. For this reason, village industries, Khadi and small-scale industries, which were the flesh and blood of Indian economy envisaged by Mahatma Gandhi, Gurudev Tagore, and all others in the National movement, have become the real victims of the model we have now followed for four decades.

Prof. A.S. Bhalla is quite right in his assessment: the strategies of industrial development in the Third World have very rarely given a prominent place to rural or small-scale industrialisation. As we have seen the Mahalnobis model's main emphasis was on heavy industry. Also it keeps the very large majority of people in the rural areas outside the scope of productive work. a paradigm shift is now needed *from "mass production" to "production by the masses"* and the chief enabling technology is Information Technology.

Prof. Bhalla is also absolutely correct in stating that rural or small-scale industrialisation has been considered independently of the overall industrial strategy. The consequence therefore, has been that the District Industries Centres which were to have given industrial initiative at the district level have languished. Gandhiji's most sacred and abiding effort to stress village industries has been ignored and these are in total neglect. So also is the sad fate of Khadi and handloom.

An even more important point which Prof. Bhalla makes is that industrial policies have been guided by balance of payments considerations and have led to the adoption of import-substituting capital-intensive strategies of industrial development.

This is an exceedingly important point. We have stopped looking within at the kind of self-effort and self-sufficiency and self-help which characterised the whole National movement and particularly the economics of Gandhiji. We are constantly running for loans to the IMF and the World Bank and deluding ourselves with the mirage of high-technology imports and bigness and foreign orientation. The time has come to remind ourselves that nothing abiding is created without self-confidence and self-help and the more we beg, the more we sink into the mire of debt. We have to go back to "Small is Beautiful" and the concept of "Good work."

Prof. Bhalla sums up his position by giving arguments in favour of the use of the new microelectronics technology, which has the potential of promoting small scale decentralised production in developing countries.

This would make small batch production possible, which would enable small enterprises to use this technology efficiently.

Prof. Bhalla concludes by giving examples of micro-electronics and small-scale production. In this he includes the Prato Textile case of Italy, Computer numerically- controlled machines in small firms in the U.K., Japan and Singapore.

These examples could have wide applications in the small towns and villages of India and make the Gandhian Village concept, which seemed at one time very much a utopia- something which is very much a reality.

Our third scholarly reference is the very talented Carlota Perez, who is Adviser to the Argentiniam Government and an Economist. Carlota has an excellent piece titled "Micro-electronics, Long Waves and Structural Change:" Long wave theory is relevant to India, because what we have had in the country these past four decades is State capitalism. And capitalist economies invariably have long wave business cycles. As Carlota rightly states we are now at the end of a business cycle which has been characterised by high oil- based energy input and also heavy in use of materials. In other words, being at the end of this cycle we are now in a "structural crisis."

Schumpeter's business cycle theory is that when we come to the ebb of the Kondratiev curve, the only way to get out of the crisis is by injecting innovation, which in turn means that *the techno-economic paradigm needs to be drastically changed*.

Carlota Perez puts this succintly by saying that now we must change from a set of *social* and *institutional* arrangements based on mass-production technologies using high-cost oil to a new system of *flexible technologies*, based on low-cost electronics.

Carlota warns however, that extrapolations from the past or the turbulent present are misleading. That is, there is no use having more of the same thing. it is no use now, for example, to go on planning the same way as we have done these past four decades with only a scaling up of investment figures. That is of no use at all. What is required is a basic change in the model itself—the paradigm which has held sway these four decades. Nor is it any use uttering homilies urging higher efficiency in production. On the contrary what are needed are totally different modes of production. Further, the present is the period of creation of those future conditions. Because paradigm shifts have great uncertainly built into them and need advanced planning.

The plain fact is that the boom of the late 40s, 50s and 60s in India has simply run its course. This boom was due to the injection of innovation made by the Mahalnobis model due to the policies of Jawaharlal Nehru. It is no use flogging this dead horse now. The plain fact is that we must now *bring about a transition in the social and institutional arrangements.*

This book is therefore, conceived mainly as a contribution for opening new paths in development thinking. I am making a case for defining the present period as a time for discursive, imaginative and speculative thinking. But that is the whole problem with the position in India today: the whole nation is caught up in turmoil, in aggressiveness, in an unimaginable thirst and yearning for greed and power, which seems unquenchable. Therefore, just at the time when tranquility is needed, introspection is needed, deep thought and mystic vision are required and an indomitable will to make these a reality, the whole nation is caught in the grip of conflict, confrontation, mundaneness, acquisitiveness and pettiness.

One may wonder why in a book devoted to the communication of caring , i.e. in which human disciplines and socio-cultural considerations are paramount, so much space is being given to techno-economic issues. The answer is really in the form of a paradox: the true nature of innovation is strictly techno-economic. But the paradox is that *the diffusion and acceptance of this innovation does not depend upon technology*, rather it depends upon the social conditions and within it the institutional framework which is available for its absorption.

As the Kondratiev curve comes to the end of the long cycle the best practice frontier is actually reached, limits to growth are encountered by more and more sectors of the economy, profits decrease and productivity growth slows down. This is exactly what is happening in India today: all the great things set off by the highly original and inspiring techno-economic innovativeness injected into the socio-economic-institutional system in the early 1950s are not only declining, but in most cases are in a state of decay. The Mahalnobis two-sector model has certainly had its day and there is absolutely no point in creating more dianasyours in the public sector. In fact, the days of the First Industrial revolution, of mass production, of the assembly line, of economies of scale in India— all these are certainly over. And there is no point wasting time over these. But what is even more grievous and painful is that the *great institutions which*

*Nehru created and nurtured are also in a state of collapse infested
with petty politics and interminable ineptness and total decline. Unless therefore, simultaneously fresh attempts at institution building
are taken up no progress will be possible.*

At this point there is a persistent search in the pool of the
technologically feasible for what would be technologically
profitable. The technological and economic spheres finally converge in synergetic fashion defining a general model to follow,
involving a new set of "common sense" principles and indicating a higher best practice frontier, designed once again to *transform* the whole techno-economic system.

This phenomenon of paradigm shift can be seen as analogous
to the appearance of a new *genetic pool* which contains the
blueprint for a variety of organism (products and processes) and
their form of inter-relation. It *diffuses* through hybridisation,
cross-breeding, evolution and new entrants. Its increasingly obvious advantages inevitably destine it to transform most and
substitute many of the old "molecules" and create a new "ecco-
system." This is precisely the work required in India today. We
must transform our economic models, our guiding parameters,
our work definitions into something totally different. At the
same time the organisation structures, which are beautifully
defined by the term "eco-system" must change.

The conjunction of characteristics to bring about this new
genetic pool holds today for *micro electronics* which is why it is
transforming both *engineering* and *managerial* common sense
towards its intensive use and gradually shaping the new *"best
practice"* frontier for old and new industries.

What the developing countries do not realise is that they are
trying to acquire what the developed world is ready to discard.
The days of mass production and supportive mass communication and alongwith it the use of intensive energy material is
gone. The techno-economic paradigm needs to be immediately
changed and microelectronics brought in to make manufacture
possible in batch production and flexible mode in a decentralised manner and communication focussed to a "class" *not*
"mass."

What we have to understand in the developing world is that
the transition to a new techno-economic regime connot proceed
smoothly, not only because it implies massive transformation
and much destruction of existing plant, but mainly because the

prevailing *pattern of social behaviour* and existing *institution* were shaped around the reqirements and possibilities created by the previous paradigm.

In the case of India as we know, the prevailing pattern of institutional structure is the pattern of bureaucratic structures, of vertical reporting systems, rigidity in controls and regulations and total disincentive for innovations, inputs of thought and inputs of creativity. The prevailing social behaviour is of official-dom, of administrative politics, manipulation, intrigue and greed.

It is no longer "common sense" to continue along the now expensive path of energy and materials intensity. On the new suggested path, the end product is going to be a flexible output of preferably information-intensive, rapidly changing products and services. Growth would presumably be led by the eletronics and information sectors, requiring massive externalities *from an all-encompassing telecommunications infrastructure*, Diversity and flexibility at all levels will substitute homogeneity and mas-sification as a "common sense" best practice, and these virtues are precisely what are most lacking in the developing countries where there is complete stratification in the administrative layers.

The biggest obstacles to the implementation of the new economic regime therefore, are the prevailing *pattern of social behaviour* and *the existing institutional structure*.

That is why, as the potential of the old paradigm is exhausted, previously successful regulating or stimulating policies do not work. This is certainly true of the Planning process in India. What at one time, under the Nehru- Mahalnobis creativity was not only meritorious but also highly inspirational, simply does not work and is totally superfluous. Depression in fact, is the syndrome of a *serious "mismatch" between the socio-institutional sphere and the new dynamics in the techno-economic sphere*: There is a shouting need *for a re-definition of the general mode of growth*, which the new Planners also, are nowhere near comprehanding.

The creation of a new environment, therefore, is most essen-tial to developing the latent techno-economic potential. Leash-ing of the up-swing therefore, is possible only when deep structural transformations are brought about.

It is salutory to recall that even for the now exhausted "mass production" paradigm, *massive transformations were rquired.*

These were achieved through massive state intervention in the economy along Mahalnobis model required in the public sector heavy industry and infrastructure. Along with this, investment was sought at international level from IMF, the UN agencies and bi-lateral arrangements.

It must be noted however, that far-reaching changes in the techno-economic paradigm and the accompanying social-institutional changes do not happen all of a sudden. *They require a lot of inventiveness, experimentation, as well as compromise.*

As an analogy: the general direction of change required to accommodate a particular technological potential is more like a waterway than like a rail-road track. *It is a wide space for innovation in social organisation and national and international institutions.*

Thus, in spite of the crisis and because of the crisis, it is essential to open new spaces for *development* thinking in terms of the future. These remarks are specially relevant to India. There is a crisis not only of resources, but *much more fundamentally of the mode of growth, central to which is the National Planning Model. The crisis can be transformed into creativity if we apply new development thinking in terms of the future.*

We have in fact, to identify the more coherent initiatives pointing towards the future and *it is upon these new trends that the appropriate institutional configuration must be constructed.*

It is obvious that in India today we are in a serious depression as well as recession. But this is not due to some simplistic reason: bad leadership or politicisation of the administration or criminalisation of politics etc. It is actually due to a very serious *mismatch* between the new techno-economic paradigm required to meet the entirely *changed* needs on the one hand, and the totally static, antiquated, fossilised "socio-institutional" mechanism of organisation and administration we continue to use on the other hand.

From the above analysis it can be seen that *socio-institutional change under normal circumstances, is extremely difficult if not impossible. An appropriate analogy is of a rocket which is to flame its way outside the pull of gravity.* This is most difficult for it, and therefore, requires tremendous *thrust* in the initial stages at the lower level.

It is for this reason that when the earlier oil-based mass production had to be introduced, *a collosal "thrust" effort had to be ushered in the form of simultaneous multi- faceted efforts including:*

accelerated demise of colonial empires, the leading role of the U.S.A. the U.N. Brettons Woods, IMF, GATT, Marshall Plan etc.

What we have seen therefore, is that the construction of a new model of growth is not such an easy matter; *in fact, it is a stupendous feat. It requires a balancing act in which conflicting forces of the old paradigm are offset by the new paradigm by the new progressive forces* and thereby, a shift is achieved towards an emerging paradigm which can cope with the new emerging social, cultural and economic problems.

This synthesis consists of an intensive process involving the *interaction of social confrontation, creativity and compromise.*

Clearly, such wide ranging changes do not occur all at once. They converge gradually and require *an enormous amount of inventiveness and experimentation as well as compromise.*

Even in the best of circumstances change is difficult to effect. So the construction of new mode of growth is paced by the level of understanding, the weight of inertia and the opposition of those who fear it. So the time it takes to create the new framework and the specific form of the ultimate outcome depend on the relative strength, lucidity, capacity to innovate *of the social forces at play.*

As far as the Third World is concerned, these countries were under colonial rule at the time of the last upswing which was the result of oil-based, energy intensive, mass production paradigm. But in the present upswing there are real possibilities of their influencing the course of events.

The important idea to bear in mind is that *once an adequate mode of growth is established,* it moulds, regulates and determines the preferred ways in which the new technological potential is a wide space for innovation in social organisation and national and international institutions.

Even socialist countries have encountered limits to growth and face the need to *transform socio-institutional framework.*

The main thing is that by a process which *combines ingenuity, innovation and creativity, the socil- institutional mechanism must somehow be radically changed if progress is to be made.*

The problem is to detect the main features of the new pattern of techno-economic behaviour *based on the potential of the new technology,* distinguishing what are merely survival tactics of those tied to the old paradigm from the more *coherent initiatives pointing towards towards the future.*

It is upon these new trends that the appropriate configuration must be constructed.

In what follows, an attempt is made to analyse the main feature of the new paradigm which is gradually becoming more and more *visible* and more and more *coherent* as organisational innovations within firms join the technical- cluster growing around *Microelectronics*.

What our planners, economists and policy—makers fail to understand is that India, unlike many or rather, most developing countries is in a position to immediately shift from the old mass-production, oil-based, energy-intensive paradigm to one based on microelectronics and digital telecommunications. Other developing countries may have to go through "stages of growth" to come to the level where they can have a predominantly service economy based on Information as the main resource. But India certainly, and this is a fact acclaimed world-wide, in view of its tremendous scientific, technical and industrial endowments, is in a position to leapfrog into the Information Society. It can thereby, *leap-frog into becoming one of the foremost advanced countries in the world.* Conversely, however, if it does not make this quantum jump its problems of population, poverty and inefficiency will sink it into a quagmire of depression, decay and abject disaster. What is totally baffling however, is that even our erudite Economists neither see this opportunity nor this threat and challenge. "Information" seems to be something that has no place in their vocabulary.

We are therefore, now witnessing in India the current scene of the tapering off of the Kordratiev curve started by the two-sector model of Mahalnobis in the forties, and going into a down-swing not only in productivity, efficiency, administration, organisational viability, but what is far more dangerous, in the total inability of the political leadership to understand what it is that we are passing through. And what we are passing through is an all round down-swing due to the *exhaustion* of the mass- production, oil-based paradigm-which is essentially what the Mahalnobis two-sector model is all about.

In fact, the new techno-economic paradigm based on microelectronics comes at a time when, if we made it the basis of new development strategies, it would solve most if not all of our national problems. The first point we need to examine is that this paradigm would replace material and enegry intensity by "Information" intensity. This has vast implications for the presently beleagurred resources position of our development effort.

The implications of the new micro electronic paradigm are not only economic, but have wide ramifications for *lifestyle* also. The first characteristic of the present state is the socio-economic characteristic of Mechanical Engineering. This involves tremendous wastage of effort and energy. "Materials" for example include transportation, and therefore, there has to be long haul of materials from where they are available to where the huge factories are. Constant movement therefore, is a characteristic of this paradigm along with tremendous consumption of energy. The Information-intensive characteristic on the other hand, places a premium on *thought, knowledge and creativity*. Not only is it on the lines of the Village-economy visualised by people like Mahatma Gandhi and Gurudev Tagore, it is also *in line with the highest tradition of metaphysics and art symbolism of Indian civilization*, which has always placed a premium on "the type of the wise who soar, but never roam."

The second characteristic is of *"flexibility"* in plant and production. In the mass-production assembly line there is no flexibility. The same repetitive, routine actions have to be carried out obssessively. If a new product is to be introduced, the whole plant design has to be changed and new machinery introduced. The Second Industrial Revolution heralded by the Information Age changes all this. Everything now is flexible. In fact, the paradigm shift is designated as one from "mass production" to "flexible specialisation". For one thing the "product" is flexible. The same machine can produce many products the hardware i.e. machine has not to be changed; only the software programming. Secondly, there is flexibility regarding place of work; work can be carried out in one's home.

Finally there is a new trend in "organisation" on the one hand "symstemation" and on the other "decentralisation".

The most important thing for us to note is the trend towards information intensity rather than materials and energy intensity in production. This *stems* directly from the very visible change in the general relative cost structure towards ever cheaper handling potential through microelectronics and digital telecommunications.

The significance of this state for *production* is to be appreciated both in terms of industrial organisation as well as mode of production.

The First Industrial Revolution basically involves setting up of huge factories, huge administrative leviathans and then the necessity for materials, energy and men to be brought to these "blast furnances". Material-intensity therefore, by definition involves huge effort and cost in transportation, because of the necessity for long-haul of materials. In existential and spiritual terms it involves a lot of movement-something contradictory to the "capacity for stillness" of Yoga— the stillness, which was central to models of great minds like Gurudev Tagore and Mahatma Gandhi. If we recall, in their models one thing which was implicit was the use of "local materials". This may have seemed romantic and utopian at that time, but now Information can in a very real way optimise the use of "local materials". From the *spiritual* point of view (and not merely the economic) the point to note is that the new model implies much less wastage of human effort on mere locomotion and restlessness. Information instead does that work. So the model has less spiritual and economic friction lossess and naturally the efficiency is much higher.

The second characteristic of the First Industrial model was its energy-intensity nature. This in main is the nature of mechanical engineering-of moving parts of wear and tear-of power engineering. In socio-spiritual terms it represents obsession with economic and political power, with consequent distancing from the Self.

The Second Industrial mode is a true and real break from the First one in the sense that its almost total reliance is on Information and through processing of that on knowledge, and may in the future lead to Intelligence that is Wisdom, or the capacity for the right choice.

A shift to Information-intensity therefore, promises not only savings in material, transportation and energy economics, but more importantly *a revitalising of our springs of knowledge, culture and wisdom. We must pursue this new model of growth persistently and assiduously.*

Thus as the potential of the old paradigm is exhausted, previously successful regulating or stimulating policies simply do not work. Typically for our Plans we now have neither resources, nor expertise, nor new "models", nor innovative approaches, nor "professional" leadership but a decadent, archaic, outmoded administrative system. So nothing works. Not only that. In fact, *the inertia and decadence of the old socio-institutional framework becomes an unsurmountable obstacle for full deployment of the new paradigm*.

The moral of the story therefore, is that the socio- institutional framework must be *changed* and *transformed* through innovation and creativity.

The present situation in India therefore, is an excellent example illustrating the points we have made above. It is patently obvious that the *techno-economic paradigm* must be changed immediately, if we are to avoid total disruption, disarray and disaster, if not total annihilation. The simple reason for this is that *India is not what it was four decades back* when Mahalnobis' two-sector model was most creatively injected through Nehru's political will. In the interim India has developed 200 million upwardly socially mobile middle class, a huge infrastructure and public sector, an incredibly dynamic and expanding private sector, the third largest scientific manpower in the world, the fourth largest army, Atomic Energy, Space exploration and what have you.

There is no earthly reason therefore, why we should continue to be slavishly doing the same things we have done for the last four decades. Why we should merely perpetuate more of the same?

The critical reason for raising this point is that whereas the earlier paradigm has abviously reaped the rich crop we have harvested; concurrently, however, a whole array of mind-boggling problems have arisen which threaten to destroy us. These can be tackled only if the techno- economic paradigm is changed.

As we have seen however, the techno-economic paradigm cannot be changed *unless and until the socio- institutional mechanism is first altered basically.*This framework as suggested by the very term consists of two parts: first, is the institutional structure. This relates to the physical and mechanical aspects of the organisation. The structure of the organisation, therefore, needs basic change. Experience in India atleast, shows that changing an existing organisation with its archaic hangups is very difficult, if not impossible; it is much *easier to create entirely new structures.*

The second aspect is the "socio" - the one which relates to *behaviour*. Therefore, not only do we need a new skeletal structure for our new undertakings, even more so we need a new "operating culture" perhaps horizontal rather than vertical reporting systems. We also perhaps need "peer relationships" based on professional sharing rather than master servant relationships of typical bureaucracies.

The most important point to note however, is that the above visible changes can only be brought about if the external apparatus for quick and efficient flow are in position. *This requires an infrastructure of digital telecommunications and microelectronics.*

Now if we recall, the genius of Jawaharlal Nehru lay in the fact that once the two-sector model of Mahalnobis had been formulated, the Planning Commission was charged with the responsibility of having it executed through provision of adequate funds and creation of appropriate public sector enterprises to bring into existence the massive super- structure envisaged by the Mahalnobis model, which, it may be pointed out, included not only public sector industry, dams etc. but tremendous investments in scientific efforts including IITs for training of engineers and CSIR laboratories for applied industrial scientific research, not to mention advanced technology programme such as Atomic Enegry and Space.

Nothing of the sort is in sight right now. To begin with the main macroeconomic aggregate model of Central Planning needs to be completely changed. Secondly, even a modelling system like Leontiff input-output needs to be abandoned in favour of models which facilitate leapfrogging. *But much more importantly the infrastructures for digital telecommunications and micro-electronic ought to come up in the same big way as that of mechanical engineering, railways and roads came up under the Nehru-Mahalnobis dispensation. Lastly an appropriate new institution like* an altogether different kind of Planning Commission needs to be created for the new task.

The actual position is dismal beyond belief. In the last three years South Korea starting from a telecommunications infrastructure as rickety as ours, has, through massive financial aid and transfer of technology built up a telecom system which, if anything is equal to if not better than the U.S. In the same period we have been tinkering around trying to make an indigenous telecom switch while the main network is in a state of shambles and disarray as bad as the most primitive country in the world. Similarly the electronics policy and effort are abyssmal.

What we do not realise is that there is nothing mystical and mysterious about these new technologies. Why do we want an indigenous switch? Why do we want to reinvent the wheel? There is nothing esoteric about these new technologies. These are really the new "highways". What roads and industrial plants were to the First Revolution, telecommunications and micro-electronics are to the Second. We must get on with the job and install these "highways" atonce, as Jawaharlal Nehru did in another context; otherwise nothing worthwhile will be achieved.

For this purpose, we also need to set up in the private sector an *independent* think tank which could be called an *Institute of Advanced Communication Policy Studies* and which should with fierce independence take up analysis of crucial technology-economic and sociological issues in this vital sector.

What our economists and engineers and planners and policy makers do not realise is that the *waning* of the First Industrial paradigm is synonymous with the waning of all that Jawaharlal Nehru's tremendous vision stood for. The direction he gave and the institutions he created must be changed 180 degrees-that is, if we wish not only to flourish, but merely to survive. Our products and services must no longer be material-intensive and energy-intensive as these were in the model that Jawaharlal Nehru set up, and rightly so at that point of time in our develop-ment. Now these need to be Information intensive. We need to take up, exclusively such activities as require information han-dling for decision making, and designing an electronic product or a software package or setting up an information intensive service to open a new market.

The point to note is that these new products and services which emerge from an infrastructure of digital telecommunica-tions and microelecronics are in fact, relatively simple applica-tions of already well known principles so that there would be neither any doubt nor any mystery about their technical feasibility. In other words, these are off the shelf technologies. Why then have we wasted the last five years trying to design an indigenous digital telecom switch and in the bargain brought to a grinding halt the growth of telecommunications infrastruc-ture-which is a pathway as crucial now as the railways or roads were a century back. Such delay can only be termed as criminal because it literally means not only crores upon crores of money lost by way of inefficiency in so many sectors of the economy, but more importantly of opportunities missed. The opportunities and therefore, the work required to gain these do not depend upon the electronic and telecom infrastructure. These ought to be regarded as given. These depend upon the innovative and experimental work which requires to be done to see how decentralised batch-mode production can be set up in agglomerations of small towns to leapfrog to the Second Industrial mode, how distance - learning can be undertaken, how a million other things can be done. This work of investigating and designing the application modes has not even begun.

The other extremely important point to note is that the early induction of Information services in the devloping situation would achieve exactly the opposite of what the "Stages of Growth" thesis would have us believe. Because "high-Information" based economy could reduce demand for crucial items like transportation, energy, distantly located materials, schools, universities etc. And the Information- mode itself could become the delivery system to replace conventional services like Education, Banking etc. Data storage and data communication systems could replace the mode of many conventinal services and thereby, render unnecessary many conventional services and the conventional "stages of growth". Simultaneously, goods produced under these conditions might become the vehicle for the consumption of increasing amounts of software and other services.

The absolute justification for following an "Information intensive" scenario is the following fact: In the midst of recession and strong inflationary pressures, the companies (the world over) most closely related to the production or intensive use of micro-electronics are showing generally high *growth rates* and their products are the only ones decreasing in prices, even in absolute terms.

As in the previous "paradigm shift" this advantage (of major expansion and simultaneously low cost) will translate into two things:

   (a)   Unusually high profit rates for these Information in-
          tensive users and producers;

(b)   Established by *growth* and attracted by diversification the users and producers will become the largest and most dynamic of the *next upswing*.

What is characterising the Indian political economic scene is: recession and an extremely high inflationary trend. It would be absolutely and criminally wrong to attribute these major setbacks in the body economic and body politic just to passing waves of a bad monsoon etc. That has got nothing to do with it. In fact, the bad monsoon itself is the result of deforestation and denuding of mountain tops - which in turn brings us to the necessity for looking to some central, basic, universal principle for why things are going wrong and such a reason ought to be in the nature of a model, a hypothesis, a "paradigm" which by its utter simplicity and straight-forwardness explains everything and puts everything in its place. And the answer is simple: it lies in the fact that the "paradigm" on which the whole edifice of the Nehru-Mahalnobis framework was built, and which has so wonderfully stood by us for four long decades is now on the down-swing and must be abandoned *with the urgency with which one abandons a sinking ship or an aeroplane which is nose-dividing*. What we need therefore, is a 180 degrees change in everythng- the Plan frame, the Econometric model, the Public sector thrust, exphasis on centralisation, supremacy of bureaucracy-all these need to be re-thought and either completely altered or abandoned.

Up-swing on the other hand, will come to only those sectors, which are Information-intensive and which rely more and more on the industrial, organisational, social and educational uses of digital telecommunications and microelectronics.

The grave tragedy of the situation however, is that the past five years have been wasted for no rhyme nor reason. Setting up telecom networks and electronic systems has an analogy to the building of roads or railway networks. Both are basically "highways-"one of civil engineering, the other of electronics. Both are routine, mundane jobs involving engineers and mechanics. There is nothing mystical, mysterious, magical or esoteric in doing this, which may require extraordinary genius. This challenge of genius really begins when these electronic "highways" and "pathways" are in position, because then we have to figure out the most challenging problems: how to use these for new forms of industrial production, industrial organisation, social needs, educational needs and the extraordinarily large demands of the "Services sector". But instead of of this area being in the hands of an interdisciplinary team of Policy analysts, some upstart engineers have held the nation to ransom by allowing no growth, ostensibly for doing R&D to design basic parts. This can only be designated as criminal because this lobby has stopped both technology transfer and flow of funds which are needed in massive amounts.

So anybody or any institution which at this point of world economic trend goes into a Information-intensive area will, by definition be going for the *up-swaing* and therefore leading to become a *"giant"*. Not only is this happening, but even existing, giants are now *diversifying* into Information-Intensive sectors.

Contrary to what we have witnessed in the U.S.A., the Information-intensive paradigm need not or rather should not lead to increase of the Services sector at the cost of the Manufacturing Sector. In fact, in the case of the U.S.A. there is actually no co-relation whatsoever. The Manufacturing Sector has not gone down *not* because the Information Sector has gone up; it has gone down for the simple reason that due to high American labour costs and lowering of productivity standards American industries have sought the easy way out and moved off-shore.

On the contrary, if there is one sector which ought to profit the most from Information-inputs particularly in the Indian situation, it is the Manufacturing Sector. For the very simple reason that Information intensity would supply what is the crying need of the Manufacturing Sector in India, namely high *productivity*. The main problem with the manufacturing sector in India is its very high ICOR- Incremental Capital-Output Ratio. That is for an "x" amount of capital investment, the output "y" is extremely low. If there is one thing which Information-intensity achieves, it is the raising of efficiency and productivity.

Secondly, as we have stated earlier, information-Intensity would decentralise production- in the batch production mode-thereby making "small scale industries" "District industries", "Village industries" not just cosmetics-but in fact, the *CORE* of the future new industrial structure. On rough estimates this would increase the present projected employment figure from 40 million estimated at present to 240 million jobs.

At present in Indian economics and planning if there is one preoccupation, or more correctly, obssession, it is with "resources", or rather their scarcity. We are therefore, constantly looking for resources outside-World Bank loans, commercial borrowings etc. We do not realise that the chief cause of our "resource crunch" is our skewed perspective- skewed as it is to the First Industrial Revolution of Europe and our conviction that development is simply not possible unless there is un-limited supply of two things: energy and materials- to wit, the Seventh Five Year Plan allocation of one-third of the total national resources to the Energy Sector. But this only shows our economic and planning myopia. If we shift our perspective and align it to an Information-intensive model, then both the energy and materials content in the economy gets drastically reduced.

We have seen some of the characteristics of the techno-economic paradigm based on microelectronics. One of the most significant of these is that the microelectronics- telecommunica-tions mode allows for "flexible" production as against "mass production."

"Flexibility" is probably the most important keyword within the new paradigm. It challenges the old best practice concept of mass production in two senses. The new paradigm makes 'diversity"in production as efficient as "homogeneity" had pre-viously been; it opens the way for the rapid evolution of products, introducing the possibility of a true innovative dynamics in time as opposed to the "minimum change" strategy implicit in mass production technologies; and it provides space for adaptability of production systems and output to specific markets and local conditions.

Implicit in this paradigm shift is a shift from economies of scale to economies of scope or specialisation. This approach opens a range of opportunities for relatively small plants serv-ing one or a set of small local markets on *specific market "niches"*, achieving high productivity levels with "economics of specialisation," not necessarily dependent on large scale. All this is a modern translation of the "Gandhian" economics we so much yearn for now.

The other point to notice, and which is of great relevance and significance to developing countries, *is the "craft" character of this new batch production mode.* This would lead to the full fructifica-tion of the "craft" potential of the new technologies.

The above discussion raises several issues for development strategies. The changes brought about by the new flexibility potential means that, on the whole, the bulk of existing plant is obsolete by international standards.

We will discuss the whole question of innovation in organisation in a subsequent chapter in very considerable detail-but some reference to this exceedingly important area needs to be made here. The process of accepting change in the technical paradigm is neither simple nor automatic, *as it requires overcoming deeply rooted behaviour patterns*, in our case the devastating administrative political nexus and its stranglehold. In fact, the diffusion of a new technological style is also a conflict ridden process of *creation of a new organisational model as regards the management of the firm*. There are therefore, many problems in the process of diffusion of *the new organisational model*.

The profound importance of organisation is hardly realized. It is for this reason that the many unsuccessful attempts at introducing electronic equipment may stem from believing that these are mere pieces of hardware, which can be incorporated into the *previous* plant or office. But this kind of mechanical introduction, which especially, most engineers and managers are infatuated with as quick "flxes", achieves absolutely nothing. Our present observation of a computer on every desk is a case in point. This is precisely the crisis in India today. *We have totally ignored organisational innovation*. All the time we are infatuated with either getting financial aid, or new technology. Not knowing that these by themselves are utterly useless, *unless these are preceeded by far reaching changes in organisation*. In fact, so powerful is the effect of organisational innovation, that if achieved, that by itself shows the path of discernment and wisdom as to how we ought to manage our finances and bring about technical change. *Organisation and therefore, human resource is the key to leapfrogging*, not a mechanical obssession with techno-economic shift. The key to techno-economic shift paradoxically is in socio-psyche-cultural shift, namely in the region of human awareness.

In reality, reaping the fruits of the new technology (Communication in this case) requires *a profound transformation* in the *organisation* of the firm and in its intercommunications both *inside* and with the *outside* world.

The present longwave transition from the materials-energy techno-economic paradigm to Micro-electronics has a very special significance for developing countries. Since the new over-reaching technology is now at its relatively early stages, *it is possible to attempt a direct entry without going through the technological stages it leaves behind.* I hope Professor Rostow is listening and foregoing his fixation "to stages of economic growth". In this sense we in the developing world are better off than those in the developed, because in the developed countries the investment into the First Industrial Revolution i.e. in Capital, Materials and Energy is so large that it is a very difficult problem for them to shift to Information-intensity. For example in Telecommunications U.S.A. is 60% into Analog and Japan 70%. For them to change to Digital is a horendous task. In other words, the new technologies allow "leapfrogging" for some of the countries which do not carry the inertia of the previous industrial structure. We leapfrogged into Atomic Energy and into Space technology and from there into Missile technology. We can now similarly *leapfrog into an Economic Development mode reliant chiefly on Information.*

It needs to be reiterated however that the key to this change in the techno-economic paradigm lies in *changes in socio-institutional framework.*

Another point which needs to be made is that for developing countries it is a question of *taking advantage of the transition to leap forward.* Where we are totally in error however, is that we think that to achieve this leap forward all we need is technology import and finance. We could not be more in the wrong. What we need more than anything else is *"Socio-institutional TRANS-FORMATION.* In a subsequent chapter on *Organisation* I will show by analysing case studies of Atomic Energy in India and the Film cultures of Prabhat, New Theatres and Bombay Talkies in our Renaissance movement that even in the absence of finance and technology, *transformation in socio-institutional framework worked magic-* magic indeed is the word-because it made the impossible achieveable.

The word *"transitional phase"* is used advisedly because we may think we have achieved a great deal when in "transition" whereas in actual fact, this indeed is nominal as compared to our real POTENTIAL, "Leapforward" is again a term used advisedly. At every attempt we made in India to leapfrogging whether this be in the Green Revolution or Atomic Energy or Space we were told India was not ready for it, not at the appropriate and required "stage of economic growth". However, we have seen that we did all these successfully. This is because India is neither Africa nor Latin America nor the Arab world. We are specially endowed in many ways: firstly the Scientific temper and knowledge came to us in the form of our ancient traditon in learning. The second extremely important factor is the greatness of the Hindu religion and the Hindu way of life-it is unique in its catholicity, openness and readiness to "absorb" even totally opposing and conflicting ideas and yet mould these into its own unique image. Lastly the great Hindu tradition of LEARNING- what has been referred to as the Brahminical tradition (but has nothing whatsoever to do with ones being a Brahmin; rather it points to an extremely ancient, perhaps the oldest tradition of LEARNING in any people. These factors have combined to make the modern Indian intellectual and elite the most formidable brainpower in the world. This brainpower however, is not only in quality, but also in quantity: such large numbers of trained scientists and thinkers are not to be found even in any other developed country of the world, let alone the developing countries. India's potentials therefore, are immense and immensureable and it is extremely unfortunate that India does not have this self-awareness and consciousness of her POTENTIAL.

We will now try to synthesise all the strands which have emerged from this discussion. It could be called synthesising of constant parameters with shifts in paradigm.

There are two parameters about National Planning on which there is a national consensus and the continuity of which we must ensure, although right at this moment efforts are afoot to dislodge these parameters. The two parameters are the following : one is that although in an open society like that in India no curb need be placed on the "market economy" of the 200 million upward mobile, yet at the same time under the guise of "supply side economics" or "Reaganeconomics " or what have you, the process of *Planned Development* must be kept in tact to ensure the well being of the 600 million deprived. Their fate cannot be cast to the vagaries of the "market economy". Which is precisely what the Reaganeconomic- wallahs are hell bent upon -and in the process holding upto to us examples of Korea, Hongkong, Taiwan, Singapore-basically satellites of the U.S. economy. We have not to fall into this trap. We can go in for rapid development, but need not cast self-reliance to the wind.

Secondly, and this to a large extent follows from our internal self-reliance in Agriculture and Industry, is our externally retaining our stand as the bottleholders of the Third World and leaders of the Non-aligned Movement. We cannot be made pawns in the game of bloc gamesmanship, but must veer our own destiny as founders of the Non-aligned movement.

On both fronts, forces are at work to undermine the Indian position.

We now give below the practical illustration of these theoretical principles in the PRATO textile experience in Italy.

The Prato Project -Bringing I.T. to Serve a Monoproduction Community

The Prato Telematics Project will be illustrated and particularly the reasons why it has been carried out, the analysis that has been conducted and *the experimental phase* that has been prepared.

First a few words about the Prato Textile Area

It is one of the largest woollen textile districts in the world. The main raw material used is mechanical wool that is wool which derives from the recycling of shoddy and discarded clothes.

It is an area of about 700 km^2, 20 km west of *Florence* with a population of 300,000 inhabitants; in this area 80% of the active population work in textile production, 66,000 employees work in *as many as 15,000 firms* only 1700 of them contact the market, *all the others are sub-contractors*.

A Central figure in the Prato Textile District is the *"impannatore"* an *entrepreneur* without enterprise, *who exerts the functions of strategic marketing, sample creation, and sale of Prato woollen products on a world basis*. Once back in Prato with his backlog of orders, it is up to the impannatore to contract the production to the various firms, organizing the different steps of production itself, checking the quality of the products he has sold at the agreed price and at the right time.

Consequently the organisational structure of Prato's production is extremely decentralized and based on sub- contacting firms; the various phases of the textile cycle are carried out by different firms in different shops; the semi-manufactured goods are taken from one place to the other several times before being delivered to the buyers.

This productivity system has obvious advantages as regards flexibility in Quantity and type of production, and is able to react immediately to market trends; from that derives the good fortune of the system.

With such an organisational structure *the role of communications is of enormous importance and the number of firms providing services (transportation, banks, custom and financial services, etc.) is very high.*

ENEA, *the Italian agency for atomic and alternative energy sources* has recently expanded its field of activities *to include the diffusion of emerging new technologies*, largely stemming from its energy experience, throughout the Italian economy.

In Prato it formed SPRINT *(Prato System for Technological Innovation)* in alliance with industrialists (the majors and the small-scale, self employed *artisans)* SIP (the national PTT), local trade associations, Municipality, banks, etc. SPRINT thus *represents a way to face the technological upgrading in a cooperative and orderly manner.*

Prato Telematics Project is the main project within SPRINT activities; all SPRINT members are directly involved in it, the works are coordinated by RESEAU *a leading Italian consultancy firm in the fields of communication and automation.*

Prato Telematics Project is born from the meeting between two different needs: Prato *requires an efficient communication and information flow in order to increase its competitiveness on international markets; Telematics needs to verify the feasibility of such requirements and to know the extents of its market.*

The objectives of telematics can be summerized as follows:

- information processing (a typical activity of informatics)
- information transmission (a typical activity of of telecommunications)
- meeting the needs of a large number of users in terms of information and services (a typical activity of consumer electronics).

All these objectives seem to fit quite well Prato's needs.

Informatics and Telecommunications are alrady present in Prato, the aim of SPRINT is to make them available to the entire community in an integreted manner and, of course, at a low cost.

The Telematics Project concern many actors and involve many problems.

1) End-users, confronted with a lot of solutions, they find out that their needs are not so homogenous as they thought. They have to undergo a careful analysis of their communication needs and choose the right solution for each need.

2) Electronics manufacturers need to sell the new apparati made available by the technological evolution.

3) Carriers have to invest a lot of money to adopt their network to the new services before even knowing whether those services correspond to an actual market.

Basically the solution to the problems is up to the end- users and can be achieved through the three following steps:

1) analysis of communication needs:

2) experimentation of those new services which are considered useful to meet such needs and evolute their cost/benefit ratio.

3) assessment of compatibility of the choice of single end-users with those of their interlocutors.

In particular, in an integrated industrial system like Prato, the choice of telematics instruments must be the result of a collective decision; otherwise there is a serious risk of non-communication.

All these consideration about telematics add sense to the Prato Telematics Project: whose main phases are the following.

The first phase was an in-depth analysis of the communications and relationships system.

The results of the analysis are the following.

1) A first important result is that 54% of all communications are limited within the Prato area. This justifies the introduction of telematics in the Prato area.

2) The traditional instruments which are being used today to communicate among the Prato actors are in order:
—telephone 57.6%

—face-to-face meetings 21.3%
—mail 20.7%
—telex 0.4%

Telephone is therefore the most used instrument, but 40% of telephone calls don't turn out well.

3)   Every year the two Artisan Associations and the Employer's Association send almost 3 million leaflets to their members to give them information, but as artisans and firms have no files of thier own, they have to call back their associations when they need some information.

4)   The cost of the **"communication"** production factor for the Prato textile industry is **2.9%** of total turnover (evaluated at 70 - 80 million dollars).

Chart n.2 represents the sum of the "visible" costs (i.e. those concerning equipment and traffic) and the "hidden" costs (i.e. the time spent by people to communicate).

It is important to underline that, for instance, it takes more time to send the same message by telephone more by telex.

The proportion between "visible" and "hidden" costs is well illustrated in the chart.

The cost of the "communication" production factor can be represented as an iceberg, whose emerging part is only 18.8%.

An expenditure whose incidence has raised to 2.9% of total turnover justifies an attempt to improve efficiency, which in the past has never been made.

Briefly the analysis of the information and communication system allowed us to outline two main needs of the Prato production system:

1)   to improve communication
2)   to meet the need of information.

It was therefore proposed, as a first experimental telematics phase, to install a videotex sytem. In fact, this seems to be the right instrument to give a significant contribution to both problems.

Actually it makes possible both to set up an electronic mailbox and supply proper services both to the producers and to the general public.

Once chosen the videotex, the services had to be designed.

It was thus set **up** by SPRINT a Technical Committee composed by the main actors of Prato, who are also the potential information providers: the Employers Association and the two Artisan Associations, plus the "Comune di Prato" (Prato Municipality) **and** Cassa di Risparmio (the main bank).

The basic services defined so far are the following:

Services offered by SPRINT:
- PRATEL: the service aims at better coordinating demand and supply of different phases of the textile production process;
- ELECTRONIC NOTICE BOARD: demand and supply notices of semi-finished products, second hand equipment, etc.;
- ELECTRONIC MAIL-BOX: a well known service;

Services offered by the Employer's Association:
- UNIFORM: information service on commercial behaviour of customers;
- INFORMATION SERVICE: possible access to all the information which the Association can provide (fiscal, industrial, relations industrial injury legislation, anti-pollution legislation, etc.)
- WAGE BILLS PROCESSING: the service consists in the trasmission of data concerning worker's presence by videotex;

HOME-BANKING and other bank services supplied by Cassa di Risparmio services offered by the two Artisan Associations:
- INFORMATION
- ACCOUNTING
- WAGE BILLS PROCESSING
- FISCAL CONSULTANCY
- TELEX SECETARIAT

MUNICIPAL TELEMATICS SERVICES supplied by the Town Council

The specification of the services is a necessary but not sufficient condition.

It has being completed by :
1)   an awareness program in the area (the project must be introduced and explained to the general public);
2)   the singling out of the first 300 experimental users that must be a representative sample of all the components of the "Prato system";
3)   a project for an educational programme addressed to both users and informaton providers.

The time schedule of the program we have set up is the following :

January-April 86 :	installation of the videotex centre by SIP;
January-June 86 :	set-up of the services;
September-December 86 :	opening of the services and progressive distribution of the terminals to the 300 users of the experimental phase :
1987 :	management, development and evaluation of the videotex experimental phase.

6

BEYOND DEAD ORGANIZATIONS

For a decade now B.G. Verghese amongst others has been leading an agitation for autonomy of the electronic media. The Prasar Bharati Bill finally seems on the point of seeing the light of the day. Its results however, are likely to be highly problematical. In fact, it will be the ninth wonder of the world if this overtly political step achieves anything constructive at all in organizational terms.

After all what is it basically that is being sought: creation of a public corporation. But is it not exactly that which sums up our developmental effort of the past four decades: "Commanding heights of the public sector" with the public corporation as its visible symbol. And what have these public cororations achieved, with the odd exception: unimaginably large budgetary deficits, ineptitude, waste, corruption, extremely low productivity and internecine warfare with the concerned, overseeing Ministry.

There is already an existing example in the official media itself: the National Film Development Corporation, which ostensibly too has a Board of Directors drawn from artistic eminence and avowed ideals which would put the most revolutionary to shame. And yet a more defunct, dysfunctional, perverse organization is hard to scan on the Indian horizon.

What makes us think Prasar Bharati is going to be any different? Already there are rumblings of the bloody battle around the corner. The present government budgetary support to the electronic media is already of the tune of over Rs. 400 crores per annum. This figure will soon double with inflation and inflated staff which is likely to plague the Corporation. Apart from the question of resources crunch, is the government which shells out this magnitude of financial support is going to willy-willy exercise "control" on policies. Premonitious of this are already visible in the overtly tactical way in which the Minister has slyly withdrawn two provisions - obviously to enable smooth passing of the Bill in Parliament. Both provisions relate to powers Government would exercise to intervene and take over charge of the Corporation.

If, on the other hand, attempt is made to make the Corporation financially free by increasing advertising revenue, the lobby on the other side of the fence is already shouting hoarse that multinationals will take over the electronic media, that is if they have not done so already. It is an open secret that sponsorship of serials by giant multinationals and other corporations is leading to vast sums being paid to Doordarshan staff under the table and this is leading to control of software and programming by these corporations.

The object here however, is not to wash dirty linen in public with B.G. Verghese and his friends. We are concerned with a much more fundamental and theoretical issue: the nature of Media organization. And the point to be realized is that organisations do not get changed if the *assumptions* on which these are built do not get changed. And cheap politics certainly changes nothing, least of all deep, underlying assumptions.

What our electronic media need is not autonomy but *CREATIVITY*. And there are umpteen examples both inside and outside government in India, where creativity has been achieved without the clarion call of autonomy. Autonomy is a gimmick, a political trick, a sedative to soothe a credulous public.

Creativity is much more difficult. It needs enlightened and unruffled leadership, creation of cadres of dedication, development of traditions, evolving appropriate operating cultures. Who is going to do this in media in the India today, when the whole atmosphere is charged with upmanship, commercialism, cheapness, manipulation and vulgarity. In organization building and behaviour, politics contributes nothing, because it only scratches the surface.

This is also the ocassion to take issue with the Joshi Committee on Software which champions an "Indian personality" of TV. Did our National movement champion an Indian personality? It did not. As we have been at pains to show in the Chapter on "Renaissance" India's unique contribution was in achieving the almost impossible reconcilliation of Western Science and Eastern Metaphysics - this universally applied to all the luminories of the Indian Renaissance whether it be a

Tagore, or Sri Aurobindo, or Gandhiji or Coomaraswamy or any other. What we have to aim at is not an Indian personality, but a *SUBJECTIVE* personality because no art is created if the operating culture is not subjective. Is Prasar Bharati going to have a subjective operating culture, in which the *Producer*, who is the life-line of this media, albiet held in utter disaffection, despise, insult and degradation - is the Producer going to have a new "avtar" in which he will breathe the rarified air of subjective purity and inwardness - which is what cultures like BBC basically have, and which therefore, make them overpoweringly invincible. BBC in its long and distinguished history has never gone to the Post Master General of the U.K. to whom it is beholden, for autonomy.

We are stating all this in order to define the purpose of this chapter. An organization is like an individual: it has a *concious* psyche and an *unconcious* psyche. But unless the unconcious is accessed and changed no abiding change is brought about in either. We examine this issue in detail first theoretically and then by application of these theoretical principles to a specific case study.

Nothing shows up more vividly the point being made in this book than our current approach to the whole area of organization and organizational dynamics. It also shows the sterility of our intellectual capacities and bankruptcy of creative ideas.

We have been engaged for quite some time now with the crusade for Autonomy for the Media. This is a wrong definition of the primary task. Tinkering with autonomy is like tinkering with the politics of the situation - it is going to get us nowhere. What rather we need to examine is: how changes in communication flow change the structure of organization.

We also hypothesise the following: the First Industrial mode extroverts the personality. It leads to massive organizational structures, constant movement due to long haul of goods and people and repetitive movements in the manufacturing process. *All this objectifies the psyche; lowers creativity.*

In the Second mode with the primacy of Information as the engine of production, we revert to organizations which are decentralised, small and located in natural habitats and therefore resemble the extended family environments of a traditional society where work is carried out in a crafts mode under small workshop conditions and *not* large factory conditions.

As advanced industrial countries move into higher stages of the "industrial revolution" approximating an Information Society they are already beginning to experience changes in *industrial organization*. The centrality of Information forces this change.

In fact, advanced industrial countries seem to be living through a period of unusual flux and instability in their basic social and *economic institutions*. Large corporations with highly integrated, heirarchical organizational structures are being forced into decentralisation of managerial authority and decision- making. *Small businesses, which were previously viewed as the vestige of an early stage of economic development, and which typically operated as subordinates of larger* corporations whom they served as subcontractors, suppliers and vendors, *are achieving a new and independent stature; they are being heralded by a number of observers as the key to dynamic economic growth and job creation.*

These remarkable changes in industrial *organization* are the result of remarkable convergence of innovations in various fields which are strengthened through their combination: micro-electronics, computerised production and control systems, telecommunications, new materials, bio- technology. *But the centrality of Information technology is visible in all this.*

In other words, as Information gains centrality in the economic and industrial process, industrial organisation seems to be at the crossroads, and the dominant mass production system of the First Industrial mode appears to be disintegrating in favour of systems of flexible specialisation. This in turn is leading to equally unexpected and surprising results: recomposition of work, *production according to the old craft model*; also in the work culture: strong social links with common shared values, where conflicts are necessarily mitigated. All these factors in the new "industrial revolution" are reminiscent of the old craftsman working in workshop conditions of his guild and close to his family.

No one of course, has chronicled the past scenario of the craftsman, the guild system and the workshop environ more creatively and eruditely than Dr. Ananada Coomaraswamy. His two exceedingly superb books are: "The Indian Craftsman" and "Art and Swadeshi". Coomaraswamy shows that an exceedingly superb *"organization"* of village craftsmen, guilds and congenial creative environment hospitable to the Arts and Crafts was crumbling before the onslaught of Industrialism.

But these concerns against the onslaught of Industrialism were not unique to Indian crafts nor to Coomaraswamy. If Coomaraswamy and his fellow Nationalists including of course, Gandhiji were concerned about the breakdown of the traditional village organisation hospitable to the Arts and Crafts, there was similar concern in England and elsewhere in the West against the threat to the old Guild system of the craftsmen descending from the Medieval period. The greatest proponent of the battle and crusade against this was the Englishman Ashbee, who was not only Coomaraswamy's closest friend but whose attempt at Guild revival and rehabilitation of English craftsmen at Chipping Campden (in the countryside away from London) was in the proximity of Coomaraswamy's English country home at Broad Campden. Other thinkers who immediately come to mind are Ruskin, William Blake and William Morris.

The point however, which we had begun to make earlier in this chapter was that it now appears that in the Second Industrial mode of the Information society the optimum industrial organization which is emerging is basically not different from the workshop conditions of the guild craftsmen - whether he be of Medieval Europe or traditional India.

This obviously has more than abundant significance for a country like India, because it would imply that in the Information mode the basic "industrial organisation" would revert to decentralisation, natural habitats, workshop conditions industry coexisting in the family environment.

This "organizational" revival obviously has implications for ecology, urbanization, village uplift and employment - but more importantly it has implications for ensuring a "subjective" approach to work - the key to all creativity. This aspect is explored in the remaining part of the chapter.

Organisation thus is the key to everything: to efficiency, productivity, creativity. The First Industrial model we have so far followed did two things.

    (a) Took away a lot of a person's energy in travel
    (b) Put him in large, dianasyor like structures
    (c) extroverted his personality
    (d) made him mechanical
    (e) "objectivised" his outlook

The Information Revolution as it is showing up in the West is revealing the necessity for smaller, workshop like organisations not different from the craft guilds and extended family organisation of traditional societies. Its blessings are innumerable: conservation of energy, minimal travel, congenial interpersonal environment, but above all a "subjective" orientation to life without which, nothing creative is possible.

Any organisation is essentially a structure, which works only when there is healthy flow of communication in it.

There are only two kinds of organisations in the world: one that make the world go *on* and the other that make the world go *forward*. To the first class belong the majority of people and organisations: those of plumbers, carpenters, garbage collectors and incidentally also high- placed bureaucrats-because all that they accomplish are the daily chores of moving files, revenue collection, law and order and that great ritual in Government "bandobast" - routine, menial arrangements for welcoming visiting nobles, either local or from distant lands.

The other type of people and organisations are quite the opposite. They are ever dissatisfied with things as they are and constantly promote change, revolutionary thought and actions and consequently minor or major upheavals.

Two distinctly opposite types of organisations cater to these diametrically opposite objectives. In the first category the external, overt, materialistic aspects of organisation is emphasised: rules and regulations, heirarchy, secrecy, vertical modes of communication or even total lack of communication, lack of any great idealism informing the objectives of the organisation and not infrequently a large dose of gossip, frustration, rivalries, jealousies, favouritism and intrigue.

The second type of organisation is highly slanted towards the *subjective orientation* in its structure and places high premium on creativity, idealism, distant vision, goals affecting the noblest in mankind and because of all this an operating culture which is manifested by high communications, strong peer relationships and a feeling of camaraderie and grand mission to carry out noble work.

It is this second category we will take up for discussion first and discuss the theoretical underpinnings which inform such structures, the "assumptions" we referred to earlier.

There are three concise characteristics of such kind of "subjectively-oriented" organisations. But it might be advantageous to note that culture is a root metaphor of these organisations. This concept will become clear in the discussion.

The first characteristic to understand is that in these organisations forms and practices are the manifestation of *unconcious processes*. One is reminded at once of Levi-Strauss' "Structuralism" and Jungian "archetypes". In other words, these organisations represent the structural and psychodynamic perspectives. The organisation is viewed as a manifestation of unconscious urges. To this writer this is the most exalted and noblest way of viewing an organisation. In the National Movement of India's Renaissance all organisations, however small and humble, were projections of unconscious urges-reaching out to light, freedom and expression.

This idealistic, subjective conception of organisation is in contradiction to the overt, materialistic forms whose objective is merely to employ the organisation as a social instrument for task accomplishment or in a rapidly and catastrophically changing environment as an adaptive organism to cope with the critical environment.

The idealistic and subjective approach to organisation is totally different: it is instrumental in releasing unconscious forces and these can create far greater wonders, even miracles, which overt manipulation of conscious forces cannot. Hence the role of charisma in leadership, of silent strength in exalted qualities of the true guide and leader; hence, also the greater strides which *genuine caring and sincerity and commitment* lead to in true direction. In a word, the true role of such organisations is *TRANSFORMATIONAL.* They totally transform the structure, the operating culture, the man-management, the peer relationships and the output of the organisation.

When we are talking of culture as root metaphor for conceptualizing organisation we are directly implying that it does not belong to two categories to which most organisations belong. One, is the "instrumental" view of organisation derived from the machine metaphor. In the developing world especially, most organisations belong to this class, because the primary task is either conciously or unconciously defined as one of a "functional" nature, of "task orientation", "mission orientation", "achievement orientation", "getting things done".

The other category widely manifested is the "adaptive" view derived from the organismic metaphor. Like any organism biologically defends itself, similarly the worker/manager constantly attempts through painful, even distressful "adaptation" to cope with the harsh, competitive and not too infrequently a rapidly changing environment. This form of organisational view is widely prevalent in the Government and political sectors, which are marked by manipulation, intrigue and even conspiracy-and mere survival is the main problem.

The concept of culture as root metaphor goes beyond these views, i.e. one of "instrumentalism" from the machine metaphor and the other of "adaptation" from the organismic metaphor.

Culture as root metaphor, on the contrary, promotes a view of organisations as *expressive forms, manifestations of human consciousness*. Organisations in this mode are understood and analysed not in economic or material terms, but in terms of their expressive, ideational and symbolic aspects. The main thrust here is to explore the phenomenon of organisation as a *subjective* experience and to investigate the patterns *that make organised action possible*.

The "subjective" approach to organisation falls into three main categories: The one based on symbolism regards culture and therefore, organisation as a system of "shared meaning". Creative expression obviously, is the mainstay of this mode. Language, ability for expression, sharing meaning with others are paramount in this mode. In fact, literary and symbolic expression are so potent that the creative expression by itself becomes a means of organisation building. Symbolic expression in other words, becomes "instrumental". We should not think of literary activity as merely avante garde, an exotic-something remote from reality. Quite the contrary, it is one of the most potent instrumental ways of achieving results-because it, through symbolic representation *shares* the meaning of the *intention* widely and thereby touches on motivation at the unconscious level. Symbolic communication therefore, is the fundamental pillar in a "subjective" approach to organisational structure.

The idea of significance of symbolic communication of course, is drawn from thinking in which culture is regarded as a system of *shared* symbols and meanings. Organisational analysis has drawn this factor and it is conceived that as in culture, an organisation essentially consists of a pattern of *symbolic discourse*.

Symbolic discourse is important is yet another way: it links *values, beliefs* and *action*. The *instrumental* significance of symbolic expression is that it helps us to interpret and understand experience and see how this relates to *action*. It is symbolic action therefore, which is at the heart of organised activity.

When we discuss activity, we atonce obviously become aware of the nature of leadership. We begin to see that symbolic organisation theorists have much in common with organisation leaders. The crucial questions for both are: (a) how to create and maintain a sense of organisation, and (b) how to achieve common interpretation of situations so that coordinated action is possible. We begin to see from this analysis that leadership can best be understood as the *management of meaning and the shaping of interpretations*. This is a *subjective* view of leadership as against the usual objective and materialistic in which leadership is synonymous with corruption, intrigue, manipulation and all efforts at overtly manipulating the environment to one's sole selfish advantage. In the subjective approach to leadership reliance is implicitly placed on the inner life-on vision, idealism, values.

"Shaping of interpretations" is synonymous with symbolic communication. It alludes to the role of creativity. Creative expression has in it the power, through symbolic sharing and empathy, to release the most powerful bonds of organisational initiative and organisational bondage.

Apart from giving a totally different approach to "leadership", this *subjective* approach, in terms of symbolic communication provides some other unique insights into the role-playing of leadership. Leadership we then see is *not* running around trying to "manipulate" the environment, trying to be on an ego trip, trying to exploit the situation through corruption or trying to use contacts for political manouvering. The reason we raise these points is because these indeed, are the characteristics of the "leader" in today's India. The leader in other words, has adopted a role which is totally extrovert, materialistic and manipulative.

But the analogy of symbolic communications indicates to us that there is a totally different and in fact, opposite approach to leadership, which in fact, was adopted universally by all our leaders in the National movement and subsequently after independence by such great scientist-leaders as Dr. Homi Bhabha and Dr. Vikram Sarabhai. This is the *subjective, human and inward-looking* approach to leadership. Here the leader supplies two main inputs: *sharing* and *caring*. As for example, Dr. Kamla Chowdhury writes about Dr. Vikram Sarabhai - "His way of management was by *caring for* people."

Another *subjective* approach to organisation is the *cognitive*. According to this approach culture is a system of *shared cognitions* or a *system of knowledge and belief*. Organisation is considered analogous to culture, a particular *structure of knowledge* for *knowing* and acting.

Cognitive emphasis leads us to view organisations as *networks of subjective meanings* or *shared frames of reference* that organisation members share to varying degrees.

From this point of view organisations become "cognitive enterprises". Thus the main functions of an organisation is that of handling and promoting "thought". This approach also shows us that if our assumptions, beliefs and norms are wrong, we get trapped in counter productive cycles of behaviour.

The understanding of organisations as cultures-structure of knowledge, cognitive enterprises, or master contracts- is strikingly similar to the *notion* of *paradigm* as it is applied in scientific communities. In other words, paradigms and cultures both refer to world views, *organised patterns of thought* with accompanying understanding of what constitutes adequate knowledge and legitimate activity.

Wrong assumption, beliefs and norms refers to the obsession of most management leaders with power, polliticking, monetary reward and status-in a word: fixation to an ego-centric approach. In such cases, the unconscious if not the conscious assumption and belief is that leadership is regarded synonymous with wielding of power, authority and ego-assertion. Such an orientation is certainly not creative and most often counterproductive, because it does not trigger motivation in the workers.

However, when we approach an organisation culture as a "cognitive enterprise" then the whole focus changes. We are then more interested in establishing peer relationships with co-workers in order to *seek knowledge*.

It is truly a paradigm shift from ego-centrism to *altruism, knowledge and expression*.

Now let us ask ourselves what is common between the concept of organisation as cognitive enterprise and a scientific paradigm. The answer lies in the fact that both refer to the world views, organised patterns of thought with accompanying understanding of what constitutes adequate knowledge and legitimate activity. The phrase "world view" is used advisedly, because the usual world view of organisation is that it is a place for gaining power, money, ego-expression, self-aggrandisement etc. But we can make a *shift* in the "world view" and then the whole view will change and the organisation become a place for *"structuring of knowledge and cognitive enterprises"*. The organisation then helps our subjective life through creativity and understanding, emotional expression and cognitive appreciation.

We will find that the conceptualisation of organisations as paradigms is useful for thinking about the processes of *strategic management* and *organisational change*.

The most important in India, even more important than technology transfer or financial resources is *Organisational Change*. Because, without that we cannot venture into anything new. There are many aspects to the kind of organisation change required in India. By far the most important is a paradigm shift from "objective" to "subjective" modes of *world view*. The "objective" view to which we are presently fixated in our administrative and management systems by and large falls into two kinds of world views. One is to regard Organisation as a social instrument for *task accomplishment*, which more often than not is the task of making money-showing profits. Most organisational structures are fixated to this view. The modernising process has come to be synonymous with greed and money-making. This is a totally "objective" world-view in which what is desirable is out there and we are constantly hunting for the "golden fleece" or if we take a cue from the Indian Ramayana then for the "golden deer" which Sita bid Lakshman to bring.

The other world view is that of Organization as *an adaptive mechanism*. To cope with the environment is becoming increasingly harsh and political and we need to be constantly manipulative and think of strategems for survival.

Neither of these world views leads to creativity or originality. For that we have to enter the world "within" and therefore, what we need are "subjective" paradigms for Organizational structure. In the "subjective" it is the cognitive, which amongst other things gives us the handle to initiate and organise *organisational change*. This it achieves by changing our world view from superfluous outer norms to "inner" realities, from fixation to greed and manipulation to *imagination, vision and the exercise of will*.

With this shift in world view a whole new world opens up to us. First, we begin to see that *thought* is linked to action. This may seem a truism, but all profound truths in nature have a strange simplicity about them. In other words the "cognitive" approach brings home to us the paramountcy of the role of "*thought*".

Secondly, there is more emphasis on the role of the *mind* than on manipulation. This remind us of Anatole Rappaport's essay on "Strategy and Conscience" - These two are at the opposite ends of the spectrum. In the "subjective" approach we gradually shift from "strategy" approach of organizing to "conscience"-approach of organizing.

Thirdly, we begin to perceive other organization members as thinking as well as behaving. We begin to get conviction that through "thought" we can reach them, touch them.

Viewing organizations as knowledge systems therefore, opens up completely new avenues for understanding the phenomena of organized activity.

The major practical consequence of conceiving of organizations as socially sustained cognitive enterprises is the emphasis on *mind and thought*. Otherwise organizations, especially as they have deteriorated in India become hotbeds of manipulation, corruption or just plain routine, meaningless, repetitive action and a lot of administrative nonsense. This change in paradigm *provides the benefit of deflecting personality expression from mere ego-aggradisement to self- actualisation.*

This cognitive view also helps us to organize *organizational change*. Because when we make "knowledge structure" the criteria of organizational vitality we can atonce size up the true nature and quality of an organization, when outwardly we seem to be overawed by its power and assets.

Another advantage in the "cognitive" approach is that it encourages a *reflective* approach, which is so rare in the world of action these days. This approach enables us to constantly examine, critique and change the social *ideational* system. This ability helps us constantly to change the *"paradigms"* of organization, whenever these get outdated and ineffective.

As for "ideational systems" three are immediately identified: the *humanistic*, the *scientific* and the *enterpreneuial*. Viewing organizations as knowledge systems opens up new avenues for understanding the phenomenon of organized activity. These questions are of practical concern to those who seek to *understand, diagnose*, and *alter the way an organization is working*.

We have discussed two "subjective" views: the "symbolic" and the "cognitive". There is another subjective aspect which could be called the "structural and psychodynamic" perspective. This has got to do with our *unconscious psychology* and the way we project it to the organization-building or organization-running tasks.

One view of culture is that it may be regarded as the expression of *unconscious psychological processes*. This view becomes relevant to organizations also if we develop *psychodynamic* approaches to organizational forms and their practices are considered as projections of *unconscious processes* and are analysed with reference to the dynamic interplay between out-of-awareness processes and their conscious manifestation.

Culture reveals the hidden, universal dimensions of the human mind. One of the characteristics of culture is that it helps us to *solve* problems with the help of symbols, ideas and categories. In this way of thinking an organization really becomes an instrument to solve problems, provided of course, it has the creativity and flexibility to *create* symbols, generate ideas and *categories talent* in such a way that contingent problems can be solved.

We are always making an error in the way we approach organizations. Our analysis always tends to deal only with the surface levels, which are in fact elements of the concious mind. These constitute the politics of the organization: the "formal structure"-hierarchy, rules, regulations, buildings, status etc. These are the outward, formal materialistic manifestations. But formal structure- pomp and glory- is a myth; it explains nothing and helps us understand nothing.

Behaviour cannot be motivated or modified just by the outward structure of an organization. That is the big mistake we make. Just because an organization has power and money does not mean that our behaviour is going to be original and creative by being in that environment which has an outward show of strength. We always attempt to explain, rationalize and legitimise behaviour in terms of the formal organization structure. But formal structure is a unrealizeable mirage.

Because to rely on formal structure is to rely too *heavily on the concious attitude*. And it is not the concious attitude alone which can make things work. The really potent forces are the *unconcious*.

This is exactly where the strength of organization models based on "structuralism and psychodynamics" lies. These models *separate the experience of phenomena from the underlying reality that gives rise to particular forms of social arrangements*. This is an exceedingly important statement and what it means is that sometimes we are hankering after a mirage which seems to be saturated with power and wealth, but on closer examination we find the seemingly forbidding edifice is resting on quicksand and it might sink into the quicksand and disintegrate and disappear any time.

This then makes us realise that what we urgently need to do is not make cosmetic changes in the existing structure, but do something much more fundamental: *change the underlying premise on which structure is resting*. This is therefore, a kind of "inner" or "unconcious" *paradigm shift* in which we change the assumptions on which we have been working so far. This kind of *inner paradigm shift* may shift us from static, archaic, obsolete *organizational* framework to one in which we "think *globally and act locally in a creative way*".

Thus we see that this kind of organization analysis which is guided by a "structuralist" or "psychodynamic" perspective endeavours to penetrate *beneath the surface level of appearance and experience* to uncover the *"unconcious" foundations* of social arrangements.

If we apply this principle to the present day situation in India, we find that the surface level of appearance and experience of most organisations tends to exhibit concentration of bureaucratic power and political manipulation-but in actual fact these manifestations are superficial and totally devoid of genuineness, strength and depth. When we dig to uncover the "objective foundations", we find that these foundations, assumptions and theories are forty years old and no longer relevant - they are decrepid, outmoded, lifeless and dead. We find that we are at the end of the Kondretiev forty years business cycle and therefore, now on an institutional down-swing, because all the assumptions are outdated and outmoded and irrelevant. Quite obviously the logical solution is not to tinker with the archaic and decrepid structure, but to *radically* shift the underlying "unconscious foundation". This, according to classical thought, requires the *injection of innovation* at this point of time. *In this innovation we should be part of the global knowledge base as well locally in a new creative environment.*

Most of us when we think of change in organization either think of getting a "new job" or of changing the visible structure of the organization, ostensibly as "efficiency" measures or "economy" measures or what have you. But this approach solves no problems whatsoever, because it is skin deep and only touches the "formal structure", the "rules and regulations". But these are a myth, because the real organization is what constitutes the "unconcious" the implied and inherent, "assumptions"-what we might term the "underlying reality" as opposed to the "seeming reality".

That is why when we think of "paradigm shift" we should not think of superficial changes but of basic shift in the *"underlying reality"*.

We begin to see now that the structuralist and psychodynamic perspective would need to penetrate beneath the surface level of appearance and experience to uncover the *objective foundations* of social arrangements.

From Public sectors units therefore, we can expect neither resources nor efficiency; only losses and virtual collapse.

We will understand the issue of *"underlying reality"* better if we take some concrete cases from the real life economic world of India today.

What is the implication of this theoretical framework of Organization building for media organizations in India. Do these have an operating culture in which the "subjective" view predominates as it must if it is to be conducive to artistic creation? Do the "symbolic", "cognitive" and "psychodynamic" viewpoints prevail or is it the mad rush of the usual objective, maniacal kind which prevails in any office? Are our media organizations operating cultures informed by "ideational systems" which are humanistic, scientific and enterpreneurial?

The answers to these questions is certainly: No. In my book "Communication and Values" I had drawn attention to this matter of organization cultures by examining the culture of the old Prabhat Film studios in Pune in the light of an organization analysis carried out on the set up of the Atomic Energy Commission of India by the late Dr. Vikram Sarabhai and Dr. Mrs. Kamla Chowdhary. It merits reiteration here because it shows how far our media organizations are from the "subjective" orientation so vital for creativity.

The first point Dr. Bhabha makes is that at one end of the spectrum are certain administrative services, actions based on past precedents and traditions providing security and continuity. At the other end, there are organizations based on research and development requiring innovation and learning. The two extremes require organizations and working cultures which are totally different. The tasks encountered by the media and communications in the contemporary world call for organizations wherein innovation and creative thinking are essential ingredients for survival as well as growth. But the question is whether we are developing such organizations.

The second point is that it is not as if there is a shortage of artistic talent or an absence of the artistic tradition in the country. In fact, we are particularly richly endowed in both these spheres. The artistic tradition of India needs no elaboration. There is world recognition for it. Artistic talent too is in plenty and just as we have one of the largest number of trained scientists in the world so too we have a large number of highly talented artists. But the problem is that the structure of our media and communication organizations are such that such talent is either not drawn upon or is mutilated if employed. The paper in question on the late Dr. Bhabha rightly states: "The general absence of the proper administrative set-up for science (same could be said for the arts and the media) is a bigger obstacle to the rapid growth of science and technology (or artistic creativity in the media) than the paucity of scientists and technologists (or mediamen and communicators)". It should be recalled here that in the analysis of the Prabhat studios it was seen that although there were serious economic and political shortcomings, the administrative culture was such that it brought out the genius in every artist.

The third point Dr. Bhabha realized is that: "Money, hierarchical status, and power are important needs for most, but to scientists and professional groups (equally applicable to mediamen and communicators) the need for creativity of working conditions and self-development are also important factors." The situation is most tragic in this respect in regard to media and the arts. The hierarchical status of the mediaman is far inferior to that of the administrator. Money-wise also he is far below. Even in the glamorous film industry, except for the glittering "stars" the condition of the run of the mill technician or worker is pathetic. In the official sector, the administrator takes the main policy decisions, not the mediaman. The position however would not be so intolerable if media and communications organizations had a creative work culture and opportunity for self-development. This is not the case. The organizations by and large are overpowered by administrative and political cultures, which subdue the creative zest of the media expert. There is little wonder that the output is pedestrian. As against this in Prabhat, New Theatres and Bombay Talkies of by gone days although there was hardly any money and even less power in the organization, the artist got the unmistakable feeling of being at the centre of things, and this in itself worked miracles. Homi Bhabha did the same under changed modern conditions. In all the organizations he created - Tata Institute of Fundamental Research, Bhabha Atomic Research Centre, Department of Atomic Energy-the scientist both in terms of salary and status was superior to the administrator. He also built organizations around individuals so that creativity and innovativeness were encouraged.

The fourth point made in the analysis under consideration regarding Dr. Bhabha is: "It was this facility of working as a policy maker, organizer, and administrator, on the one hand, and participating in the scientific work at the "coalface" level on the other hand, that provided him the on-going understanding to motivate and manage his research workers." The analysis goes on to state that in research and development tasks "the chief executive, besides policy-making and administration, should maintain direct contact with his professional role." It is in this regard that the condition of mediamen is pathetic. They have the worst of both worlds. Neither do they play a role in policy-making and administration nor do they maintain their professional role and skills and knowledge. Gradually they gravitate to the lowest common denominator, victims of the corroding administrative politics and out of touch with their professional discipline. Dr. Bhabha in his organizations achieved exactly the opposite: his scientists were top professionals as well as top administrators. His was a unique experiment in creative administration that should have been taken as a model and applied everywhere. But this was not to be. In Prabhat also we see in the remarkable figure of V. Shantaram, one who was skilled in everything. He was a professional of the highest order but also an able manager and administrator.

Finally the analysis (by late Dr. Vikram Sarabhai and Dr. Mrs. Kamla Chowdhary) states that in such developmental tasks in which research is a vital component what is needed is a shift from "experience based knowledge and skills to highly *conceptual knowledge*. The understanding of this change means the recognition of socio-technical systems rather than a mechanistic organization structure." The term "conceptual knowledge" is used advisedly, because it is the basis of all scientific and artistic activity. What the media culture lacks most is the almost complete absence of "conceptual knowledge", which can only come from scholarly activity, research and R & D effort. Socio-technical systems as against mechanistic organizations means that multi- disciplinary task-forces should be quickly available for re-grouping in project management mode.

We now have a lot of talk about autonomy for the electronic media. In that sense the Atomic Energy Department under the late Dr. Bhabha had no autonomy because it was very much a part of the Government. Yet the operating culture was highly creative. Creativity depends upon the extent of subjectivity in the operating culture and that in turn on the quality of leadership.

We are expanding our communication and media organizations indiscriminately, but making them totally devoid of the "subjective", which alone can bring the blossom of creativity. Otherwise we are merely extending the arid zone of the robot and the technotronic monster.

7

BEYOND MASS MEDIA

This Chapter is treated in five parts:

(a) An introduction in which we stress that the crucial question is not of 'largeness' of the Mass Media through constant expansion or of the much touted "autonomy" but of usage for social, economic, behavioural purposes.

(b) We are at a DIVIDE where now we have to shift from mass media to class media.

(c) The implications of this are illustrated in some Indian and some U.S. case studies.

(d) A survey of the Indian Mass Media scene is presented.

(e) A theoretical framework for National Policy formulation in this area is presented.

In this book we have stated again and again that like the "Transport Corridor" which was a must of the 40 year old Energy-intensive model, if we now had a national "information corridor" based on digital electronics and telecommunications it could lead us to a new kind of spatially-distributed, decentralised political economy characterised by widely dispersed batch-production units (almost in a crafts cum extended family mode) with unimaginably fruitful consequences for employment generation, ecological preservation and almost complete stoppage of migration from rural to urban areas.

Lest readers feel that this is a figment of the imagination of an over-idealistic author, mention needs to be made of the fact that this concept has already been proved in India in the Mass Media situation. This author worked for years with the late. Dr. Vikram Sarabhai in an endeavour to create a Mass Media Corridor through Satellite Television. Dr. Sarabhai was backed in this effort by the late Dr. Homi Bhabha, who formed a Committee which ultimately lead to other developments, which catapulated India into the Space Age and a Domestic Satellite in geo-stationary orbit.

The effect of this Mass Media corridor are there for all to see. It has opened up in a very short period an unimaginably large Rural market for consumer goods, which normally would have taken a hundred years. Two articles are reproduced at the end of this chapter (one from 'India Today' and the other from the 'Times of India') which show the astonishing magnitude of the effect of this 'corridor' on consumerism.

It is of course, an altogether different matter that the ideals of the architects of this 'corridor' (namely Dr. Bhabha and Dr. Sarabhai) were 180 degrees the opposite to what has actually happened. They, like Gandhiji, wanted the village manufactures, culture and self reliance to come up through this latest technology. But the perversion of these values through perverse use of technology, advertising and commercialism are there for all to see.

This does not however, diminish the force of the argument being made in this book: the unimaginably powerful effect of an "Information Corridor" which can be expected on the political economy of the country.

To take up the earlier argument: look at the Mass Media in India and their inanity and ineptitude speak for themselves. Research tells us that "of people who listen to radio 85 per cent listen to Vividh Bharati" — i.e. to the jingle and junk of an unholy alliance of jungle — beat "filmi" music and crass advertising.

Television has been high-jacked from the great idealistic dream of Homi Bhabha and Vikram Sarabhai who envisaged community-access programmes of values and culture to be produced by villagers, tribals and the deprived. Instead now Delhi uplinks on its National programme the glittering glamour of totally worthless consumer products backed and abetted by 'serials' which have neither message nor meaning nor relevance to the crises of the times we live in.

The film industry — biggest in the world — churns out also the biggest garbage in the world. The parallel movement in cinema for which the National Film Development Corporation was created has been controverted 180 degrees and now imports pornographic films through Non- resident Indians — an arrangement not comprehensible in terms of logic.

The output of the Films Divisions — again the largest documentary films producer in the world — is hard to beat in inanity, crassness and total lack of knowledge of the medium. If one of these films comes up for viewing after the 9.30 p.m. English news on TV, it is a proven cure for insomnia.

Last but not the least is the video revolution which in its ultimate analysis is showing 'blue' films to tribals, remote villages and distant hill folk — who till the other day were singing their own centuries — old folk songs and keeping time to the rhythm of community folk dance.

This Indian media spectacle of vulgarity, inanity, corruption and debauchery is overseed and lorded over by a handsome lot of six I.A.S. Joint Secretaries to the Government of India, who in keeping with the high-traditions of their stiff-necked service are inaccessible, irrevocable, incorrigible and irreverantly irreversible.

The question that naturally arises from this night-mare of the dangerously "largest media array in the world" is: What are our priorities? What are our policies? What does our political will wish to achieve?

Lenin knew the answers to these questions. Russian film of which he was the father was to be used for the Bolshevik Revolution — and that is how came to being the series of films made under Lenin's supervision and of the emergence of Podofkin, Eisenstein and others.

Mao knew what he wanted: hence Madame Mao's operas electrifying the Chinese people.

Even Americans, with their innate love of the Dollar know exactly what they need. The American media has only one purpose, only one grand design, only one message above all others: "Live", it says to its audience, "constantly live beyond your meeans. Live on credit, be profligate, consume even when you do not need to, constantly devour the environment, burn up calories — eat, eat, eat — buy, buy, buy." And that is why the American economy stays in tact.

When it comes to India what is it that we want our Mass Communication to achieve. No answer is available. When tissues multiply and proliferate without reason they are cancerous. Our Mass Communication is a cancerous growth eating into the body politic and body economic and to it can be traced the materialisation of life, the errosion of values, the destruction of culture and the consequent cults of aggression, vice, violence and uncontrolled consumerism spreading like wild fire in the country.

Development Communication on the other hand has meant inanity, aridness and blantly self-congratulatory messages on the dubious functioning of a bureaucracy and government totally ignorant of and insensitive to the potentials of the vital forces of communication. In fact, Developmental Communication has come to a point where it can well be equated with non-communication or even counter communication — it certainly inspires no one, and does not lead to any mass mobilisation nor mass motivation.

The burden of this book is that after four decades of developmental effort we are in every sphere at a *DIVIDE*. So we are at a divide in mass media also. We have certainly created an horendous infrastructure. The point we are raising here when we plead: "Beyond mass media" in fact, is a plea to go beyond the infrastructure and start a new phase where we divert energy and investment from endless expansion of the media to *its intelligent, worthwhile and wise use.* In this we are beyond doubt criminally deficient. The question we must face in desparate seriousness is: what is the use of being the largest feature film producers in world, the large documentary film producers in the world, the largest TV audience in the world, the largest video boom in the world if all this "largeness" is spelling our doom and destruction? Are there any institutions monitoring this doom? Has academics any interest whatsoever in understanding and analysing this catastrophy? Are the creative people concerned about the direction the media is taking? Are they activating about it? Does the government have any sensitivity about this issue at all? Or is it wrapped up in the ghost of autonomy only? To whom is the media accountable in this country? Is there any research whatsoever on the havoc it is causing?

The time has come to call a halt to this cancerous proliferation and to take stock of ab initio principles: where is our media heading for? What do we want it to perform? What do we want it to achieve?

Commentary on Case Studies

The basic point which is being made in this chapter is that we are at a DIVIDE in our media philosophy and working. We have to immediately *shift* from mass media to class media. We have had forty years of mass media — blaring a generalised message to an unknown, anonymous audience, to what we might call: "whomever it may concern", and parenthetically: not concern. This section is treated in two parts. In the first part it is shown how mass media with its unconcern and total insensitivity to specific requirements and special attributes can unwittingly destroy an entire "class" of society. In the second part we show the opposite: *class media* can achieve the desired results.

In the first part we will examine the highly tragic and suicidal effect our Television today is having on Rural India. The origins of television in India trace back to our decision to have a National domestic satellite system in geo-stationary orbit and the names of two geniuses: Dr. Homi Bhabha and Dr. Vikram Sarabhai are associated not only with the electronic and space infrastructure they sought to create, but also with the aims and objects of the way this infrastructure was to be used.

The Homi-Vikram media model as I like to call it, was the first attempt since Independence to create an Information corridor, essentially for Rural India. There were to be a series of agro-nuclear complexes in the rural areas all over India with an atomic reactor as the nucleas to generate power. The waste was to be cycled into a fertilizer plant and the fertilizer into agriculture. Electronics was to be a key cottage industry. And the complexes were to be linked through satellite communication.

This was their vision of going *forward* to Gandhiji's Village India in an atomic-electronic-space mode. The television software was to be largely prepared in the villages in community- participation mode through mobile recording units and uplinked from several dishes placed in rural areas.

This whole dream and vision has been 180 degrees controverted and shattered. On prime national time Delhi uplinks serials interspresed with commercial advertising which has had the most unexpected and phenomenal impact on Rural India. The Ad agencies and ratings companies for example, have evaluated that the Mahabharat at any given time was seen by no less than 300 million persons at a time. This figure is much larger than the population of most countries in the world. The biggest rating on U.S. television is the Bill Cosby show which is only 50 million; Mahabharat was 300 million — by far the largest T.V. viewing in the world. Ad agencies have reaped phenomenal sale of products advertised during this prime time and this according to them is largely because of the rural market. *T.V. advertising in fact, has opened up a tremendous Information corridor in Rural India* — to the extent that the 'India Today' issue of July 15, 1990 has carried an article: "The Call of Consumerism" which shows in detail how Village India is getting "hooked on to a whole range of consumer products" and as a result tremendous rural markets are opening up. This is worse than getting "hooked on" to drugs, because what the villagers are now increasingly buying is not only expensive and worthless but largely poisonous and dangerous. For example, from the old "datun" for brushing teeth, Colgate boasts that the villagers are now switching over to Colgate toothpaste — caries and the Dentist are not far away now! Similarly chocolates and soft drinks are replacing healthy preparations of "gur" and "lassi" or fresh sugarcane juice. We are told for example that Rural India now buys 60% of the toilet soap in India. NIRMA incidentally, thanks to T.V. alone has become the single largest selling detergent *in the world*. The situation is summed up by ad men who state that while urban markets are saturated and static, rural markets are growing at the rate of 60% a year.

Much more sinister and suicidal than the blaze of consumerism in Rural India is the change in basic values and lifestyle and character which is sought to be created. Writing on a South Indian retailer named Venkateswarlu, the "India Today" report is forthright: "Inspired by the beautiful women who daily sing the praises of toilet soap, Venkateswarlu's sons now use LUX". But tomorrow these very seductive women might make Venkateswarlu's sons take to something even more expensive and incredibly more forbidden. If our T.V. is now making charming, seductive, partially — clad, gay singing women enter the minds of our young men in the country and replacing them for the traditional gods and their consumer jingle are replacing the village deities mantras, is it not cause for consternation, alarm, premonition of impending doom.

Coming back to our theme of mass and class media — What has happened therefore, is that consumerism of the most blatant kind intended for elitist, upper middle class, urban audiences, by being indiscriminately blared on the mass media has unwittingly hit a totally unintended audience: the deprieved rural poor. But being as powerful a medium as T.V. is, it is making this poor, deprived rural person predisposed to things, products, titillating suggestions and twinkling, glamorous body — bare women whom he will very soon not be able to give up at any cost. Is the experience different from drugs? Is this the dream of Bhabha and Sarabhai fulfilled? Are we entering Gandhiji's Village India? Through the public's own money, a public communication network has been created to systematical destroy public interest.

Now we take up the second part in which we show how *class communication* if properly handled can achieve the exact target desired. This will be illustrated throgh a number of *case studies on class communication* given in the later part of this chapter.

The first is on the use of traditional media — folk songs and drama for Family Planning messages to women-folk. Although this is an impossible area in which we have totally failed, when the target audience was segmented, the message specific and the channel humane — it had the desired effect.

The next two cases drawn from American media show that when a message is "segmented" using all the discipline of the marketing mode, it is successful. The most outstanding example of course, is the T.V. serial "Sesame Street" for the pre-school child in the U.S.A. Joan Cooney the founder of the Children's Television Workshop noted that on the average the American child is exposed to more than seven hours of T.V. viewing a day. Utilizing this "captive" audience and with the aid of a highly competent inter- disciplinary team and taking almost two years to do the homework a T.V. format for a one hour programme was created which had very very sharp behavioural objectives and used the very expensive techniques of advertising and of comic strip effect presented in animation. As the Educational Testing Service, Princeton University evaluated, Joan Cooney achieved the impossible: the 3-year old pre-school child unattended by any teacher gained as much as 80 to 90% knowledge and behaviour change after seeing one hundred of these one-hour programmes. This is the wonder that *class communication* can achieve. We have nothing whatsoever comparable to this exactitude on our media. However, large our media might be, it utterly lacks "class" concentration - i.e. specificity and segmentation.

The other case study of the "marketing" technique in class communication is the American movie "Jaws", which through this "specificity" approach ended up earning U.S. Dollars one million a day.

The key to the success lay in delaying the release of the movie till a "social reality" of the dread of the shark had been created through a media campaign including commentaries in newspapers, television campaigns and above all Jaws on the cover page of TIME magazine as the cover story.

The next case study: "Social consequences of Mass Communication — Public concern over mass entertainment in the U.S.A." apart from voicing concern about the inordinate increase in sex and violence viewing in the U.S.A. mentions the views of highly distinguished scholar Herbert I Schiller on mass communication and the Third World. This is an admirable example of class communication having its deadly effect. According to Schiller it tantamounts to *cultural dominance* of the Third World. The Western media software which is exported to these countries is of such a kind that "the communicated news and entertainment supports a value system essential to *their* (i.e. Western countries) commercial purposes".

Finally there is a case study of "Role of Television advertisements in conspicuous consumption" and it clearly shows that so powerful is the channel and the marketing technique that it forces (one should say *drugs*) the poor to buy expensive and more often than not, not only worthless but positively harmful things.

The question this analysis is leading up to is: if the media channels which we have at our disposal are so powerful and if the *"class communication"* techniques are so effective, then why do we not move over to them for our Development Communication purposes at this point of the *DIVIDE*.

CASE STUDIES — INDIAN AND AMERICAN

Some effects of media on social change in India

TRADITIONAL MEDIA:
FOLK SONGS and DRAMA

In India, as elsewhere, folk media reflect the ethos of the people. They are characterised by the spontaneity that springs from the emotions of common people in their natural surroundings. Folk songs reflect the traditions and customs of a community. India has a variety of folksongs which are linked to ceremonies and activities in various regions. Through a study of folk music, deeper layers of the culture are revealed enabling glimpses of underlying needs, motives, attitudes and values of individuals.

Several successful attempts have been made by various agencies to modify folk songs using a participatory approach, songs have been modified to include sex discrimination, intrahousehold relationships and authority structure within the family and these then provided relevant issues for conducting group discussions. It has been observed that while using drama for communicating messages on immunization, rural women composed songs describing the symptoms of common childhood diseases, and the schedule for immunization. In the process of developing the song, singing it repeatedly and rhythmically the message was reinforced effectively.

The areas taken into account for modification of folksongs were rejoicing at the birth of a girl child, options to girls to select life partners, emphasising education for women, and the small family norm. The folk tunes were retained and only the words were changed.

Thus folk songs have been effective in spreading messages and specially in improving the image of women.

Case Studies on the Social Effect of the Media in the U.S.A. — Sesame Street

Formative Research in the Production of Television for children

There is currently in the United States unparalleled interest in the systematic use of broadcast television to promote the social, emotional, and intellectual growth of young children. Support for this movement lies in the recognition that television is ubiquitous, reaching into 99% of all United States households, that young children are exposed to upwards of 30 hours of television fare each week; that while they learn a great deal from what they watch, there have been far too few significant attempts to plan program content in order to address important areas of learning and development systematically and that no other approach can promise to deliver so much to so many at so small a unit cost. An important feature of this movement is its emphasis on "formative" planning and research, whereby important objectives are first clearly identified and systematic audience tests are then carried out in order to evaluate progress towards their achievement during the actual course of program's production.

Thee Children Television Workshop (CTW) was created in 1968 to produce a series of 130 hours long broadcast television programmes for preschool children with special emphasis on the needs of the urban disadvantaged child. The result — is the "Sesame Street" series. During a pre-broadcast period of nearly a year and a half, and through the current season, the producers have made extensive use of formative field research to improve both the programme's appeal and its educational quality. The formative research methods applied in the production of "Sesame Street" have been reapplied and extended by CTW in planning and producing its second major programme series, "The Electric Company". This series is designed to teach selected reading skills to children 7 to 10 years of age.

The CTW Operational Model

The principal activities undertaken: If there is a single most critical condition for rendering such a model of researches-producer cooperation effective, it is that the researcher and the producer cannot be marching to different drummers. The model is essentially a model for production planning. More specifically it is a model for planning the educational (as opposed to the dramatic) aspect of the production, and the formative research is an integral part of that process. The activities included in the model in their approximate chronological order of occurrence are:

I. *Curriculum Planning*: As the initial step towards establishing its educational goals, CTW in the summer of 1968, conducted a series of five 3 day seminars dealing with the following topics:

1. Social, moral and effective development
2. Language and reading
3. Mathematical and numerical skills
4. Reasoning and problem solving
5. Perception

The seminar included: psychologists, psychiatrists, teachers, sociologists, film makers, television producers, writers of children's books, and creative advertising personnel. Each senior group was asked to suggest educational goals for the prospective series and to discuss ways of realizing the goals on television.

Behavioral Goals: The deliberations of the seminar participants and the recommendations of the CTW board of advisers were reviewed in a series of staff meetings from which a list of instructional goals for the programme emerged. These goals were:

I   *Symbolic Representation*
A   Letters
B   Numbers
C   Geometric forms

II *Cognitive Organization*
A   Perceptual Discrimination Sources
B   Relational Concepts
C   Classification

III *Reasoning and Problem Solving*
A   Problem Sensitivity and Attitude Towards Inquiry
B   Inferences and Casuality
C   General and Evaluating Explanations

IV *The Child and His World*
A   Self
B   Social Units
C   Social Interactions
D   The Man Made Environment
E   The Natural Environment

Specific goals under each of these broad headings were stated, in behavioral terms, so that they might serve as a common reference for the programme producers and the designers of the achievement tests. Appropriate coordination of production and evaluation thus was assured.

— Existing competence of Target Audience
— Appeal of existing materials

— Empirical production
— Production, Aiming and Progress Testing of the Series
— Summative Evaluation

Impact of Media on Social Reality — The Movie "JAWS"

The mass media constitute a dominant force in the construction of one's knowlede of the environment. Mills states: "Very little of what we think we know of the social realities of the world have we found out first hand. Most of the "pictures in our heads" we have gained from these media—even to the point where we often do not really believe what we see before us until we read about it in the paper or hear about it on the radio. The media not only give us information; they guide our very experiences. Our standard of credulity, our standards of reality, tend to be set by these media rather than by our own fragmentory experience."

The media have the capacity to expose certain aspects of an environment and to create strong vicarious experiences. By August 1975, for example, 50 million people had seen the movie Jaws, whose plot is about the life and times of a great white shark that terrorizes a beach resort. One of the more interesting aspects of this movie is the way in which it was marketed and the subsequent events that perpetuated the marketing process.

This sequence was:

(1) The movie was adapted from a best seller book
(2) The paperback's logo was used in the advertising campaign.
(3) Reporters were lured to the movie location everyday for 5 months.
(4) Release of the film was delayed until the summer months
(5) Television campaign coincided with the wide release of the movie and consisted of a prime time blitz.
(6) There was a marketing of Jaws T shirts, pendants etc.
(7) A Time magazine cover piece occurred during the week of the movie's release
(8) The movie immediately started making $1 million a day
(9) Because of the stunning success, the movie became news, and the Media contributed to the publicity with

news stories. Newspapter features were written about audience reaction. Many shark experts emerged and their commentary was sought for both newspaper and television.

(10) Shark sighting became more news worthy and it was not uncommon for newspapers to mention 'Jaws' in their reports.

The example illustrates just how much focus can be placed on a single event in the environment and how the reinforcement process can restructure one's reality.

Role of Television Advertisements in Conspicuous Consumption

Television is a 'massinformer', 'masseducator' and 'mass persuader'. It is a vital link through which advertisement messages reach the consumers. The effect of the growth of advertising on the daily lives of the consumers can best be studied through mass media, the nature of advertisements they carry and the role they play in influncing the tasks and preferences of the consumers. Here television is very significant as revealed by the recent experience of the advertising industry in the early eighties.

In a poverty ridden developing economy like India, there is no room for false standards for consumption. With these considerations in mind a study on the Role of TV advertisements on conspicuous consumption was conducted by a research group in Delhi.

The investigation was carried out in the metropolitan city, Delhi, over a sample of 100 families selected from all parts of Delhi in order to get a representative sample.

The findings revealed that as regards televiewing frequency, pattern and duration children of all age groups, majority of homemakers and male heads watch television. Majority view all the peak hour-transmissions, thus getting maximum exposure to advertisements. The home makers topped the list followed by children.

Most of the products advertised on TV were being purchased by the respondents even when they considered many of these commodities unnecessary. They attributed the introduction of the product or reinforcement for purchase of these commodities to TV advertisements.

The selected five brands of food products popular with all income groups included three brands of chocolates, eclairs, noodles and soft drinks. There was an increase in the total number of families purchasing each of these brands over the past one year and TV advertisements played a role in either initiating, reinforcing or increasing consumption.

The initial demand and increase in demand has been most by adults followed by children in age group upto 10 years and then 10-15 years. The factor responsible had been TV advertisements in 95-100% cases.

In terms of income group, the middle income group had the highest purchase of all the popular brands. All the respondent families purchased soft drinks and 64% opined that TV advertisements had increased the amount of purchase of soft drinks by children.

Thus, television advertisements do play a significant role in encouraging conspicuous consumption either by informing about a new product or reinforcing the familiarity and increasing the preference for most of the products they promote, and in turn convince to purchase or purchase more. Most influenced group was that of children of all ages; they being the most vulnerable consumers are baited into the purchase of most products not necessarily for their well being.

This research survey drew attention to the need to introduce and strengthen consumer education for the masses to make them alert and wise buyers and dissuading them from purchasing products indiscriminately.

The need of the hour is to blunt the destructive edge of the double edged weapon — Television. Advertisers should also have some social and educative perspective and not mislead or deceive viewers.

**Social Consequences of Mass Communication:
Public Concern Over Mass Entertainment in the U.S.A.**

Violence

Many people in the USA are concerned, even anxious, about violence and sexual activities portrayed by the mass media, especially in entertainment. This content offends some persons standard of morality or good taste. Public concern also reflects persons' fear and belief that 'bad' content has harmful, social, psychological, and moral effects (especially on young persons) and leads to antisocial behaviour.

Gallup polls taken about the effect of violence in massmedia, in the mid-twentieth century found that about seven of every ten Americans believed juvenile delinquency can be balmed at least partially on crime comic books and television and radio programmes.

Media presentation of sex and violence have been the subjects of several federally sponsored commissions on the effects of mass communications, in addition to numerous other less programmatic investigations. The Secretary of health, education, and welfare authorised the formation of a surgeon general's "Scientific Advisory Committee on Television and Social Behaviour to investigate scientifically the harmful effects, if any, of televised crime and violence, particularly in leading to antisocial behaviour, especially in children. The results were published in 1972 in six volumes. The Committee summarized its interpretation of the numerous studies:

A preliminary and tentative indication of a causal relation between viewing violence on television and aggressive behaviours; an indication that any such causal relation operates only on some children (who are predisposed to be aggressive); and an indication that it operates only in some environmental contexts?

In 1982 a follow up report reviewed the preceding decade of research on television and behaviour. Some of these recent studies report a statistical relation between the amount of violence watched on television and aggressive attitudes or behaviour. But other studies have found this relationship weak. There are differences of opinion, as to whether there is a significant connection between people's usual exposure to violence in the mass media and their subsequent aggressive, even delinquent behaviour. If there is such a connection could it be interpreted as causal, contributory or even deterrent?

Sociologist Leo Bogart says — The entire history of mass communication research has shown the tremendous difficulty of teasing out specific effect from the tissue of surrounding social influence.

The invisible effects of individual incidents of TV violence might add up to patterns that would leave their traces upon the culture even when specific episodes could not be related to specific effects." The significant question, he suggests," go beyond the short run relationship between television violence and aggressive behaviour in children. They concern the long-run influence of the mass media in shaping our national character."

Sex and Pornography: Public opinion is divided about the presumed effects of viewing or reading mass communicated erotic entertainment. Surveys in the 1970s and 1980s report that more than half of American adults i.e. at that time believed that erotic media content led people to commit rape. Around a third of the public believed that the sexual materials in mass communication make people 'sexcrazy' and two thirds of American adults agreed that erotic materials get people excited. At the same time, six of every ten adults say that mass communicated sexual materials are informative; about half think that they improve marital relations; more than half say that they provide people an outlet for bottled up impulses.

To study the issues, the U.S. Congress created a commission on obscenity and pornography, which reported to the President and to the Congress in 1970. The Commission established an Effects Panel to review and evaluate existing research on the effects of exposure to sexual stimuli from the mass media, to design and implement a program of new research, and to summarize and evaluate the total findings for the Commission. The panels investigations included a variety of studies.

The findings suggest that exposure to erotica had no independent impact upon character and there is no substantial basis for the belief that erotic materials constitute a primary character deficit or that they operate as significant determinative factor in causing crime and delinquency.

Social Values and Cultural Influences

Some authors argue that mass entertainment has important social consequences when it crosses national boundaries. They maintain that the cultural values and messages contained in imported mass communicated entertainment (in news and information) can pollute and displace local culture, especially in small or developing countries. Even the very style of the supplier's mass communication production, its technology and values, influences the communication systems of these countries.

Communication scholar Herbert I Schiller for example, argues that mass communication has become a mechanism for the cultural dominance of Third world nations by multinational corporations (mainly Western) seeking world markets for their goods and services. These countries export mass communicated news and entertainment that supports a value system essential to their commercial purpose. He further states that ruling groups in some Third world countries collaborate in this venture by importing Western goods, services and technology, and communication programmes and techniques. He calls the process *cultural imperialism*.

Other authors also have expressed concern that mass communication from abroad may endanger the cultural values of a society and its members. Most criticism seems directed at the apparent mass communication dominance of Western societies especially the United States and other capitalistic nations. Concern is raised also about the impact of mass communication exported from the Soviet Union and other communist societies. Their news, information, and entertainment reflect the Communist view and also threatens the culture of societies that import them. *"Cultural- invasion"* can thus come from many political directions.

Commenting on this situation, *Everette Desms* asserts: "It is said that Media imperialism results in cultural imperialism and implants Western ideas and values, thus upsetting natural, evolutionary development. At its core, this argument is ideological. Those on the Left decry the existence and impact of cultural imperialism and those on the Right defend the contribution of Western communications enterprises in developing countries. The reasons for the dominance of American content are obvious. The American argument is that they produce more programming and make it available more economically than any other nation in the world."

The public fear of cultural invasion and subsequent cultural pollution, perhaps even cultural dominance, has itself had social consequences, as in laws restricting the amount of foreign programme that can be broadcast by domestic television stations, restrictions on foreign ownership of imported motion picture films, and other measures. Such concern also lies behind some of the issues surrounding reactions to the possibility of international direct satellite broadcasting and nation's rights to control the flow of information and entertainment within their borders versus beliefs in the right to a free flow of information and communication throughout the world.

Soap Opera Portrayals of Sex, Contraception and Sexually Transmitted Diseases in the U.S.A.

In 1986, a full page newspaper advertisement for the planned parenthood federation of America carried the headline 'They did it 9,000 times on television last year. The advertisement went on to state that television is a major influence on teenagers about sexuality and responsibility. It may now be a more important influence than school, parents or even peers. The problem is that television is putting out an unbalanced view (about sex) which is causing more problems for teenagers and society.' The second advertisement stated "Todays' TV message is this 'GO FOR IT NOW GO FOR IT AGAIN DON'T WORRY ABOUT ANYTHING." But there is plenty to worry about.

Asking the question "Is TV sex gitting bolder? In an article in TV guide, the guide states: "network censors agree that Television is indeed on an upward curve of permissibility that has steadily increased the amount and types of sexual behavior that can be shown."

In survey of 1,400 Cleveland parents, television was considered to be the highest ranked source (after the parents themselves) of sexual learning for their children and, in particular, a source of inaccurate information about sex. Other studies have indicated that the majority of married men and women believe that there is too much sex on TV and that adullts are uneasy about children being exposed to televised sex.

For more than a decade, beginning with Franzblau, Sprafkin and Rabinsteins study of 1975-76 prime time programs, communication scholars have been analyzing the sexual behaviour portrayed in network TV programmes. In a 1981 study, Sprafkin and Silverman found a sharp increase in the amount of sexual content in prime-time network TV programs.

Focussing specifically on afternoon soap operas, Greenberg, Abelnan and Nevendorf concluded "Soap Operas have more sexual content than do prime time programmes, but the types of intimacies portrayed differ. Loury, Bove and Kirby's study of soap operas from the 1979 season found an average of more than six sexual behaviors per hour. And, like several earlier studies, they found more than three instances of sexual behaviors involving unmarried partners for every instance involving partners.

Nuclear War and its Consequences on TV News in the U.S.A.

Because the threat of nuclear war is potentially too politically divisive and too frightening to the audience to be 'newsworthy' television may be a 'silent willing partner of the government in keeping nuclear issues below the threshold of national consciousness."

Many political activists have hoped that concentrating the media's attention to issues of war and peace would galvanize public interest, stimulate public debate, and force changes in public policy. The nuclear arms competition between the United States and the Soviet Union, with its ever-present threat of a catastrophic nuclear war, has stimulated this hope in many. For example, Edward Hume, screen writer of the ABC TV movie *"The Day After"* which portrays the destruction that would result from a nuclear attack, hoped the film would "wrench" public dialogue "back to the surface" on the "Value of defending this country with a nuclear arsenal." Similarly, Carl Sagan hoped to provoke a wide-spread public response to his theory of *nuclear winter* — which would make nuclear war a suicidal undertaking by revealing it in the popular Sunday Magazine supplement Parade.

The low level of public knowledge about the most basic aspects of the nuclear regime, however, discourage those who seek to politicize nuclear issues. Manoff has argued that the maintenance of the nuclear regime depends on just such an ignorant and politically inert public. Producing such a public requires a quiescent press which in order to protect national security maintains a strong deterrent in the face of the 'enemy' avoids politicizing the nuclear issues by failing to undertake vigorous adversarial journalism of a type that is lauded in other contexts.

With the threat of nuclear war serving as a cantus firmus to modern life, it could be argued that the media should be filled on a daily basis with images and information about the nuclear threat. Critic Richard, Pollak has argued for establishment of a 'peace beat' that would make nuclear news a staple of journalism, in the way sports, politics and crime have been ceded

a permanent place. Given the event- pegged nature of U.S journalism, however, it is unreasonable and experimentally futile to
expect such constant attention when in journalism terms, nothing new is 'happening.'

The journalistic "taboo" against reporting repetitive stories,
which Gans has noted, seems particularly true of this story. The
constant iteration of the horror of nuclear war and the production of nuclear weapons is not likely to interest or mobilize the
public in the absence of clear, practical, uncomplicated actions
that could be pursued to reduce the threat. Journalists and
public alike may have long since fallen victim to paralysis of
the mind or, in Robert Siftors' words, a *"psychic numbing'* that
militates against daily journalistic attention regardless of the
level of threat.

The nuclear threat does not, of course, however spectrally
over us, cause disregard. Events do occur that have news value
in the traditional sense and provide an opportunity to examine
how the media respond to the challenge of making real the
nuclear threat and educating, if not energizing, the public. The
year 1983 saw the unfolding of three such events of potential
interest to journalists, each of which could have been the news
peg for a serious examination of the nuclear threat.

One— the theory of nuclear winter-is based on scientific discovery.

Two— televising the fictional film "The Day After" is a cultural event.

Third— discussion by members of the Reagen administration
of the possibility of fighting and prevailing in a limited nuclear
war—is a strategic event that throws light on war fighting
policy.

A study was done to see how network TV news responds to
these three stories :

The responses of the network TV were found to be minimal.
The paucity of network coverage overall suggests that television
was uninterested in using nuclear winter of "The Day After"
to discuss nuclear war and its consequences.

Risk Analysis and the Construction of News

The news media commit fundamental errors of attribution in
their coverage of risk situations, by treating them as novelties,
failing to analyze the entire system, and using insufficiently
analytical language.

From almost any point of view, a journalists' definition of a good news story means a catastrophe for someone else. And therein lies a problem as far as the media's role in risk communication is concerned.

Most scholars agree that the media have some social responsibility to warn the public of impending dangers, be they natural or technological, but how the media interpret that responsibility has yet not been precisely described. Along with other institutions, the media do seem to alert the public about immediate hazards, even if not with thorough going accuracy. But how they should participate in the long term raises more fundamental issues. Some have argued that the media should not only warn of impending events but also educate the public about their ramifications, others, considering scholarly work that documents the media's capacity to educate the public about risk as equivocal, conclude that they should not have a significant role in this larger arena of risk communication.

One reason for this more negative assessment is the 'highly selective, often sensational, and sometimes inaccurate media reporting of risk and regulatory actions to control them. A more deep rooted critique argues that the mass media, as instituions, do not or are unable to adequately explain the scientific and political complexities of various form of risk. On scientific issues with political overtones, such as nuclear power, fluoridation etc., dialogue seems essential. The public's fantasies, thoughts and questions may not be most effectively answered by the mass media.

What should the public expect—or not expect from the news gathering process, not only in short term warnings but in longer-term education about the political choices surrounding risk?

Lommon's definitions of news-outside of the "human bites dog" category-generally include the elements of timeliness, consequence, prominence, rarity, proximity conflict, change, action, concreteness, and personality. That is, news *generally focuses on discrete events not on the underlying issues that gave rise to them.*

But this definition of news is not context free. All journalism, including objective reporting, is a creative and imaginative work, a symbolic strategy; journalism sizes up situations, names their elements, structure and outstanding ingredients and names them in a way that contains an attitude toward them. "News follows certain well understood stylistic and cultural patterns. In fact, news of disaster tends to be portrayed as melodrama — a form of communication that relies heavily on plot predictability and stereotype.

All these aspects of news preclude an essential characteristic of risk analysis—the assessment of options, one of which "includes a threat to life or health among its consequences." News stories recount events, not usually options. Further it is difficult to define the appropriate context or a relevant historical, social or governmental context which may be 'dropped' from all but the lengthy stories for fit or other news values. And news may discuss options in a highly stylized form that is not easily interpreted.

For example, death and injury tolls appear near the beginning of news stories about disasters, because they are considered a shorthand form of conveying both the magnitude and human cost of an event. But these top-heavy journalistic accounting seldom include crucial comparative data-lives lost per thousand, additional cases of cancer in the next twenty years— that would provide a context for interpreting the numbers. Such news reports decontextualize the issue, omitting any mention of the benefits gained by the assumptions of risk while focusing instead on the "body bount" be it corporate, governmental or human.

Scientific experts and risk analysts find body counts an incomplete way of assessing risk, even though lay people tend to perceive risk in these terms. Thus in its traditional selection and ordering of information, news does not report risk but rather the negative consequences of assuming that risk.

The language of News—that is, the words and pictures used to convey information—also leaves room for interpretations, especially in the absence of background and conflicting information. Rather than using the precise mathematical formulae of risk analysis, news offers the richness of words and the symbolic content of pictures. The televised *Challenger* explosion brought into millions of living rooms a vivid illustration of the risks of space exploration. What was omitted from those visually compelling reports was the accepted calculation of its risk: the chances of a shuttle explosion were variously placed at between 1 in 25 and 1 in 100. Challenger exploded on the 16th flight.

Because news is based on the concept of novelty rather than situational analysis, car accidents, the product of a well known risky system, seldom become major news stories, while leaks of methyl isocynate in Bhopal or the partial meltdown of the Chernobyl power plant do. Because news is event- centred it seldom looks at the system in which a given event is embedded. What would be considered a 'normal accident' to the professional risk analyst, becomes the Challenger disaster to the public viewing the nightly television report. And because the journalistic rendering of risk uses images that carry with them such strong cultural and emotional overtones, the translation of the mathematical precision of risk analysis is problematic. Add to these structural elements the professional demands to 'humanize' individual stories and news reports of risks make what Fischhoff has called the fundamental attribution error: 'the tendency to attribute too much responsibility to people for their actions and too little to the social and environmental constraints shaping these behaviours."

Indian Media Scene

(1) *Print Media* : The significance of the print medium to rural areas is practically negligible owing to low literacy rates. But even in urban areas the developmental role is questionable.

All these remarks are applicable to the Indian Press today. The papers are full of all kinds of information-weather and transport disasters, drought, political defections, economic data, etc. Yet, we do not know what to make of it all. Even the editorials and signed articles are for the most part irrelevant, and anything but insightful.

As against this, Japan has a Press which is "intellectual" and Britain, a broadcasting system which is "literary" and U.S.A., a Public Broadcasting system which attempts seriously at "community" access. Our present-day journalism by and large can only be described as write-up on political happenings presented in unimaginative form.

This spate of undigested information, however, has not been without its negative side. The number of newspapers, weeklies, journals, monthlies, quarterlies, reviews, etc. has increased exponentially since Independence. This naturally has made the "awareness" level go up and with this has excessively gone up the material expectation of people. The "information" explosion has excessively raised aspirations and put people in the rat-race of cut-throat conflict and competitiveness.

To this "information" overload, totally detached from human feelings and a meaningful feedback, can be attributed the increasing neurotic fears and compulsive behaviour in our society. Instead of religious and philosophical literature and mythology as of old, people now are always reading newspapers, magazines, advertisements and this has a profound effect on making them shallow, hollow, neurotic and compulsive.

Finally, the whole area of traditional culture and the unorganized rural sector of the country finds no echo in the print medium. These remarks are not restricted to official programmes of rural development, but to the magic and mystery that is India, to that ancient civilization, which still exists, to its arts and beliefs and metaphysics. In the cruel turbulent world of political economy, there is no breathing spell for what constitutes the real life of India.

To some extent of course, this is not a uniquely Indian phenomenon; it is world-wide. Its roots can be traced to modernisation and speed and particularly to two factors which have emerged as the enemies of literature and informed journalistic writing : rapid technological change and the fury of public event. Their impact has led to a universal "crisis" in letters.

Through literature as well as informed journalism we are able to cope with the present to apprehend subjective reality. It is the true path to inner communication.

Technology and politics, however, have appeared as monsters in the path of this health-giving communication. Advanced technology compresses time and motion and accelerates the rapidity of event, to which perturbation is added by the exploitativeness of political action. This has had two effects. On the one hand, journalism is getting cluttered with too many happenings, information overload and undigested ideas, which create confusion and consternation in the public mind. On the other hand, the man of letters is increasingly denied the detachment, distance and leisure required for creativity. By the time a literary work appears, its import is irrelevant to the burning issues of the day.

What has happened therefore, is that a cleavage has been created between journalism and letters and its sharpest manifestation is in the USA, where both activities are highly professionalized.

As a result, two things have happened. First literature has increasingly lost its significance in our lives. Second, the wisdom of literary introspection is denied to public events and decision-making.

But the problem is not insurmountable and in some countries new kinds of writings have come into existence which attempt to cope with this problem. The most outstanding example of course, is of the New Writing in the U.S.A. which has helped bridge this yawning gap between journalism and literature, public affairs and judgement, rapid change and introspection. It is to the American writers, therefore, that credit must go for creating an entirely new climate in writing which goes by the generic name: New writing.

In order to be able to understand the significance of public affairs, the complexities of events and their political, economic and socio-cultural implications what is required is not merely information but wisdom. And wisdom requires a different kind of writing—one characterized by introspection, judgement and subjectivity. Therefore, the kind of writing we require more now is interpretative writing, which explains to us why affairs are happening the way they are happening. What is required is also "subjective" reportage so that the writer gives us a vision of the happenings from the "inside" and makes the events "alive" for us and gives us a "feel' for the situation. Increasingly we also require investigative reporting because with the complexities of public events increasing, the underlying causes of these happenings either get concealed or camouflaged.

It is for the investigative reporter to lay bare the reality and expose the intricacies and subtleties of the situation. We also need writing of travelogure because India is a land of variegated cultures and an extraordinary richness in civilization. All this cannot be sensed just sitting in Delhi.

Unfortunately, however, there is none of the New writing — interpretative, subjective, investigative, travelogue. The fixation to an antiquated model of colonial writing to which has been added mere politics and intrigue is what is available. In short, as in many other spheres, it could be called the politicisation of journalism.

In stark contrast to this the experience in the social sector in Rural India has been a total failure. After four decades of development effort, we neither have a "theory", a conceptual framework, nor success in practical communication. From the Eighth Plan onwards, therefore, a very concerted effort must be made in the Social sector to find out a viable theoretical framework and also what *Communication strategies* will provide us with a breakthrough.

(2) *Radio :* The radio hardware has a 3-tier set up. The megawatt transmitter at Nagpur with repeaters all over the country provides the National channel, which broadcasts national programmes beamed at the whole country. The Medium wave transmitters serve regional purpose. Now the most important point to note is that at the third tier we have gone in for FM (Frequency Modulation) mode as against AM (Amplitude Modulation) mode of the Medium Wave transmitters. The reason for this is to avoid the "Megawatt race" in which India finds itself, surrounded by very powerful Megawatt transmitters of Voice of America, B.B.C., Pakistan, China and American transmitters in Sri Lanka beaming towards India and drowning our Medium wave.

But this calamity can be turned into a blessing because FM transmission has a radius of only about 25 kilometres and therefore, is ideal for Local Radio, which in a *community- participant* mode of transmission would be ideal form of communication for Rural Development.

Instead of this however, the All India Radio plan is to connect these FM transmitters in relay mode for regional coverage and use for Commercial broadcasting of Vividh Bharati—which in fact, would be the very enemy of Rural Development with its consumerist jingle and urban-oriented programmes.

(3) *Broadcasting Policy:* The only thing that can be said about India's broadcasting policy is that we have never had one. The British seem to have paid only minimal attention to broadcasting in India even when education was of supreme importance to them. Three possible reasons can be advanced in explanation.

The First Industrial Revolution was one of the Guttenberg press. It was the written word which symbolised it. In terms of communication, it meant the primacy of the print medium. The audio-visual media were considered inconsequential and treated as an exotic. It was only during the Second Industrial Revolution that radio, television, satellites and computers have come into their own, and communication, instead of being tagged onto transport, has found its rightful place along with the information system.

Secondly, there was the problem of getting radio receivers, particularly for community listening. British attempts with battery operated sets in the Peshawar area, for example, failed miserably.

Finally, the type of people, beginning with Lionel Fielden, the first British Controller of Broadcasting, who happened to man the radio medium in India, had extraordinary talent and a sense of "nationalism". Thus, the British did not evolve any policy.

Paradoxically, the most creative era in Indian broadcasting was the British period. People like Fielden, the Bokhari brothers (Zulfikar and A.S.), Mehra Masani, K.S. Duggal, Somnath Chib, Iqbal Singh, P.C. Chatterjee and a host of others had exceptional intellectual and artistic talent. There was no attempt even during this period to define a policy, but in retrospect one could say that the these outstanding broadcasters helped create a cultural atmosphere most hospitable to the arts.

The real trouble in Indian broadcasting system began after Independence when the venom of politics entered it. Certain people demanded broadcasting time on a communal basis.

With the expansion of the network and increased industrialisation and the impetus given to electronic manufacture, we have entered what might be called the third phase of broadcasting—that of the obsession with hardware. Any planning for broadcasting now boils down to inordinate demands for hardware expansion.

In conceptual terms, then what we have done is to subvert the communication revolution. Instead of making use of the new concepts of cybernetics and information theory as tools of development and education, we have succumbed to the technostrategic syndrome, In this syndrome, the media have taken the macabre form of 'gamesmanship' and 'steermanship', of politics and manipulation. The task of giving messages has become an exercise either in gimmickry or deception.

It is time to change all this. The Government should take positive steps to formulate a cogent and coherent broadcasting policy. This should include needs identification of the target audience especially in rural areas, utilisation in terms of infrastructure and inputs, creative software programming, matching hardware with appropriate technology, an adequate and relevant organisational structure, and a free operating culture. To this should be added an open system situation, continual monitoring and remodelling, attempts to formulate a policy framework and adequate planning mechanism.

The task clearly is stupendous if not altogether impossible, given the kind of work culture we have in this country. But this is the challenge we have to face.

(4) *Television :* The television hardware again is in 3-tier mode. The up-link from Delhi via satellite covers the entire country and provides the National programme. A combination of up-linking from State capitals and microwave provides the regional programmes. But here again in TV as in radio *Local TV* is not engineered thereby denying local community-access programmes ideal for Rural Development. This *Local TV* could be very easily provided through the LPTs—Low Power Transmitters spread all over the country-each with a transmitting radius of about 25 to 30 Kilometres. Each could be provided with inexpensive TV production equipment and community participation ensured in programme production.

The end result is that Television which is definitely the most effective and persuasive medium of mass communication is not being used for Rural Development despite, the huge outlays Government is disbursing for this medium.

5. *Satellite-Mode Transmission :* The great visionary-scientist, the late Dr. Vikram Sarabhai gave leadership for the idea of a domestic satellite system essentially for the purpose of Rural Development. According to his system configuration earth stations were to be provided all over the country in remote rural areas. The TV Programme production was to be done in the rural areas by TV mobile vans all over the country. The earth stations were to up-link to satellite and the signal was to be received in remote villages in DRS- (Direct Reception via Satellite) mode by chicken-mesh antennas hooked to a community receiver in a village.

This stupendous vision of Dr. Sarabhai for "Television for Rural Development" has been totally shattered, controverted and vitiated. We are doing the exact opposite. We are using highly expensive satellite technology for multinational advertising, elitist urban-oriented essentially entertainment serials and last but not least: cricket-matches—to the utter neglect of rural development.

(6) *Film* : India has not only the largest feature film industry in the world but also the largest documentary film industry. Yet the impact of both on development is highly questionable. Documentary films made by the Films Division used to be dubbed in sixteen Indian languages and then shown all over rural India by the Field Publicity unit of the Ministry of Information and Broadcasting. But this practice has been stopped. Also, the National Film Development Corporation was created to promote a parallel cinema to make high quality films. In its earlier incarnation as Film Finanace Corporation, it did meritorious work but the parallel film movement is all but dead now. We can only boast of the number of films made, not the care they show for values, ideals and inculcation of progressive norms.

India's fabulous film industry is a testimony to the genius, courage and preserverance of a few outstanding persons (producers, directors) who working against the heaviest odds, with little help in terms of finance or technology, have put India on the world cinema map. In the earlier years, these were the leaders of New Theatres, Bombay Talkies and Prabhat and later individuals like Shantaram, Bimal Roy and Satyajit Ray have kept up this tradition. The Indian film, therefore, is solely and exclusively a product of private enterprise.

When the S.K. Patil Enquiry Committee was set up in 1949, some persons who deposed before it urged nationalisation of the industry, but Patil and his colleagues rightly saw absolutely no reason for such a step.

The question of the Public Sector's role in film, however, has come up from time to time and its most obvious expression is the Films Division, which came into being in 1948 under the aegis of the Ministry of Information and Broadcasting. The rationale for this step was that apart from the entertainment output of commercial cinema, the government must take steps to ensure that films of an "educational" nature are made and distributed for the moral edification of the viewers. It has been a struggle and a losing battle for the Films Division all along, but it did attain its high water-mark under the late M.Bhavnani and later Ezra Mir in the 1950s.

From time to time, the government made efforts to bring in talented leadership from outside. One such attempt was a stint by James Beveridge of the National Film Board of Canada and the other by Jehangir Bhowanagry of UNESCO, Paris. Both, however, returned to their respective jobs somewhat chastened and disillusioned.

The attempt by the Films Division to have its own theatre in Delhi for exclusively showing its own documentaries proved an abysmal failure. Nobody was interested in these didactic films.

After World War II, we see two main trends in Indian cinema, which continue to dominate the scene till today. One is the Bombay Hindi commercial world, which by now has become a colossus—an industry with an annual investment of hundreds of crores of rupees in films, not to speak of the incredibly large capital investment in theatres, studios, laboratories, etc. With notable exceptions the material churned out is of abysmally poor standard, sentimental, perverted and inane. Its financing system is highly speculative and totally devoid of any order or sense. With the exception of Satyajit Ray, who has appeared as an unexpected star on the firmament, albeit totally disowned by the masses, the general standard of film making bears no semblance to the glorious days of nationalism of Prabhat, New Theatres and Bombay Talkies.

The other trend has been the steady expansion of the Films Division. But here too we have travelled far away from the glorious days of Bhavnani and Ezra Mir and the heroic attempts of Bhowanagry and Beveridge. The medium has been reduced to blatant propaganda and a peculiar sort of pompous, affected recital of events in an artificial pseudo-scholastic style, bordering on boredom and disbelief.

To a large extent, we are faced with this extremely sorry state of affairs because no heed was paid to the recommendations of the Patil Committee and matters were allowed to drift.

Out of these two trends of total unrealism—the one sentimental, the other affected—as if by some magic has emerged a trend of the younger film makers: Basu Chatterjee, Shyam Benegal, Girish Karnad, M.S. Sathyu, B.V. Karanth, Basu Bhattacharya and others. And as if by some magic again, they seem to comprehend and capture reality.

It is in this new emerging context that we have now to explore the problem of feature versus documentary film. An analogy which would help the analysis is from the world of letters. A new kind of expression has come into existence, variously called the 'The New Writing' or 'New Journalism,. Its exponents are Truman Capote, Norman Mailer and others who have synthesised journalism and literature.

It is the change in our environment, in the world we live in, which has necessitated this synthesis. The two overpowering forces in modern civilization are the technology push and fury of public event. Both literature and journalism in their original form are inadequate for the task. History is made so fast by the fury of public events that the calssical detached man of letters tends to become irrelevant and his literary output tends to be bracketed with history. Daily journalism, on the other hand, cannot muster the introspection, quietness and detachment needed for understanding and wisdom. A resolution of the problem has been attempted by the emergence of the new kind of writer, who is essentially a man of letters, but takes up for his subject some of the most compelling issues of the day. He treats in literary style burning issues of the day.

Benegal's Manthan appears to be something similar, and may be regarded as a forerunner of what might be called the 'New Film'—a film which treats of social urgencies in the style of a feature film. The end-product is a synthesis of the documentary and the feature.

The professional background of the new genre of directors starting with Ray is totally different from the traditional filmmaker, and astonishingly relevant to the task in hand. Benegal provides a unique combination of gifts. First, work in commercial advertising, then in advertising films, documentaries, educational television and finally entry into the world of feature films. It is not surprising that two of our foremost producers, Benegal and Ray, started life in advertising. Others of the new genere have come into feature film-making from an earlier stint in documentary work.

This tends to support our thesis that the need of the hour is rapprochment between journalism and literature, between functionalism and art. Little wonder that our foremost directors are those who have been and continue to be concerned with the compelling exigencies of modern life. However, the New Film, now coming into its own, is not what is generally considered an 'Art Film'. On the contrary if anything, it tends to be closer to public urgencies, to reality and to the documentation and narration of episodes, which evoke thought and concern about contemporary pressing problems. In this sense, the 'New Film' movement in India today, whether expressed through Sathyu's Garam Hawa, or Benegal's Manthan, or Karanth's Kaadu, is totally different from what has come to be established as the art film in the West.

It is quite apparent that these films of Karanth, Chatterji, Karnad, Benegal and Sathyu are not only of high intellectual and aesthetic standards, they are also doing well at the box office. How is this explained? We have probably to look for the reason in the emergence of a new kind of audience.

A number of factors have contributed to this. First is the vast increase in population with the result that about 150 million people live in the large and metropolitan cities. Secondly, the rate of literacy and education has gone up. In sheer numbers, the jump is exponential. Together with these two is the increasing modernisation and change in values and life styles. No systematic research has been done on the subject of cinema audiences, but from the somewhat limited premises, it can be safely surmised that better taste has evolved and a large number of the populace now demand better quality in everything. These are the people who have become increasingly sick of the junk and tinsel churned out by the Hindi cinema and have found in the 'New Film' the relief they were seeking.

Telecommunications

Along with the development of large Digital switches to handle very large metropolitan telecommunication traffic the primary thrust of C-DOT (Centre for Development of Telematics) of the Department of Telecommunications was to focus attention on development of Digital RAX-"Rural Automatic

Exchange" of about 80 lines for expanding communication to village India. The argument given was that this RAX system is better suited to our villages than any other system in the world because it can face unpredictable varying climate, withstand high temperature without the need of air-conditioning and most important of all: run on low, fluctuating electric power or even batteries. The slogan was: "One RAX a day" (same as for LPT's in TV) i.e. one RAX would be installed in a village everyday so ultimately to cover all the 500,000 villages in India within a short period of time. Instead however, the whole programme has got grounded because attention has been diverted to fancy hi- tech electronic projects and in the bargain the village has been given the go-by.

We see a uniform pattern emerging in the development and usage of our Communication Technologies: the ultimate casualty is Rural Development.

Distance Learning

A corollary to this kind of envisioned Rural Telecommunication is that it can do wonders for far flung rural communities by making possible Distance Learning of all kinds. It can be engineered for long distance education programmes through picture transmission in *slow-scan* mode. This kind of mode is particularly relevant in the nation's drive to eradicate illiteracy, in agricultural education to farmers, training extension agents and for imparting social welfare, health and family planning education.

Computer-Communication Systems

The National Informatics Centre under the Planning Commission is setting up a nation-wide computer communication system called NICNET essentially with the view to covering all districts in India. It will have four headquarters: Bhubneshwar, Hyderabad, Pune and Delhi and these in turn will be connected via satellite to computers located in every distric in India. This will make it possible to readily access at District as well as at National level information relating to land resources, health records, education levels, quantum of jobs, agricultural status etc.

From the Rural Development point however, the question is how to use this system for planning and implementation in *decentralised* mode through Information Technology. The technology may conceivably come, but a lot of spade work will have to be done to work out the systems configuration for utilising this information in a decentralised mode.

Fibre Optics

This is the latest communication technology which communicates through light beams travelling through fibre glass. One optic fibre has the miraculous capability to handle millions of communication signals. Already some companies like ONGC have installed this technology and they have large surplus capacities. As the link essentially charters rural areas the question is how to use the surplus capacity for Rural Development purposes.

Facsimile

This essentially is transmission of picture or matter in picture mode through Digital ISDN mode of telecommunication.

Communication Policy Planning

This paper suggests that eventually an adequate instiutional mechanism is necessary for the formulation and implementation of *Communication Policy at National Level in India.* The broad conceptual framework for this purpose is discussed.

Environment for Public Policy Analysis

The problems that the government faces cover a broad spectrum of complexity—at the one end there are the routine problems while at the other end there are problems dealing with a rapidly changing environment, involving choice among a large number of poorly defined alternatives.

For issues that lie towards the simpler end of the spectrum, most agencies have well-developed internal coping mechanisms. For complex issues, few agencies have adequately developed internal analysis mechanism. Also, the tasks to be assigned to outside specialists usually cannot be precisely specified. Help in resolution must come from the new institutional mechanisms. But what characteristics must these mechanisms have? Policy orientation, influence, breadth of character, interdisciplinary character and eye to the future and a systems approach.

Policy Orientation

The fundamental orientation of such an institution must be towards production of policy relevant studies. Management and staff members should percieve the need for, be motivated toward and receive rewards for production of policy relevant research. Policy orientation should not be appended to a higher priority concern for production of scientific research, or profitable products or for the training of students. Nevertheless, the research programme must include supporting basic research in sciences, technologies and methodologies.

Influence

The second essential characteristic is influence. There are two consequences, which are not directly observed but which are important. The first is the need for continuity or an association that exends over a long span of time rather than the span of a single task-order contract. Good policy research is based not only on the analyst's skill, but equally on the awareness of the specific characteristics of the agency he is working with. Moreover, continuity is the precondition for trust.

The second consequence of the need for influence is the complementary need for independence. The institution must be able to think about "unthinkable" and "forbidden" topics., to be able to reject received institutional dogma, and to be believed by an independent outside observer. It is essential for the policy-analysis organisation to complement its influence with independence.

Breadth of Charter

The third essential characteristic is a broad charter. Its charter should, in general, encourage it to examine the full range of subjects consonant with the responsibilities of the concerned agencies rather than narrow, specified tasks. And the choice of specific topics should rest primarily with the policy analysis organisation, rather than the contracting agency.

These conditions are of equal importance to both the policy-analysis organisation and the contracting agency. The importance derives from the nature of good public poli~, analysis, which much more resembles scientific research than it does procurement of the usual goods and services.

Inter-disciplinary Character

Policy issues faced by government agencies fall less frequently than in the past into the domains of a single academic discipline. Public policy analysis organisations must be able to mobilize the highest skills of people trained in a wide range of disciplines from engineering to sociology, from computer science to medicine.

Each of the successful Policy Analsis Organisations has recognised and operated according to these principles. Experience has suggested that this dual staff organisation inter-disciplinary study teams and discipline-oriented departments- is essential for long term organisational success.

True inter-disciplinary studies demand intricate merging of insights and methods into a study that responds directly to policy issues. There are four pre-conditions of such research: the right problems, the proper leader, appropriate methodology, and adequate incentives.

The most important single factor determining the true inter-disciplinary character experience is the quality of the project leader. Such a person should combine a fundamental concern with the policy problem, recognized excellence in some single discipline and solid understanding of the achievements, approaches, and vocabulary of several other disciplines.

The institutional framework in which research is conducted must provide the proper finance, professional incentives and rewards for achievements in inter- disciplinary research.

Future Orientation

The effects of public policy decisions taken today are reaped for many years into the future. Public policy analysis must therefore look to the future to seek the context in which to examine many of today's issues. Activities must have time reference that range from the present to twenty or more years into the future.

Systems Approach

The final essential characteristic is the concern for the whole and not just for the parts of the problem. The systems approach consists in nothing more than the common sense observations that in investigating a problem, one should examine all those agencies and modalities whose actions affect it. However, this warrants frequent repetition because it is so often and so casually overlooked.

ANNEXURE-1

The Call of Consumerism
("India Today" – July 15, 1990)

With villagers getting hooked on to a whole range of consumer products, a vast new market has opened up.

PROTAP Roy is senior vice-president, marketing, at Godrej Soaps Ltd. If you walk into his office these days, it's just possible that he'll be quietly muttering to himself: "India lives in its villages." No, Roy is not about to discard his pin-striped suit for a khadi kurta and his executive briefcase for a jhola to walk into India's poor benighted villages, spreading sweetness and light.

If India's villages excite him, it's for quite un-Gandhian reasons. They represent the hottest new market for his company's soaps—and by far, the fastest growing. The figures are cheering. Rural India buys an unbelievable 60% of the toilet soaps sold in the country. Even more alluring, while the urban market for soaps is more or less stagnant, the rural market is growing at a staggering 60% a year. So if Roy says "Jai Kisan" with gusto, he has very good reasons for doing so.

It isn't just soaps that are turning on India's villagers. They'are also getting hooked on a whole range of other consumer goods—toothpaste, colour television sets, scooters, washing-machines, fans, refrigerators,sanitaryware, air-coolers, the works.

All at once, a new market has opened up for India's corporate world: Bharat. From remote hamlets in eastern Bihar to the prosperous sugar belt of western Uttar Pradesh, from the wheat fields of Punjab to the rice paddies of Kerala, from marginal farmers to rich landlords, villagers are flocking to buy consumer goods—and buying them with a venegeance.

The numbers tell the story. The rural market for packaged consumer goods crossed Rs. 1,500 crores in 1988, more than double the figure five years before. Over 20 per cent of colour televisions produced in the country are sold in rural areas. As are 48 per cent of mono-cassette players and 48 per cent of mopeds. The list is endless.

Expectedly, companies are rushing to grab a piece of the pie, setting up special divisions to cater to the new market and designing products specially for rural areas. Cadbury's for instance, is developing chocolates that won't melt easily in the heat. And LML Ltd. recently introduced a scooter with a more powerful engine—aimed at the farmer, who can use it for transporting goods. Says P.B. Bharda, vice-President (sales and marketing) of soap manufacturer Tata Oil Mills Company Ltd. (TOMCO) : "We realised that if we needed to jack up our sales there was no alternative but to go rural. The competition in the urban market is too hot."

Advertising agencies like Lintas, Clarion and Ulka are cashing in on the boom by setting up separate rural advertising cells. Says Sumit Roy head of Lintas rural marketing unit : "After the middle class urban consumer boom, what we are seeing today is the rural middle class boom. It had to happen."

The surprises never cease. As Pratap Roy of Godrej will tell you. A couple of months ago, Roy travelled with his company's van to Islampur, a remote village in Maharashtra. After the usual hoopla—music, announcements of free gifts—the van made its way to the few shops in the village. There was a surprise in store for him : every shopkeeper wanted to lay his hands on all the bottles of hair dye he had. Soon he also discovered that farmers didn't want the dye for themselves. They were using it to colour their cattle to make them look younger and healthier.

Union Carbide found that its slick plastic torches, which were all the rage in the metros, had no takers in the villages. Farmers preferred heavy brass torches. Says Union Carbide Managing Director G.P. Gokhale: "With the brass torches, they feel they are getting value for money."

Other companies are modifying their products to suit rural tastes. Texla drew a blank with its television sets with grey and black cabinets: farmers had no use for sombre urban shades. It introduced a new range—in bright red and yellow. Now farmers are grabbing all they can get.

Yet other companies have tried to anticipate rural tastes and push their wares accordingly. Dabur distributes religious texts like the Hanumanchalisa and Ramcharitmanas or calendars with religious themes along with its ayurvedic products. "It works wonders in the villages of India", says S. Ramachandran, general manager, marketing. The strategy also worked for Texla, which cashed in on the popularity of the Mahabharat serial by naming its sets Arjun and Yuvraj, Radio manufacturer Murphy discovered that the name Murphy Munna went down well with rural consumers.

One company which succeeded in targeting the same product in different markets simply by changing the packaging is the West Bengal-based KMP Oils. In Muslim-dominated Uttar Pradesh, the company's hair oil is sold in green packs. In Orissa, the same packs come in purple—the colour is considered auspicious in the state.

Another effective corporate strategy has been to sell products in smaller packs to suit, presumably smaller, rural pockets. Hindustan Lever found that retailers in villages were cutting its large 100 gm soap into smaller pieces and selling these. So it introduced a small 75 gm soap. Now, is planning to sell Wheel detergent powder in sachets. It has encouraging precedents: Godrej's Re 1 sham-poosachet has been a runaway success.

That, of course, doesn't mean that only cheap brands sell in rural markets. Usha found that sales of its economy models were falling sharply in rural areas. Farmers prefer Usha's premier "Century" brand, though it is priced 20% higher. Says Vinod Dhawan, Vice-president of Cadbury's: "It is a myth that cheaper products sell in rural markets. The rural consumer is ready to pay for quality products".

And bent on getting every paise's worth too. For Lalitaji of the Surf advertisement now has her rural counterpart. Only, not one, but many. And each with a different taste. There's Lalitabai in Maharshtra, Lalitaben in Gujarat, Lalitbehn in the north, Lalitabon in West Bengal, and in the South, Lalitamma. It's for her family's pocket that companies will now have to fight.

Khan, a shopkeeper: "Television has changed our lives." Nissar has no complaints, of course, business is booming: he sells a dozen cakes of soap every day.

But marketing in rural areas—as companies are discovering entails more than just beaming slick commercials. Says S.K. Wadhwa, executive director of sewing machine manufacturer Usha International: "Their reach is limited. You have to create excitement so that villagers remember your product." Usha's solution was to run sewing schools in villages which offer short-term tailoring courses for women.

Other companies have been equally innovative. Brooke Bond adopts tea stalls which tempt villagers to sample its product by offering free cupts of tea, Geoffrey Manners participates in village melas where its salesmen, dressed in white aprons to resemble doctors, extol the virtues of Anacin. In Andhra Pradesh, Philips dresses up people to look like its bulbs and batteries and parades them through the village.

All this is a far cry from the antiquated marketing methods of the past, when companies used to have a few big stockists and catered to expanding markets by increasing their number. The strategy worked. But only up to a point—it made no sense to have a stockist in a village with a population of 1,000 where the demand for a certain product would be a dozen units a day.

Hindustan Lever's answer is to use a fleet of vans which regularly visit remote villages with a population of less than 5,000 at regular intervals to restock small shops with its primary products—Lifebuoy and Wheel soap. The strategy is called Operation Harvest. Says Sidharth Sen, marketing director (detergents): "We are just tapping the rural market. There is a lot to learn."

Colgate Palmolive has supply vans which offer free samples and screen video films on oral hygiene. These are supplemented by bicycle vendors who go to villages where the vans can't reach.

The Delhi-based Jain Studios and the Dalmias have a fleet of video vans which screen films and Chitrahaar in villages. Space on the vans and video-time is available for hire and companies are flocking to take advantage.

In their rural marketing drive, companies have come up against several problems. For one, the rural market is not a homogeneous one. LML found that the south was more receptive to its scooters than the north. Says Marketing Manager Rakesh Jayal: "People in the south are more willing to accept a high-tech product than the north. They're more brand conscious, more restricted to a few pockets, has spread all over the country. And with the Government ensuring that agricultural prices don't crash, the farmer has money to spend—all of it tax free. One statistic is revealing of the surplus money that farmers now have in their pockets: in 1960, the average rural household spent 81 per cent of its income on food: today it spends less than 70 per cent.

The consequent splurge effect is visible all over the country. In Shamli, a mandi market in the heart of western Uttar Pradesh's sugar belt, Neeraj Goel finds buyers even for the washing-machines that his shop stocks. Television sets are, of course, passe. Says Goel: "I sell 60 sets every month, and the demand swells during the festival and marriage season.

In Perunna village near Changanacherry town in Kerala, Babu Alex has a shop selling swanky sanitaryware. Some taps cost more than Rs. 3,000, but that hasn't kept customers away. Business is thriving and Alex now has a computer to aid him in speedy and accurate billing. In Jaridih village in Bihar's Dhanbad district, a paan shop displays thermos flasks of a myriad brands. The shopowner says he sells a dozen flasks every day. It's hard to believe, until the shopkeep explains that many families have as many as six members working in the mines.

Television, with its alluring commercials, has, of course, contributed in large measure to the splurge. To see how well it has succeeded, move to Andhra Pradesh, to the house of M. Venkateswarlu, a small-time paddy farmer in Guntur district. Among his prized possessions is a televison set.

The change it has wrought is evident. Inspired by the beautiful women who daily sing the praises of toilet soap, Venkateswarlu's sons now use Lux. For washing clothes, the family has taken to Rin — the commercials imply you can't do without it. The pearly white teeth of the models in the tooth-paste advertisements too have taken their toll: after a long debate, the family abandoned charcoal for Colgate.

It is a long way from Guntur to Asagarh, an adivasi village on the Bombay-Ahmedabad highway. But as far as the effect of television goes, its inhabitants might be part of Venkateswarlu's family. Asagarh's thousand residents make a living cultivating wheat or working on the local chickoo farms. A decade ago, mention of washing soaps or chocolates might have evoked blank stares. Today, reputed soap brands vie with each other for a place in the adivasis' toiletry. Potato chips are in high demand. And some adivasis will smoke only a Wills cigarette. Says Nissar.

ANNEXURE-2

ECONOMY (TIMES OF INDIA)
INDIAN VILLAGES ARE CATCHING UP ON THE
CONSUMER BOOM

Indian villages are witnessing a slow and silent revolution. Consumer items from shampoos and refrigerators are slowly becoming a regular feature of village homes. As recently as a decade ago it could not be conceived that VCRs, washing machines, pressure cookers and mixies would be used in the villages. Today, the widespread usage of these products in the villages is a reality.

A number of factors have propelled a boom in the sale of consumer goods in rural markets. The benefits of the so- called Green revolution, have augmented the purchasing power of the farmer. Further investment in rural areas as part of developmental expenditure on road building, irrigation projects, etc. has also contributed to the increase in buying power of rural India. The incentives and tax-holidays offered by the government in backward districts led to the dispersion of modern industries in the rural areas. This, in turn, has provided employment in the villages and created a market for consumer products. The spread of banking operations through a network of branches in the rural areas has also aided the penetration of monetary economy in the villages. Another factor in rural prosperity has been remittances from abroad such as that by Indian workers in Dubai or Nigeria.

The appeal of consumerism has been spread by Doordarshan, which took a host of consumer and "convenience" products to the doorstep of the villagers. Advertising of television particularly in its colourful version has given exotic products a live and real appeal.

Improved literacy and education also augmented the desire for consumer products in the villages. Educated villages are becoming more conscious about their health, appearance and personality. They thus have a tendency to purchase products like shampoos, toothpaste, perfumed hair oils, etc.

The influx of consumer products is changing the attitudes, outlook and value-systems of the rural consumers. Age-old beliefs and cultural values are vanishing. The feudal caste system is giving way to a class system based on incomes and material possessions. The Brahmin is no longer held in awe. It is the villager who owns a VCR or a colour television who is held in esteem.

In the last decade, more villagers are in the monetary economy than ever before. This includes those villagers who are daily wage earners with incomes around Rs. 5 to Rs. 8 per day. Such villagers, tend to make daily purchases of their requirements of products like common slat, cooking oil, matches, soaps and detergent powder. Companies manufacturing products like tea, soaps, etc. specially produce small packs to cater to the demands of such marginal consumers.

Rural consumers rely substantially on the recommendations of the retailer in deciding the products, they buy. Over a period of time they develop faith and confidence in the retailer's judgement. The rural retailer is therefore crucial in the success of a new product in the villages. Manufacturers have begun making special attempts to ensure that the retailer is convinced about the quality and performance of the product. Over the years, the rural retailer has become astute and has realised his own potential in pushing certain brands, on which he earns extra margins or incentives. Manufacturers of well known brands of matches tea, soaps and detergents give the retailer a margin of about 5-8 per cent and advance credit for about a week. However, companies which market new brands have to offer margins upto 15 per cent and credit upto one month to the ruler retailers.

Sales of consumer products tend to increase sharply immediately after the harvest when the farmers are flush with funds and spend them on textiles, radios, jewellery, etc. Some of the augmented purchasing power is also expended in conspicuous consumption like lavish weddings, alcohol, clothes and parties. Villagers tend to postpone major expenditure like marriages, purchase of two-wheelers, tractors and land upto the post harvest season. The excellent harvest in 1988-89, is estimated to have resulted in an increase in foodgrains production by 32 million tonnes and oilseeds production by 2 million tonnes. It is estimated that the purchasing power of the farmers increased by Rs. 10, 000 crores merely on account of this increase in foodgrains and oilseeds production.

However, producers of consumer goods have yet to develop exclusive marketing strategies for the rural areas. They do not have the infrastructure, the resources and the knowledge to publicise products exclusively in the rural areas.

Use of the cinematic image continue to be a major mode of advertising on village hoardings and shop-boards. The Hindi cinema is a powerful entertainment medium in the villages and film stars are adored and idolised. Astute distributors show their products being used by well-known filmstars to increase their franchise. Amitabh Bachhan blows rings of smoke from "Chavi" beedies and recommends them. Jeetendra eats "Tasy" biscuits and suggests that other follow his example. Sridevi relishes the "Sweety" brand of ice-cream and advises others to do so too.

One of the major impediments to the expansion of the consumer products network in the villages, is the paucity of related information. Precise information about the size of rural markets, their potential and consumption patterns is not available. Even the population figures of various villages are a decade old. Research into the buying habits, product preferences and consumption pattern of rural dwellers is virtually non-existent.

This paucity of information occurs in a situation where the rural consumer can no longer be taken for granted. With an increase in his purchasing power and awareness levels he is becoming more discriminating and quality conscious.

Another impediment to the rapid proliferation of consumer products in the rural areas is the absence of all- weather roads to transport goods. There are 5,76,000 villages in India, of which 79 per cent have a population less than 1,000. About 80 per cent of these villages are not connected by all weather roads. There is, therefore, a tendency among manufacturers to concentrate on the larger villages, feeder and mandi towns and semi-urban centres.

Last but not the least, lack of adequate finance is another reason for poor inventory levels of stocks with the rual retailer. The public sector banks can play a critical role in the development of rural markets if they increase their credit to rural and small town dealers and stockists, to enable them to improve their level of inventories.

These measures along with a strengthening of distribution networks will go a long way to enable to realisation of the collossal opportunities that rural markets present.

8

BEYOND INAPPROPRIATE TECHNOLOGY

It is said that war is too serious a business to be left to the generals. Technology certainly, and Communication technology in particular, seems too serious a business to be left in the hands of technocrats — these nonchalant adventurers, sychophants and ego-trip operators. These technologists have certainly done an admirable job of making a complete mess of our Communications systems, particularly Telecommunications technology, with the result that the nation is 20 years behind the state of the art and caught up in a morass of bureaucratic muddle, technological confusion and political criminality out of which it is going to be exceedingly difficult to extricate ourselves. We are in a Telecommunications mess of the first order.

The first very important concept to understand is that technology is one thing and *innovation* through a shift in the techno-economic paradigm quite another. One has very little to do with the other. Technology per se, something to which our technocrats are pathologically fixated, has no value whatsoever of its own. What is needed for Development is *NOT* technology or new technology, but *INNOVATION* through a shift in the techno-economic paradigm.

This will become clear if we understand the conceptual framework underlying it, which has been admirably spelt out by J.A. Schumpeter in his theory of Business Cycles. According to Schumpeter when we are at the end of say a 40 or 60 years Business Cycle everything including the supporting institutions are on a down-swing. At that point it is necessary for an entrepreneur to introduce an *Innovation*, not infrequently based on a new technology but not necessarily so, which leads to a new techno-economic paradigm which in turn then begins to pervade the entire economic activity.

Excellent examples of this are both the pre and post Mahalnobis model phases. In 1947 when we got independence we could produce almost nothing either in Agriculture or in industry. The Nehru-Mahalnobis approach was correct. In terms of Keynesian economic thought it was rightly felt that government should take the economic initiative and pump massive dosage of captial and finance into the economy. It was further decided that the bulk of this investment be made in capital-intensive, heavy industry in the public sector in order to lay the foundations and basic infrastructure of the economy. Now it needs to be noted that there was nothing very esoteric about the technology - it was not some fancy, latest, cutting - edge technology; it was off the shelf state-of-art technology; in some cases, even outmoded, discarded technology. But even that worked because the significant factor was not the technology; the significant factor was that the combination of the parameters mentioned:

   a)   Large investment into the economy by the government;
   b)   Concentration in heavy engineering;
   c)   Building up a massive public sector and infrastructure
all these combined to make a dramatic shift in the techno-economic paradigm which catapulated the country from a primitive aggrarian state to ultimately an extremely significant industrial power backed by world-rated technical and scientific manpower. This is an admirable example of the application of the Schumpeter model in which diffusion of innovation through entrepreneurship leads to changes in the techno-economic paradigm and this in turn to an upswing in the entire economy.

Now we are at exactly the other end of the spectrum. This very Nehru-Mahalnobis model is in a down-swing. All the institutions created as a result of injecting this model are in a down-swing and in advanced stages of deterioration and decay. This fact is not appreciated by our politicians and bureaucrats who either politicise techno-economic issues or tend to think that administrative measures can circumvent the crisis. Actually the need of the hour is injection of a new technical innovation, as we did in 1947 and shift to a new techno-economic paradigm. As we shall be at pains to show in this chapter, this shift has now to be towards diffusing Information Technology if we are to be able to cope with the myriads of problems on hand.

At this point it will be valuable as a theoretical frame if we fully understand the implication of the Schumpeter's model. According to Schumpeter, *innovations* are the originating cause of the cyclical fluctuations in the capitalist society. An innovation is the commercial application of new techniques of production, new materials or perhaps basic new methods of doing business.

Schumpeter assigns the role of an innovator not to the capitalist but to the enterpreneur. The enterpreneur is not a man of ordinary managerial ability, but one who introduces something entirely new.

Schumpeter's model starts with the breaking up of the circular flow, with an innovating entrepreneur for the purpose of earning profit. In order to break the circular flow, the innovating entrepreneurs are financed by bank credit expansion. Since the investment in innovation is risky, they must pay interest on it. Once the new innovation becomes successful and profitable, other entrepreneurs follow it in "swarm-like clusters". Innovation in one field may induce other innovations in related fields. The emergence of a motor car industry may in turn stimulate a wave of new investments in the construction of highways, rubber-tyres and petroleum products etc.

Cyclical process: Since investment is assumed to be financed by creation of bank credit, it increases money incomes and prices and helps to create a cumulative expansion throughout the economy. With the increase in the purchasing power of the consumers, the demand for the products of the old industries increases in relation to the supply. Prices rise, profits increase and old industries expand by borrowing from banks. It introduces a secondary wave of credit inflation which is superimposed on the primary waves of innovation. Over optimism and speculation add further to the boom. After a period of gestation the new products start appearing in the market displacing the old products and enforcing a process of liquidation, readjustment and absorption. The demand for the old products is decreased. Their prices fall. The old firms contract output and some are even forced to run into liquidation. As the innovators start repaying bank loans out of profits, quantity of money is decreased and princes tend to fall. Profits decline. Uncertainty and risks increase, the impulse for innovation is reduced and eventually comes to an end. Depression ensues and the painful process of re-adjustment to the 'point of previous neighbourhood of equilibrium', starts. Ultimately the natural forces of recovery bring about a revival. Once again equilibrium is restored. Then some enterprising entrepreneurs begin with a new set of innovations, others follow, and a new boom begins.

Entrepreneurs are the key figures in Schumpeterian analysis. They bring out economic development in spontaneous and discontinuous manner.

Now that a down-swing has set in the Nehru-Mahalnobis model we must try to understand that the onset of depression indicates the increasing degree of mismatch between the techno-economic subsystem and the old socio-institutional framework, and the need for a full-scale reaccommodation of social behaviour and institutions to suit the requirements and the potential of a shift.

But are we making any attempt at all towards:

a)   Diffusing a new technology which would bring about a basic change in the existing techno-economic paradigm? This paradigm is energy-based and has unlimited consumption of rare and high cost oil as its base.

b)   Are we creating new set of institutions (as Nehru did) to meet the totally changed conditions in India today? The India of the 90's is certainly not the India of 50's.

c)   Are we creating new operating cultures and social behaviour to cope with the changed times and the new needs?

The answer to all these questions is an emphatic "No". The whole area of technology and economics has been totally politicised - witness the composition and antics of the new Planning Commission under the new dispensation - activists and agitators totally divorced from a capacity to structure new ideas or formulate futuristic strategies based on progress which has overtaken the world in the form of the Information Society. These barefoot planners are itching to go back to the spinning wheel and join company with Rousseau's Noble Savage.

There is another reason which forms an impediment to the establishment of the new techno-economic paradigm, which in our case has to be established by Information Technology.

The massive externalities created to favour the diffusion and generalisation of the prevailing paradigm act as a powerful deterrent to change for a prolonged period. It is only when productivity along the old trajectories shows persistent limits to growth and future profits are seriously threatened that the high risks and costs of the new technologies appear as clearly justified. Both the Industrial and Agricultural scenario in India form obstacles to change and to diffusion of the new Information Technology. Because of the closed economy of controls and so-called indigenous production we have entrenched in the country, industry never had it so good because the most third rate quality goods can be palmed off at the most exorbitant rate to a captive public groaning under incredibly soaring costs and incredibly poor quality. With no competition, no imports, no quality-control, no check on prices and no responsibility to the customer the whole of industry has turned profligate, reeling with black money and in no mood whatsoever to desire change and innovation.

The Agricultural scene is equally distressing. The rapidly proliferating Green Revolution, absence of taxation and now increased pressure to write off electricity bills and farm loans has created an indulgent middle class in Agriculture, which is equally profligate, consumerism-oriented and in for fun and frolic.

The temper of the nation as a whole is towards profligacy and debauchery. In the interim 600 million go without food and attempts at introducing innovations in techno-economic management are going to go unheeded.

It is against this national scenario that we contemplate the introduction of the Information Technology paradigm. The technological regime, which predominated in the post-war boom, was one based on low-cost oil and energy-intensive materials, (especially petrochemicals and synthetics), and was led by giant oil, chemical, automobile and other mass durable goods producers. Its 'ideal' type of productive organisation at the plant level was the continuous flow assembly line turning out massive quantities of identical units. The 'ideal' type of firm was the 'corporation' with a separate and complex hierarchical managerial and administrative structure, including in-house R&D and operating in oligopolistic markets in which advertising and marketing activities played a major role. It required large numbers of middle range skills in both the blue and white collar areas, leading to a characteristic pattern of occupations and income distribution. The massive expansion of the market for consumer durables was facilitated by this pattern, as well as by social changes and adaptation of the financial system, which permitted the growth of 'hire- purchase' and other types of consumer credit. The paradigm required a vast infrastructural network of motorways, service stations, oil and petrol distribution systems, which was promoted by public investment on a large scale already in the 1930s, but more massively in the post-war period. Both civil and military expenditures of governments played a very important part in stimulating aggregate demand.

Today, with cheap microelectronics widely available, with prices expected to fall still further and with related new developments in computers and telecommunications, it is no longer 'common sense' to continue along the (now expensive) path of energy and material-intensive inflexible mass production.

The 'ideal' information - intensive productive organisation now increasingly links design, management, production and marketing into one integrated system - a process which may be described as 'systemation' and goes far beyond the earlier concepts of mechanisation and automation. Firms organised on this new basis, whether in the computer industry such as IBM, or in the clothing industry such as Benneton, can produce a flexible and rapidly changing mix of products and services. Growth tends increasingly to be led by the electronics and information sectors, taking advantage of the growing externalities provided by an all-encompassing telecommunications infrastructure, which will ultimately bring down to extremely low levels the costs of transmitting very large quantities of information all over the world.

The skill profile associated with the new techno- economic paradigm appears to change from the concentration on middle range craft and supervisory skills to increasingly high and low range qualifications and from narrow specialisation to broader multi-purpose basic skills for information handling. Diversity and flexibility at all levels substitute for homogeneity and dedicated systems.

The transformation of the profile of capital equipment is no less radical. Computers are increasingly associated with all types of productive equipment as in Computerised Numerical Control machine tools, robotics and process control instruments as well as with the design process through CAD, and with administrative functions through data processing systems, all linked by data transmission equipment. According to some estimates computer-based capital equipment already accounts for nearly half of all new fixed investment in plant and equipment in the USA.

The deep structural problems involved in this change of paradigm are now evident in all parts of the world. Among the manifestations are the acute and persistent shortage of the high level skills associated with the new paradigm, even in countries with high levels of general unemployment, and the persistent surplus capacity in the older 'smokestacs', energy-intensive industries, such as steel, oil and petrochemicals.

Summing up we find that we are dealing with three totally different categories: one is "change in the techno-economic paradigm" which is the most significant and important and unless this change pervades the entire economic activity, there is no basic change in the pattern of development activity and growth. In order to achieve this techno- economic paradigm the basic input is "technical innovation". As we have seen what is so important is not capital but *innovation* and not an ordinary capitalist, but an *entrepreneur* who with his vision, skill and energy promotes an innovation. Then again this innovation has not to be confined in a pocket, but has to be widely "diffused" so that it impacts on the total economic and developmental activity. Last and least important of the three is technology. As we have seen in the case of the Mahalnobis model, the technology we introduced into India was not necessarily the latest or cutting edge; in fact, some of it was obsolete. But that did not matter. What mattered was the change it brought about in changing the techno-economic paradigm from a primitive aggrarian state to a highly modern and technologically advanced state.

Applying this pattern to Telecommunications, the end product which ought to have been visualised is how at the earliest to make a shift from the rural - urban divide and agriculture industry divide to a new kind of economic functioning where through Information we would have decentralised manufacturing in batch production mode, distant learning systems, distant health care systems etc.

For this the technical innovation needed was of providing an 'Information corridor' at the earliest possible.

The choice of Information technology was the least important and the most inconsequential.

Instead the exact opposite has been done. All the time has been infructuously spent in a so-called indigenous CDOT switch and so the opportunity never arose to get the country to a different techno-economic mode.

The questions being raised are totally wrong. The question is not whether the CDOT switch at Dehi Cantonement or Alsoor is working or not working, the question is: Why did we go in for this switch development in the first place? Why did we embark on this enterprise to re-invent the wheel? Why have we wasted five years and put the country 20 years back?

When the British consolidated their position in India did they first try to develop ab initio a new kind of road 'bitumen' or a new kind of piston for a railway locomotive? No, certainly not they got on with the job and criss- crossed the whole country with P.W.D. (Public Works Department) roads and an incredibly large railway system. They did this because they knew clearly that they could not exploit the country economically if they did not have these 'pathways'.

Similarly in the execution of the Nehru-Mahalnobis model we did not wait to develop ab initio all the technology required for heavy industry. Nehru, in fact had the wisdom and sagacity to get technology from as wide a spectrum as possible. So we collaborated with Russians, Germans, British, etc. for different heavy industry plants and for different I.I.T's. The result was that technologically and scientifically we got off the ground very rapidly.

The Koreans for example, did the same thing in Telecommunications. They started later than us, but collaborated with three foreign technologies: AT & T, IIT and Fijutsu and now have a telecom system which rivals the U.S.

What is coming out of this analysis is that our scientists and technologists are narrowly concerned with technology only, and at that, are enamoured with cutting-edge technology. From the Developmental point this has no meaning; what we need is diffusion of innovation and wide dispersion of a new techno-economic paradigm which takes the country to a much higher level of economic functioning. In the chapter on "Beyond Mass Media" we have seen what wonders have been wrought by the Information corridor created by Satellite television and the advertising and marketing which goes with it. If we similarly had by now built up a corridor with the newer interactive technologies represented by microelectronic-telecommunication, computers, electronics we would have been able to use those for development purpose.

We cannot afford to waste any more time. If we are now openly thinking of deregulating areas like steel production and electricity generation, there is no earthly reason why Telecom munications and Electronics which are so profitable enterprises should in fact, become a burden on the budgetary support. These should be immediately deregulated and all future expansion in Telecommunications, Computers and Electronics should be in the private sector only.

The question which we need to ask however, is: do we know the 'human' - i.e. social, economic and political implications of these technologies. If not, then a lot of work needs to be done in this area.

To reiterate the position: all that our technologists and scientists are doing in the Communication hardware field is to either reinvent *technology* or aim at cutting-edge Technology; the obssession is with technology: either we must make an indigenous CDOT switch or a Fifth generation computer. The exercise is useless, because preoccupation with technology leaves no time or energy for bringing about a technical innovation. For example, in the last five or ten years have we done any work of an R&D or Systems engineering nature to establish how these new communication technologies will be used:

(a) for the optimisation of efficiency in the Bulk sector
— Electricity, Oil, Transport, etc.
(b) For the Rural sector:
(i) Distance Learning Systems
(ii) Distance Health Systems
(c) For the Rural sector

In any case, who is to do this work? The Communication and Information Ministries do not regard this as their work. The only notable exceptions are Atomic Energy and Space, where the Application aspects of the technologies have been given foremost importance and institutionalised.

Secondly, the user Ministries and bodies are either not aware or not competent to carry out such prototype develop ment for optimal usage of the latest Communication and Information technologies.

Finally, we have to go a step beyond technical innovation, and see how the central economic model can have a major techno-economic paradigm shift in which in the new economic dispensation Communication assumes centrality. This requires the

Economist to come into the Information-Communication picture at the national level. Such work is conspicuous by its total absence.

What this analysis reveals is that, contrary to usual assumption, the technologist has the least role in our leap-frogging endeavour. Far more important are the Users on the one hand and Economic Planners on the other - and both these are conspicuous by either their absence or indifference. Equally important is the problem of requisite institutional mechanisms to bring these various parties together.

Major inventions and developments achieved so far:

(a) **Communication satellite**

Satellites have provided telephones, televisions, teleprinters and fascimile links throughout the world.

(b) **Low cost satellite: earth stations**

The satellite receiving equipments were, few years ago, rather expensive. Planer micro waves circuits make it possible to produce satellite receiving equipments enmasse at very low cost.

(c) **Demand-assigned multiple-access equipment**

Modern satellites have very high capacity for communication channels. Those can be shared by geographically dispersed users in a highly flexible manner, some of the channel capacity being allocated to users according to their instantenous needs.

(d) **The helical wave guide**

It is some sort of pipe now already working which can carry 25000 or more simultaneous telephone calls or equivalent information in digital form over long distance.

(e) **The Laser**

This means of transmission now in the developmental stages has a potential of carrying many millions of simultaneous telephone calls or their equivalent.

(f) **Optical fibres**

It is a thin flexible fibre made of extremely pure glass which can carry thousand times as much information as a pair of copper wire. Optical communication through fibres can be packed into one flexible cables thus affording their means of many thousand communication channels.

(g) **Large-scale integration (LS)**

It is a form of ultra miniaturised computer circuit that probably marks the beginning of mass production of computer-like logic circuitry. It offers the potential of extremely reliable, extremely small, and, in some of its forms extremely fast logic circuitry and memory, if large quantities can be built, this equipment can be produced at a very low cost.

(h) **On-line real-time computers**

Computers capable of responding to many distant terminals on telecommunication lines at a speed geared to human thinking. They have the potential of bringing the power and information of innumerable computers into every office and eventually every home.

(i) **Microcomputers**

Mass producible miniature computers at low cost.

(j) **Video-telephones**

through which subscribers see as well talk to each other.

(k) **Large TV Screens**

that can occupy a wall, if necessary.

(l) **Cable TV (CATV)**

A cable into homes with a potential signal-carrying capacity more than one thousand times that of the telephone cable.

(m) **Voice answerbook**

Computers can now assemble human voice words and speak them over the telephone. Voice answer-book and push- button telephone set makes every such telephone a potential computer terminal.

(n) **Millimetre Wave Radio**

Radio at frequencies in the band above the moicrowave band can relay a quantity of information greater than all the other radio bands combined together. Chains of closely spaced antenas will distribute these millimetre wave signals.

(o) **Data broadcasting**

Information can be broadcast in digital form at VHF or UHF frequencies for reception on home TV sets, special terminal or portable devices.

(p) **Pulse code modulation**

All signals, including telephone, picturepnone, music, facsimile and television can be converted into digital bit streams and transmitted, along with computer data, over the same digital links. Major advantages accrue from this.

(q) **Codeus**

Circuits which convert signals such as speech music and television into a bit stream, and convert such stream back into the original signal Codeos will become increasingly inexpensive and efficient.

(r) Computerised switching

Computerised telephone exchanges are coming into operation offering many new services and computer like logic can be employed for switching and concentrating all types of signal.

(s) Data Banks

Electronic storage for huge quantities of information that can be manipulated and indexed by computers capable of disseminating in a fraction of a second.

These are the major inventions so far having vast potentialities. In the next decade, we can make a forecast, a plausible realistic production, of the state of things to come.

Forecast for the next decade (1990 onwards)

(a) Semiconductor logic and memory circuits will be available at a much lower cost.

(b) Cost of microprocessors drops to about $ 10.00 each. Pocket machines with little or no memory become available with substantial memories. Programme libraries for pocket programmable machines grow impressively.

(c) Data processing machines continue their prodigious growth, with some of the fastest growing segments being related to data transmission. Mini-computers and micro-computers become available in large numbers.

(d) Facsimile mail and document transmission increase in popularity and drops in cost. Electronic mail and message services become an important field for the value-added carriers.

(e) The effect of distance on transmission drops and the tariffs become independent of distance.

(f) Privacy and security of data transmitted and stored become a major concern.

(g) Several domestic satellites in the 12 GHz for broadcasting (and 12-14 GHz for communication) bring radio and TV to every home in many countries.

(h) Frequency-division multiple-access (FDMA) is employed to enable users in geographically scattered locations to share the satellite transponders on a demand basis. Later as digital techniques come into being with satellite, time division multiple access (TDMA) is used. TDMA will enable users to request voice or video channels of widely varying data rates. These demand-assigned multiple access techniques make it economical for areas without a high traffic volume to have a satellite earth station.

(i) Satellite usage will fragment into two types: first augmentation of common carrier network by means of a small number of large earth stations, and second, by passing common carrier networks with large number of small earth stations.

(j) Intelsat V takes over the international traffic increases rapidly.

(k) PCM transmission in telephone networks comes into being. Data order voice on microwave links enables nation-wise data transmission at a very fast rate (1.5 mbps).

(l) Data transmission costs a small fraction of which it costs today. The drop in cost will lead to a massive growth in data transmission applications, with many new types of application, vast terminal networks, and in some cases many thousands of terminals connected to one computer centre. Data banks with 1013 bits of directly accessible storage become fairly common. Such storage is used for photographs, drawings, and documents in image forms as well as for digital data.

(m) Computer voice input systems permits a user to speak to a computer over the telephone, using limited vocabulary of clearly separated words. The Computer responds with spoken voice words.

(n) Telecommunication is extensively used in medicine, Information from all manner of patient instrumentation is transmitted to specialists or computers.

(o) Picturephone gains popularity.

(p) CATV starts using optical fibre cable television systems, delivering television in a digital form.

(q) Hi-fi music starts its new carrier with digital quadraphony giving distortion-free and noise-free music with brilliance and clarity.

(r) Extensive use is made of millimetre radio links in the suburbs and cities for distributing all types of signal.

(s) Satellite technology spreads rapidly especially for private and governmental networks. These networks share transponders by using multiple-access techniques. (FDM or TDMA). More powerful satellites are launched and the cost of domestic satellite receiving station drops considerably. The number of satellite broadcasting to developing countries increases.

(t) Electronic payment and cash transfer through computers are introduced in a wide scale.

(u) The concept of open university catches on and major international exchange of programme material is introduced.

(v) High fidelity television becomes popular. Three dimensional television is demonstrated using large wall screens.

(w) Major strides are made in industrial automation with the widespread use of 'intelligent' robot machines.

4.   The above gives some thoughts on the technological developments in the field of communication in the next decade or so. We have not identified any special problems for close scrutiny and study. But one thing is sure: The scope for innovation in this field is immense and few technologies can have a more profound impact on the future of society.

9

BEYOND DIFFUSING INNOVATIONS

Tones and tones have been written on the question of diffusing innovations. And in the Indian context the extent of this work done in the Family Planning area far exceeds perhaps that in any other country. Everett Rogers is one of the more prolific scholars. And yet what has been the result: after being the first country in the world to have a regular Ministry of Family Planning, after all possible kinds of formulations on innovation theory, after putting together one of the most ambitious Family Planning programmes in the world, the Indian Government after forty years of effort has now officially declared that the Family Planning programme is a failure.

The other illustration given in this chapter is of diffusion of knowledge in Agriculture, and here the point made is that this has had hardly anything to do with communication; the Green Revolution is the wise and resolute Indian farmers' response to disequilibrium economics.

This leaves us intellectually at base zero in innovation theory after forty years of aimless effort. What is going to be our agenda for the future in this field?

Have we no scholars, no thinkers, no capacity left for conceptualising, no feeling for theory, no heritage for observation, classification, formulation? The innovation diffusion area is a blatant example of Indian intellectual bankruptcy.

Rural Communications in India presents a paradox. Rural development could be regarded roughly in two broad areas: one, Agricultural growth and second, the social sector including health, family welfare, nutrition, womens' literacy etc. It is highly paradoxical that in India's past four decades of development effort whereas diffusion of innovations through practically all communication channels has been highly successful in the Agricultural sector, it has been an abysmal failure in the Social sector. This paper purports to set out the present position in these two diverse sectors, examine the success and failure of communications in the two sectors and then on the basis of this somewhat cursory examination, project for the future the direction of detailed studies and investigations required in order to bring social progress in our rural areas in line with agricultural growth. It is perhaps this imbalance which is at the bottom of the present rural unrest.

We will first take up for study communication in the Agricultural sector. Undoubtedly the first step in this direction was the Community Development programme. Although the programme brought out into strong relief the rural sector, it was inadequate for any breakthrough in the Agriculture sector for the very simple reason that Agriculture needs a highly specific, technical approach, whereas Community Development by very definition was a very general type of programme.

Breakthrough in Agriculture in the form of the Green Revolution only occurred with the very specific technology of Agriculture and to this was added a very *determined demonstration of economic benefits for the diffusion of these innovations*. The upgradation in "technology" consisted of upgrading the already existing canal network in the Punjab, setting up of fertiliser factories, diesel pumpsets for pumping water where canal water was not available, making available High Yield Variety seeds, manufacture and supply of tractors and other mechanised farm equipment.

This by itself however, would have achieved nothing. It was really the diffusion of these innovations through extension channels, and the acceptance of these ideas by farmers, which brought about the Green Revolution. This was achieved by setting up on the lines of the U.S.A. a chain of land- grant type of Universities as for example, at Ludhiana, Pantnagar, Jabalpur etc. with attached Extension Service, which carried the message of the new people. Alongwith this IADP-Intensive Area Development Projects were set up, which actually demonstrated the yields achieveable with the new seed varieties, fertilizer, water and other inputs.

Now coming to the sociological analysis of the issue, it will help us in our understanding if we regard the acceptance process in Agricultural diffusion as "adaptation" rather than "adoption." This is an extremely important point and we must dwell on it a while to clearly understand it. This concept incidentally, negates the views propagated by earlier sociologists and communication specialists like Daniel Lerner (of M.I.T.) Lerner's "adoption model" had four steps which were indispensable if "adoption" was to take place. These four steps were:

urbanisation

media exposure

literacy and

adoption

To this Lerner added a fifth component which he termed "empathy". This represents psychic mobility or in the case of our Punjab peasant, his capacity to empathise with new ways of working, new technologies for adoption and new styles of living. In other words, according to Lerner and his tribe, "adoption" of new agricultural methods was not possible unless there was a fundamental attitudnal, behavioural and lifestyle change in the farmer. According to Lerner this in effect, meant not merely modernisation, but very explicitly Westernisation which meant by implication that the "traditional" man is incapable of growth and development unless he first adopts the Western value system. Lerner puts this blatantly and if one may state, uncouthly by stating that the process of modernisation is defined as *the common behavioural system historically associated* with the urban, industrial, literate and participant societies of Western Europe and North America."

The Green Revolution apart from being a great technology lesson is equally a great lesson in the sociology of modernisation. It has made complete nonsense of "modernisation" theories like those propounded by people like Lerner. These theories missed out on two very important points. The first is that they overlooked the fact that the "traditional"farmer can be as "traditional" as they come, but still be an "economic" man. He does not have to give up his traditional attitudes and lifestyle in order to learn what makes "economic" sense. He recognises economic sense when he sees it. This economic lesson is in line with the political lesson political scientists like Myron Wenier (again M.I.T.) have learnt the hard way namely:the traditional Indian villager-illiterate as he is—does not need to become literate or to learn the English language to become politically wise. He has demonstrated this in seven National general elections, namely, that he is innately politically wise - and with his judgement he has either brought in or thrown out a political aspirant and for that matter, the government. So coming back to our argument, when the traditional Punjabi farmer saw new technologies which made economic sense, he went in for them unhesitantingly.

The other point on which people like Lerner missed out is that in order to use a modern technique it is not necessary to give up one's values and belief systems, as people like Lerner have been at pains to stress-wanting the whole world to be of one belief - namely that of the industrial, competitive, strife-ridden West-hell bent on competition, greed and manipulation.

The Green Revolution is rather a lesson in "adaptive" behaviour towards modernisation. One can "adopt" ones traditional culture, but "adapt" modern techniques for ones well-being. In fact, the Green Revolution is a lesson in the Economics of "Adaptation," and shows how Development can be regarded as an adaptive process.

Let us further explore this difference in "adaptation" and "adoption". It would seem appropriate to name the archetypal decision maker in disequilibrium the "adaptive man". Adaptive man is an agent who makes short term plans, not because he is irrational, but because he is seldom prescient, that is: obviously not possessed of fore- knowledge; he is cautious in adapting to a changing environment because traditional experience suggests that caution is often a wise tactic in the game of economic survial; he responds to feedback from the market and the behaviour of other agents because the task of estimating competitor's behaviour far exceeds the capacity of the largest and most sophisticated economic modelling centre. .

What we must not forget is that the Development process and particularly the Agricultural sector, is full of uncertainty and any form of "transition" is replete with risk. Several strategic aspects of realistic, adaptive decision making must be incorporated if the transition of development is to be understood. These strategic details are essentially decision tactics for uncertain decision making, adaptation in response to feedback, learning for multiple goals.

The Green Revolution therefore, throws new light on the magnificence of traditionality rather than the usual lable that such people are obscure and opaque. On the contrary, it shows that the Punjabi farmer in the modernising process retained the best of both worlds: he continued to "adopt" values and lifestyle (he did not give up the village) of his ancient world, but simultaneously showed the sagacity, cunning and discrimination to take the risk of "adapting" very high technology in the extremely uncertain world of Agricultural disequilibrium. This throws up the Green Revolution in a new light as far as the communication process goes. It has shown in the process of diffusion of innovations, the "adoption" of traditional values on the one hand, simultaneously "adaptation" of the latest and most sophisticated and expensive technology.

In doing this it reaffirms the appraisal that the whole process of modernisation in India has always been one of *"modernisation of tradition"*. Unlike many other emerging countries, in India there is never a sharp distinction of one thing being traditional and the other modern. On the contrary India updates herself continually by winds of change from elsewhere while never giving up the anchor of her ancient belief, perrenial philosophy and metaphysical truths on which she is anchored and which she has deeply "adopted." But with this stability she then 'adapts" herself to the latest, the most modern, *the most risk-driven and the most uncertain.* The story of the Green Revolution therefore, is the story of the simultaneous acceptance of two diverse and almost disparate messages: *the certainty of tradition* and the *uncertainity of technology;* And the Punjabi farmer comes out as master of both.

The most outstanding case of diffusion of innovations in India since independence is the Green Revolution, particularly in the Punjab. A critical analysis of this is attempted below. It will be seen that it does not fall into any of the models which communication specialists, especially American have been espousing. It is rather a case of Development as an adaptive process dealing successfully with economic disequilibrium.

This is proof, if proof is needed that we need altogether new theories of the diffusion process in the Indian context. The task assumes urgency especially in the area of Family Planning, which is dealt with later in the chapter.

Development As An Adaptive Process

The Green Revolution in the Punjab

Punjab is one of the fastest growing agricultural regions in the world. Appreciation of the importance of agriculture in the process of development has been greatly enhanced by the green revolutions that have begun to transform the economies of diverse countries, such as Costa Rica, Israel, Nigeria, the Phillipines, Thailand, Tanzania and Yugoslavia. Even for countries with high population densities such as India and Pakistan, the recent advances in agricultural output have raised new hopes.

The Punjab is one of the smaller state of the Indian Union, with only a tiny fraction of the total population and land areas. Its net area under cultivation, however is greater than Taiwan, a country often cited as an example of rapid agricultural change.

Of greater importance is the areas rate of agricultural growth. From 1952 to 1965 - a period that we might appropriately call the transition and take off - the Punjab's agricultural output grew at an annual rate of more than 5.5% - comparing favourably with the most rapidly developing agricultures of the world and being the highest among the Indian States. One of its 11 (eleven) districts, Patiala achieved a growth rate of almost 11% annually.

The Punjab is unique among Indian states. The study bears special significance to the future agricultural development of a large part of the world. The Green Revolution in Punjab is a - Technological change. The pattern indicates that technological change is task-oriented. It does not consist of the total replacement of a traditional technology (bullock - labour intensive) by a modernized (tractor, tubewell - labour saving) technology. It consists rather of a task by task replacement.

This leads to a period of transition during which labour - saving and labour intensive technologies continue to be juxtaposed in a "hybrid technology". The composition of this hybrid technology depends upon the cost and input - structure of various individual operations and their proportionate change over time. The vast structural changes that look place in the Punjab were reflected in - changing factor proportion.

There are two indices that outline in broad terms the Green Revolution as it occured in Punjab:-

(a) the rapid rise in output and factor productivity &

(b) the commercialization implied by a growing marketed surplus and explosive adoption of non-farm inputs.

Green revolution was a state of rapid transition from age-old production methods to a modern technology. It involved rapid accumulation of capital, a transition from traditional to modern agricultural practices and an extreme change in the structure of labour utilization.

There was the fact, that decision makers (the Pubjab farmers) were responding to technological and market conditions that were changing out of equilibrium. The broad historical forces, institutional developments and modifications of the economic infrastructure that have shaped the region have been taken for granted.

Economic-development, is of course a multifaceted process. Its study requires an understanding of how decision makers behave and how markets and non-market environments interact with that behaviour and obviously, the development of new institutions *and simultaneous decay of old ones constitute an important and a fruitful area for investigation.*

The development and transformation of socio-economic infrastructure of markets, transportation, energy, irrigation and administration - all play a crucial role in shaping the environment, sometimes enhancing, sometimes hindering the developmental process.

This transformation showed various input-output ratios, input- land ratios and input-labour ratios. Land, labour and financial capital use per unit of output declined. Machine use per unit of output increased as it replaced the use of draft animals.

As output per cultivated acre increased, labour and labour-bullock labour use per - cultivated acre declined. Total financial outlay showed a slight increase only after 1963, the real increase was confined to an increase in the use of new power sources. This was shown by the increase in diesel and tractor hour use per acre.

The green revolution involved the introduction of new high yielding crop varities, the use of fertilizers and the use of irrigation. It was the rapid mechanization accompanying the process of change from traditional to modern farming.

The model shows that choice of technique is made task -by-task. During the period (1952-65) investments in non-farm produced capital goods have been concentrated on tractors for land preparation; sowing and transportation; tubewells for irrigation; and power threshers for threshing winter crops. The traditional bullock and labour-intensive practices had been rapidly replaced for these specifc tasks, while other tasks continue to be performed in traditional manner. This is a period of transition during which labour - saving and labour displacing technologies continue side by side presenting a picture of a "hybrid- technology". Such an occurence is not uncommon in periods of transition where components depend upon the detailed cost-structure of operation and proportions change over time. *Aggregate indices of technology, a common input of macro-economic growth and development models*, are incapable of capturing the dynamics of this transition and disequilibrium.

The composite impact on farm sector labour-utilization of two conflicting forces:-

(1) a reduction in the demand due to the adoption of task specific labour saving technologies and

(2) an increase in the demand for labour due to the increase in yields and total output as a result of increased double cropping, increased area sown to high yielding varieties and the use of chemical nutrients. The net effect on total labour use was 5% higher in 1965, than in 1952, despite the rapid mechanization described earlier.

The General features of agricultural transformation in the Punjab during 1952-65

(1) A rapid growth in output and productivity.

(2) A rapid adoption of the green revolution package (new seeds, fertilizer, and water) especially after 1960.

(3) Rapid, task-specific mechanization in an apparently aggregate labour surplus environment.

(4) A structural change in the demand for and the composition of inputs and the consequent changes in factor proportions.

(5) An increasing commercialization of farm production through forward (output) and backward (input) linkages with non-farm sector.

Conclusion

The Punjab model has tracked the agricultural development in a Developing country through a transition from traditional to modern technology in a way that shares many common characteristics with the process as it is occuring elsewhere. It has displayed how, in spite of vast institutional differences that distinguish them from their counterparts elsewhere, *peasant farmers are amenable to economic incentives and respond rationally once appropriate account is taken of their decision milieu.* It has shown that, despite a continued belief to the contrary, *traditional agriculture can develop rapidly within the framework of a decentralized market-oriented economy,* given that policies that facilitate appropriate developments exist outside the farm sector.

The path of transformation was characterized by changing relation factor scarcities and proportions, the adoption of new mechanical and biological technologies and a steady increase in commercial rather than subsistence production.

The unprecedented increase in total output in the region has been accompanied by substantial structural changes in investment-pattern, farm technology, labour use, and market-orientation.

The central theme of this study has been - economic development *as an adaptive process.* The process has been described as a cautious suboptimizing response by individual economic agents - the Punjab farmer in particular - to a changing economic situation, conditioned by strategic decision making and an external environment. The aggregate implication of this conception of development has been (inspite of lags and constraints on change) the rapid transformation of traditional agriculture. The transformation involved the growth of marketed surplus, the accumulation of industrially produced capital goods, increasing use of off-farm inputs, especially fuel, fertilizer and electricity and the adoption of high yielding varieties. It also involved a decline in traditional farm practices, a drastic change in seasonal workloads, and, more generally, the disappearance of more or less self-sufficient subsistence activities.

The sixty-four million dollars question we raise is: where is Mass Communication in this most spectacular of all diffusion achievements we have had. Green Revolution is an excellent example of the thesis of this book: we have to go "Beyond Mass Communication."

We end the discussion with a query? Why has not the same success met us in the Social sector - particularly Family Planning? In fact, the past four decades record in communication in that sector can only be called an abyssmal disaster. The population has risen from 300 to 800 million and is well on its way to becoming one billion. We can only formulate questions, not answers. Is it that this sector needs basic "adoption" rather than "adaptation" that is a lifestyle change to a modern industrial culture? Or is it that the traditional person would accept limiting the family if the "economic" aspects were made evident as these were in the case of the Green Revolution technologies? Or is it that a value change in favour of limiting family size can be brought about within the ambit of traditional culture? These are vital areas of investigation for the future.

We will now have a detailed look at the position of Family Planning Communication in India.

A glass half full may be described as both half empty and half full: Neither description is wrong. It is a question of one's perspective. The highly complex issue of the population question in India is a parallel to the above analogy. Critics have not been wanting in downplaying the positive aspects of a population as large as that of India's. But how many have really probed the pertinent issues? The same hackneyed arguments have come up again and again - arguments which reflect obssession with growth in ABSOLUTE NUMBERS. Why not, instead be obsessed with the "PRODUCTIVITY" of this huge population?

It is generally perceived that population is bad if in excess; that all growth indicators are brought to a standstill if so; that a country's "D-DAY" is not far away etc. No country other than India, may be China to a certain extent (and that too relatively) fits in all these criticisms."PER SE" there is nothing wrong absolutely nothing-with growth in numbers. Labour is an asset and a resource. But the crucial issue in India is how much of this asset is being utilised as a resource? India was the first country to initiate a family planning program, on a NATIONAL BASIS in 1952-5 years after independence. This very fact of an early realization of a population "explosion" speaks volumes of Nehru's farsightedness. Family planning is the idea, programme or act of preventing births and of avoiding their consequences. It is in the context of such an assumption that the entire issue of family planning in India should be considered. Many countries have initiated family planning programmes—some have been more successful than India. But they have learnt from India's mistakes. Being the first one to initiate a family planning policy India herself never had this opportunity. This is an aspect to be borne in mind at all times whenever we consider the issue of either success or failure of the social sectors in India- the predominant one being population.

To understand this complex issue of our population and related population control measures, a cursory look at the various stages of implementation of a National Family Planning Programme would be useful. After the initial stimulation of interest in the problem, the actual execution of the remedies started. The "CLINIC" was the first phase—where the Ministry of Health designated medical men to administer family planning as any other health service through existing health clinics. After initial enthusiasm, this phase did not show highly encouraging results simply because clinic services reached a minute proportion of their target audience.

Once the "CLINIC ERA" failed, a major policy decision was taken when the national programme was re-oriented to a "FIELD" approach. As with all bureauracies, a lot of time elapsed between the "CLINIC"era and the "FIELD" era- these years in India witnessed large growth rates of 4.5% per annum.

Under the "FIELD"approach, rather than waiting in the clinics for clients to appear in large number, the family planning staff or the so called "bare-foot doctors" actively pursued them in their places of work or at homes. To make matters worse, an average extension worker in India (like the village midwife) had a ratio of 1 :6000 or even: 10,000 in certain places.

The failure in India of the above phases (ranging from 1952- 70 (exposed the complete obsoleteness of the "Classical Diffusion Model" so energetically propounded by Rogers. Rogers derived his model as a pararrel to the one in agriculture where "extension agents" were necessary to actively promote the "adoption of innovations." The family planning field workers emerge as the counter-part of the extension agent. Now criticisms of the failure of this phase in India is fundamentally wrong because here one is talking about *"BEHAVIOURAL MODIFICATION"* among millions who have superstitions and beliefs in their blood since times immemorial. It is not a question of using a ball-point pen instead of an ink-pen or viceversa. Here we are talking about FUDAMENTAL changes in the attitudes of Indians—more so among those who are the targets of family planning programmes. In the face of insurmountable problems, the Indian Government left no stone unturned to bring about certain changes- changes which Indian men and women are very sensitive to. Roger's S-Curve has not worked in our society because it is a marketing strategy. His is an advertisement-oriented approach. It is simply due to this fact that it has taken India 15 years to market "NIROH". It is no use if boards and placards and other advertisements are showered upon people. They will simply not accept it. Selling a contraceptive in India - on the basis of Roger's model- is selling of a product. But here we want something much more than that. We are talking about behavioural modification and not just the selling of a product. Roger himself admits that his work is based on research in the USA. How can one - in criticising the second largest population - use an advertisement model for population and that too in a society as complex as India's. We have not gone into the cultural perspective of the man whom we are telling not to produce more children. Therefore, it is superficial marketing strategy.

This is precisely what has happened in China. The Chinese Government's decision to impose "ONE FAMILY ONE CHILD" Policy has "boomeranged" on its face. WHY? Firstly, China's power structure now is much more decentralised than it used to be in 1979-80 when the policy was first introduced. Decentralisation has brought with it the associated problems of loop-holes in the effective implementation of the family planning programme.

Secondly, in 1979-80, the target audience for China was its farmers : when the programme was first initiated, the economic condition of the average farmer was far from happy. But cooperatives and limited free-market mechanisms in the agricultural sector has improved the lot of the Chinese farmer. Now the same farmer who saw logic and rationality in restricting his family to only ONE CHILD does not bother.

(NOTE: Both these changes are a direct result of Zhao Ziyang's inclination for a relatively "open" style of ruling as deeply contrasted with Deng Xiaoping's autocratic style).

The above two illustrations go to show that a "MECHANISTIC" approach does not work even in a totalitarian state like China, leave alone India. One of the reasons for Mrs. Gandhi's ouster from power in the 1977

General Elections was the issue of "forceful sterilisation". The Emergency had many unpopular 'features: Yet there are serious grounds for singling out the sterilisation drive as among the most potent cause for the forfeit of popular support by the Congress party. In all the states where sterilisation excesses were on a wide scale Congress was radically defeated; indeed Mrs. Gandhi's supporters only managed to do well in the South where the sterilisation drive was not said to be unusually forceful. Ironically the Southern states of Andhra Pradesh and Karnataka registered lower birth rates in the whole of India in that period.

It is difficult to account in any other terms for the result in Uttar Pradesh, one of the states most marked by sterilisation incidents, where Congress powerfully dominant before, lost every single seat including those of Mrs. Gandhi's and her son — the latter strongly identified personally with compulsion in family planning. What seems most surprising in retrospect, even though few had predicted the extent of the defeat, is not that Mrs. Gandhi lost but that she had been confident of winning. Perhaps historians will conclude that this was the first election IN THE WORLD in which family planning was A—if not THE——deciding factor. The Emergency experience also goes to show that a "CAFETARIA" approach simply does not work.

In India the distinction between "HARD CORE RESISTER" and the "RECEPTIVE" audience is not possible if one is to follow Rogers. In a country where children are perceived as economically valuable; where children are perceived as means of porviding retirement benefits to their parents in old age; and where children are perceived as contributing to parental prestige, distribution of a few contraceptives is not going to solve the problem. India has to adopt "BEYOND FAMILY PLANNING" policies.

In such a context, what role does communication have in our society? Is it going to be a channel for bombarding the people with slogans of "SMALL FAMILY HAPPY FAMILY" or is it going to be somethings more than that? Even perfect methods of contraception and abortion - welcome and important as these may be - will not alone solve the problem of the "population boom". This is because the idea of the small family norm takes decades to catch up by the people. We have been independent for 41 years. Countries like South Korea, Mauritus, Singapore etc. may have witnessed large scale successes in planned population growth; but let us not forget that these countries do not have a complexity of the magnitude of India. With all our problems, We have done quite a lot.

Let us invert the pyramid. Instead of going in a jeep to carry out sterilisation and vasectomy, let us decentralise the industries —and decentralise them towards the villages. More than ever before, Gandhian economy is most pertinent and needs to be applied for. To Gandhi, the teeming millions of India were an inexhaustible source of human labour —a source which can and has increased our material wealth. Decentralisation of industries towards the rural sector will automatically improve the standard of living. Once the standard of living goes up, population will also decline. This is what is exactly happening in our cities as of today. The ratio of the socially upward mobile vis-a-vis the others are increasing.Indians are beginning to realize the opportunity costs of a larger family vis-a-vis a smaller one.' It is this realization that has led to a proliferation of nuclear families in our cities. Information technology is the springboard for higher labour productivity. Higher labour productivity will lead to higher standards of living and higher standards of living will lead to reduced growth rates of population. This has happened in Western Europe, this has happened in the USA, this has happend in Australia. This can happen in India. It is pure Economics.

This is not to suggest that India is problem-free. The demographic projections for 2000 A.D. are far from bright. The 1981 Census data shows that 14% of the total married women in the rural areas and 10% in the urban areas are in the age group of 15-19. Similarly, per cent of married women, who are aged 35 and more, are 27 in the rural areas and 20 in the urban areas. To compound the existing demographic structure, the number of couples will also be large. The Census of 1981 showed that population had increased by 27.24% since 1971. With this growth rate population will double in 35 years. The year 2000 A.D. will also witness India overtaking China in absolute numbers (if equilibrium is maintained). All these projections underline the fact that sterilisation methods will not be successful.

Communication technology must promote "beyond family planning policies" and provide a motivational basis for lower fertility. India needs to do her own research to suit her characteristic conditions. What is needed is an understanding of cultures, a communications strategy based on behavioural sciences; a research policy in behavioural modification. There is lot of scope for anthropological studies. Our basic flaw has been that we have looked at sheer numbers; have deduced "Draconian" implications from these numbers and very pessimistically projected population policy as India's failure. The attitude has to be just the opposite. There is a tremendous need for change. There is enough evidence to show that the couples need assurance of survival of their children before they decide to limit their family; It is also known that couples that accept fertility regulation in the early stages of marital life tend to have smaller family size. To tackle a problem as large as our ours is not humanly possible. More than anything else SPACING METHODS are required and spacing needs communications. The problem has been wrongly defined. As a result the whole demographic situation is skewed. The solution has to be employment intensive growth in the villages. However, the cure should not be worse than the disease. Population in India WILL stabilize - may be at a higher level.

Stabilization of this population is a challenge for Communications in India. The cities have faced the challenge quite well, the villages need to. The whole of India has to and will be able to. The question is of TIME.

We stated the thesis in the beginning that the course of events in India shows that whereas diffusion in the Agricultural sector has been successful, in the social sector this has not been the case. In the social sector nothing is as important as Family Planning and success has eluded us in this sector. We examine two case studies here of investigations made by a research organisation in Delhi which are illustrative as well as instructive.

Case Studies of Diffusion of Innovations in India

To explore the stages in the acceptance of the family planning programme in a village of Kanjhawala block, within the framework of the "Adoption Process."

Model :

Family planning is a national policy in India. The importance given to the programme is evidenced by increase in the budget allocation towards this programme in the successive five year plans. Various researches have indicated that the factors influencing acceptance, rejection or discontinuance of family planning

may be different from one region to another because these are
the function of a variety of social, educational, economic and
cultural factors. Empirical evidence indicates that the conceptual
framework of the adoption model is appropriate to measure the
extent of acceptance of the programme.

A study was conducted in the Nangloi village of Kanjhawala
block, Delhi State. The village had a subcentre of the Primary
Health Centre and considerable work in connection with family
planning had been done. The *findings* of the study indicated
that the percentage of respondents at the awareness (100%) interest (98.5%) evaluation (71.42%), trial (25.71%) and adoption
(4.28%) stages, gradually decreased. However, although all were
aware, none of the sample were fully aware of all the aspects
of the programme. A maximum percentage mentioned that
family planning meant "planning for smaller families." Also, a
majority of the respondents heard about family planning from
neighbours.

It was found that the middle class were most aware of the
programme; whereas in the later stages of adoption they were
not among those who were highly interested or motivated. At
the interest, evaluation, trial and adoption stages there were no
significant effects of caste. Percentages however revealed that
there were more users of contraceptives in the lower age group
(below 30 years).

At the interest stage, the literate group and the respondents
with large families showed a keener interest in the programme.

It was found that the people who had evaluated the
programme belonged to the older age group, were from nuclear
families and had more than four children.

In response to a question on opinions and feelings towards
acceptance of the programme, most of the sample favoured the
acceptance of birth control practices though a few felt that they
favoured the programme for other people but did not approve
of it for self practice. It was interesting to note that these respondents were from the low (below 30 years) and high (above 40
years) age group. The former gave the reason that they wanted
more children and the latter were resigned to the will of God.

The evaluation of the effects of contraceptives was mostly
negative. Diverse effects on health due to the use of the loop
were expressed.

Responses to general questions indicated that most of the respondents had unscientific and incomplete knowledge of the different types of contraceptives. This was one reason why there was a lack of proper evaluation of contraceptives. Further it was found that in many cases the wife was willing to accept contraceptive practices but the husband did not agree.

II. *A study of some of the socio-cultural factors associated with the Adoption and Non-Adoption of family planning among Rural women in Delhi territory (1968).*

The population problem arises out of the limited resources to provide for the basic necessities of people, despite the pace with which the economy has progressed. It is the poorer sections of the community that bear more children due to extreme poerty, ignorance, illiteracy and other sociological factors. An understanding of cultural barriers is essential since the socio-cultural setting of a community is to some extent the cause and consequence of poverty and ignorance. The success of the family planning programme in India will ultimately depend on the impact it makes in the rural areas where most of the Indian population lives. Removal of socio cultural inhibitions towards family planning is a prerequisite to solving the problem.

The study was conducted in the Mehrauli block, Delhi State. The sample was selected from the total population of married couples with wives in the age group 25-45 years. The group was divided into adopters and non-adopters, according to whether the couples had used atleast one of the contraceptive methods. The sample comprised of women only.

The findings revealed that there were no significant differences between the caste groups and adopters and non adopters. There were, however, a greater number of non adopters in the higher caste groups, and also in the age group below 40 years.

A large percentage of adopters (98%) as well as non-adopters (97%) felt that the ideal size of family should be 'as decided by fate or karma". 70% of the adopters and 44% of the non-adopters felt that women had a right in deciding the size of a family.

Of the total sample of 120, 83 desired a son, while all felt that a son plays an important role in the family, 56% fiftysix per cent of the adopters and 87% of the non-adopters felt it was necessary to reproduce till a son was born, 52% of the adopters

and 67% of the non adopters felt that a women having no sons
would be looked down upon by the community. Further, about
64% of the total sample felt that chances of divorce were maximum if a woman could not bear a male child.

All respondents considered a woman's main role as
reproducing and bringing up children 48% of the adopters and
76% of the non adopters felt that more children added to their
social prestige. 38% and 71% respectively felt that more children
meant security in old age, 36% of adopters and 70% of non
adopters flet that socio cultural barriers obstructed family planning.

All the adopters and 86% of the non-adopters had heard
about family planning. The awareness of the loop was maximum (60%) vasectony (26%) and condom (25%) being next, 51
respondents mentioned knowledge of no method whatsoever,
66% of the non-adopters felt that family planning publicity
should be encouraged. The reason most commonly stated for
not adopting family planning methods was *ignorance*.

Smokeless Chulhas

In the social sector another innovation which has been tried
is of diffusing the idea of "smokeless chulhas" in villages. But
this also has had disappointing results. We take up detailed discussion below:

In order to achieve progress, it is essential to have a clear
understanding of technical change as a process, in which an
innovation is introduced into another culture by a change agent.
During its implementation there is a reaction by the members
of the recipient culture and ultimate rejection or acceptance of
the innovation takes place.

The adoption of innovations is an expression of the behaviour
of an individual. Studies conducted in India have revealed the
importance of variety of social, psychological and economic factors in adoption of new practices. They have emphasized that
knowledge of factors positively and negatively related to the
adoption process would be very useful wherever an innovation
has to be introduced.

In this connection Dube states that

"Not all improved practices are accepted atonce, many are
rejected, not because people are traditional minded, conservative

or primitive but because innovations in all their ramifications do not fit into the total cultural setting of the community."

Hence, the nature of the innovations must be in line with the culture in which it is introduced.

In India, various, studies have been conducted in the field of acceptance of farm practices where it is commonly observed that farmers even in the same village and the same neighbourhood adopt innovations in varying degrees. The social environment, cultural milieu and personal factors determine farmer's differential behaviour in this matter. For a long time, economic advantage of a practice was considered to be the only basis for its adoption. But this view does not hold good anymore.

"If economic considerations were the only basis of acceptance" says Wilkening "improved practices would be adopted as rapidly as their economic advantages are demonstrated.

The other factors such as social, personal, cultural and psychological also influence adoption.

Ten studies have been done on the adoption of home practices such as the smokeless chullha. The introduction of this practice into the rural homes is an ideal example of diffusion of new ideas into the community, and their failure.

The Improved chullah was supposed to have an enormous impact in removing drudgery from women's life as it:-
- takes away smoke through the chimney and protects the women from its hazards
- a clean and bright environment can improve the health of the whole family
- It is easier to clean pots, pans which have been spared of the black soot at the bottom.
- an improved chulha consumes less fuel and hence there is saving of both labour and time in the collection of wood.
- It helps in improving the quality of life.

Popularizing this improved chulhà was not an easy task for the Government.

The Department of Non-Conventional Energy Resources under the Ministry of Energy, launched a nationwide product on the demonstrations of improved chulhas in the year 1982. The target of this programme was to construct improved chullahs in over 10 lakh of rural homes in the year 1985-86. More than 4 lakh chulhas have already been installed in various villages in Haryana, Rajasthan, Punjab, Uttar Pradesh and Maharashtra. It is proposed that 5 lakh more chulhas will be installed during the Seventh Plan period and the expected net annual saving in fuelwood thereby would be to the order of 42 lakh tonnes valued at Rs. 29.4 crores.

There was need to support such programmes by substantial research, not only on the fuel efficiency characteristics of chulhas but on the several socio-economic and cultural practices of people; relating to the use of these chulhas. If a project involves huge investments preliminary investigations and acceptability tests are called for before launching a new innovation, but this is where the scheme failed.

A study done in village Kirari Nangloi block proved this. A preliminary survey of hundred families covered under the DEDA's demonstration project on smokeless chulhas revealed that only in 34 families the chulhas were in order. Only 20 of them actually used the chulha for their day to day cooking. The remaining 14 either used kerosene stove or gas and did not use the smokeless chulha which was reduced to only a showpiece. 66 of the families had broken their chulhas. Even the 20 families who were still using the smokeless chulha were not fully satisfied with the model and desired some modifications.

The problems faced by most homes were:

1) pot hole size small so unfit for large families
2) 2 pot chulha cumbersome and wasted space
3) Takes more time and unsuitable for baking chapatis
4) Inadequate height
5) The orientation of the chulha is in many cases was not correct, where the chulhas faced south, they were broken saying that since it faced Lanka it was inauspicious.
6) The families did not properly understand the use and principle of the chulha. They thought there were too many do's and dont's in the chulha.
7) The chimney would choke with soot and ash and for want of expertise left unclean.

Thus more improvement was required in the chulhas. A proper follow up after their construction and proper discussions with the users is an essential part of introducing new innovations.

Another innovation attempted in the social sector: digging of sullage borchles has met with failure. We take a look at the analysis. All in all the social sector, which reflects lifestyle, also reflects horrors of gloom and dismay and is responsible for exceedingly low quality of life in rural India as well as urban slums. The great challenge is: how to change social behaviour, attitudes and lifestyles?

From the discussion so far we have seen that "caring" is really no different from what has been termed "self realisation" in Indian civilization and which also has been termed as the only worthwhile purpose in life. To my mind, in modern psychology the concept coming closest to it is that of Maslow's conception of what he terms "self- actualization." He has built up a scale of eight points by which success in self-actualization can be measured. Let us apply these to the Communication scene in India.

The first characteristic of self-actualization is that it implies the individual experiencing fully, vividly and *selflessly* with full concentration and total absorption whatever is to be done, and not in manipulating the situation. It also means becoming totally absorbed in something and to forget the inner defences and complexes. The key word in all this is *selflessness*. The present generation suffers from too much ego and self consciousness.

The question we have to, therefore, ask ourself is: does the communication media in India today foster a sense of selflessness, an attitude of dedication to a task, an attitude of self-abnegation for something higher.

The answer definitely is in the negative. Its whole effort is to pamper the ego by fostering consumerism, selfishness and a continual area of ego-assertion. The media foster in us a sense of urgency for progress - a euphemism for selfishness and ego-orientation.

The second characteristic is the factor of "choice" in life. In fact, life could be regarded as a series of "choice-making" events. On each occasion it is open to us to make a progression choice or a regression choice. On one side are choices based on safety, fear, defence; on the other side, growth choices. Growth choices are choices towards self-actualization.

The communication media do not give a fair choice, obssessed as they are with negativities only. In fact, anything positive is not considered as news at all. But positive is is not to be confused with propaganda.

The third characteristic is, in our decision-making, to listen to our own genuine inner voice - "the impulse voice" - and not to introjected voices of others: father, mother, friends, society. This determination is a path to self-actualization.

Do the media help us to do this? The fact is exactly the opposite. Their voices are slanted towards consumerism and the Establishment, not listening to the "still, silent voice" of the conscience.

Fourth, taking *responsibility* for our actions and the result of those actions. This is a big step towards self- actualization.

Here again the media are leading us astray because they are becoming increasingly irresponsible.

Fifth, acting with courage is another step towards self- actualization. Courage implies having the strength of our convictions. One cannot do this unless he first has the strength to listen to himself, *his own self*. Then only he will have conviction. Taking such a stand involves daring to be different, unpopular, nonconformist.

The media easily achieve the opposite. As the word suggests *"mass media"* is based on the disposition of the *masses* and hence on the lowest common denominator of culture and values. These are being constantly bombarded on innocent people who introject these alien values and therefore, become confused as to where the truth lies, and end up having no ability to have strong convictions.

Sixth, self-actualization is as much the process as the end result. We are immediately reminded of Gandhiji's conviction that the means are as important as the ends. Self- actualization therefore, means working to do well the thing that one wants to do, irrespective of what we want to do.

Do the media inculcate such high-minded one-pointedness, and single mindedness of purpose. Through their aimless shabby, sloppy presentations these achieve exactly the opposite. Obscenity, irrelevance, disdain for reality, cheap fantasy, violence, sex, character-assassination in a word, all negative attributes characterise the media. Can these make us conscious about right means? Certainly not.

What Is Caring ?

Can any one honestly say today with the poet Robert Browning "God's in heaven and all's right with the world"? On the contrary what has man made of man?

Today, the dire need of man is not so much of more material goods as it is of peace and poise within and love and harmony around. All the world over, man is shaken by emotional complex and psychic anxiety. Fear and frustration have taken the place of his optimism and self-confidence. Hope, cheer and joy have become rare commodities in his life and he fills this growing void with cheap entertainment and bizarre literature which present crime and violence as man's heroism.

In the home, the sense of mutual belonging among the members of the family has been weakening fast. Marital ties are gradually losing their sacred ethical hallow and assuming the form of a contractual relationship between man and women to satisfy their biological needs. Affection and love, service and sacrifice which alone make a 'sweet home' are giving way to discord and hisharmony. Parents are called upon to keep a careful watch over their college going children, lest they turn drug-addicts. A survey of students behaviour conducted by the Indian Council of Medical Research (ICMR) in 1977 revealed that 20 to 23 per cent of the University students boys as well as girls in Delhi, Chandigarh, Calcutta and Bombay were addicted to sedative drugs or alcohol.

Looking at social life, there is hardly any country in the world today which is free from political strife, economic exploitation of the weak by the strong, labour management fights, dishonesty and corruption in administration, crime and violence in most of the fields of social activity.

The international scene shows that most of the countries live under the shadow of internal revolts or external aggression. Every country - big or small - is directing a good part of its resources to pile up nuclear or other deadly weapons of warfare. The more powerful countries are vying with one another to impose their own political and economic ideologies on the weaker countries, through persuasion or aggression. Time and again, war clouds thunder in some part of the world or the other, sounding a threat of world conflagration every moment.

The net result is as the psychologist Dr. Samuel Sandweiss tells us "The world today seems to be in the grip of a supreme moral and spiritual crisis. People everywhere are feeling frustrated and helpless and are anxiously wondering what is in store for humanity. Never has there been so much distrust, hatred and violence as is witnessed today in almost every country."

But Who Cares?

The question is: what is generating these malevolent forces causing so much degradation of life and degeneration of man all the world over? How can such virulent and corrosive forces come into play and gather strength when the horizons of man's knowledge pertaining to almost all the dimensions of his life are expanding beyond his wildest dreams of only a century ago? In fact the present era is hailed proudly and joyfully as the "Heroic age of inventions." 'Age of the Adam' 'Space Age,' 'Jet Age', 'Computer Revolution' etc. All the various sciences together have opened up new universes for man to probe into and come out with discoveries bearing on man's health, wealth and welfare.

The overwhelming progress of science, its conquest of space and time, sound and light, the continuous flow of goods and services from new inventions of mechanical devices making life materially rich and physically healthy and happy all these made science appear as a great power capable of giving man's life an ideal mould and direction in all respects. In fact, man began to look up to science as an omnipotent power capable of solving all his problems and having the potential to give him all that he needs and seeks. This mechanistic faith making man less significant than the mechine made him more insensitive to fires instinct and impulses in his nature which constitute the main springs of humanism. With this growing insensitiveness, the matter based outlook and philosophy, materialistic success became the be all and end all of life. Materialism became the beacon light guiding and inspiring man's onward march. It seems as though the anti- Vedic view of life of the ancient Charvaks had come back to life, urging man to lead a life of luxury, no matter how he earned his fortune. As a result, altruism, charity, selfless love, spirit of self-sacrifice and allied finer qualities and values of life lost their place of importance in man's view. In their place, egotism, selfishness, opportunism and acquisitiveness became the hallmark of 'wise-living'.

In short, in the new order of life and living, Mammon became the most adorable God, materialism the faith, the almighty dollar its priest and self-interest the highest mode of worship.

The picture of modern life consisting of different contradictions and confusions is very well caught by the well-known poet T.S. Eliot:

"Endless invention, endless experiment,
Bring us knowledge of motion, but not of stillness,
Knowledge of words, and ignorance of the world,
All our knowledge brings us nearer to ignorance,
Where is the life we have lost in living?
Where is the wisdom we have lost in knowledge?
Where is the knowledge we have lost in information?
The cycle of heaven in twenty centuries,
Brings us further from God and nearer to dust."

Science by ignoring the inner 'being' of man has made him lose the precious traditional values of life, without making any provision to create new ones suited to the present age of reason and rationality. Does this not justify Dr. Einstein's view that science has succeeded more in pushing back the frontiers of man's ignorance than adding to his store of knowledge of life.

What the common man may not be aware of is that in the course of its quest of Reality, and particularly the fact that since as it probes deep into the material phenomena, he is treading into the realm of spirituality. In the meeting of these two major streams of knowledge lie the best hopes of rescuing mankind from the impending cultural and moral collapse and then putting man on the pathway to enduring peace and progress.

If caring is what characterised the Indian National Renaissance in the early part of this century, and if four decades of so-called Development with its mass production and mass communication syndrome has resulted in a totally perverse, noncaring society, we have to look for communication systems "Beyond mass communication" to rectify the malaise.

10

BEYOND SLAVISH RESEARCH

Ideally there ought to be the closest link possible between research on the one hand and theory on the other. Research ought to refine theory and theory ought to guide research. Yet one cannot think of one single instance in the last forty years in our country where theory building has been attempted on the basis of research in the communication area. This points to our intellectual infirmity and lack of purposive thinking in the communication field. And that from a people who down the ages have been leaders of philosophic thought, model building, classification of knowledge and sheer genius in abstract formulation. Where has that skill gone? Why has inertia, ineptitude and mental slavery overtaken us? We now live on the crumbs of other people's theories, of Western lands which are irrelevant to our needs and aspirations.

The second point is that research should ideally provide corrective to executive action. We cannot think of even one instance in recent years where executive action has either been challenged or changed by research inputs. Glaring examples of executive action which needed second thoughts and therefore, executive restraint are the following:

(a) Conversion of TV LPTs— Low Power Transmitter into HPTs— High Power Transmitter, thereby altering the whole character of TV broadcasting.

(b) Not using radio FM transmitters as Local Radio

(c) The onslaught of advertising in the broadcast media

(d) Totally wrong utilisation of prime time viewing on TV

(e) Letting the Film industry disintegrate without any executive intervention.

The next point is that Policy Research is totally unknown; we only have micro communication research where a very localised effect is examined. These researches are totally useless from the point of view of inputs for Policy formulation.

When we have no clear policies it means we have no idea of the objectives we wish to achieve. When policies themselves are in need of formulation or re-formulation; then improvement of planning or managerial functions, which aim at implementation of existing policies, is not only useless but often counter-productive. First, the implementation exercise diverts energy and resources from the primary task of policy analysis, and secondly, it results in doing more efficiently the incorrect thing.

What we desperately need is POLICY research — that is, conceptualisation of research in terms of structure, organization, professionalisation, socialisation and participation. Critical research which gives us insights into the macro aspects of Communications treated as a crucial component in society dealt with as a cybernetic model. Communications should be regarded as one of the fundamental pillars of the entire social system and must be studied in terms of its relationship with other social factors. In the absence of such Policy research, decision- making in the Communication sector is adhoc and we proceed to build the system like blind men, totally unaware of needs, implications and consequences.

Policy is one aspect, the other equally important is Economics. Our services sector in India is now contributing more than 50% to the G.N.P. Yet there are no studies on the Economics of Communication and Information Economics is a totally neglected subject. Research work needs to be done not only on the Sociology of Communication, but also on its Economics. Research in the field of Information Economics is most important.

Another point is that we are moving from linear systems to interactive systems in which the networking mode is most important. We must now take up research in "network" systems.

Another point we have to encounter is that of the U.S. supremacy in this field. The Communication discipline is essentially a North American phenomenon; Europe having devoted itself more to the sociology of knowledge. American supremacy effects us, as in our open society their ideas and models are bound to percolate. Here there are both the positive and negative sides. On the positive: The American approach and research is characterised by great rigour in the discipline. On the negative side: (a) the cultural orientation is not only irrelevant to India, it could be disastrous and (b) American research suffers from the "fallacy of instrumentation." It tells us too much about too little whereas our primary problem is to determine macro-directions and macro-policies.

Next, even the West have discarded the old Development Communication models attributable to Schramm and Lerner and Rogers. New thinking on the subject is discernable. Have we done any research keeping the new emerging paradigms in mind? We certainly have not and it is called for urgently.

The frontiers of Communication research are going beyond the national to the international as well as multilinguals. Are we ready for this widening of our horizons? It could certainly provide comparative estimates, which will put the problem in a wider context.

The present communication research in India is confined to Government-sponsored agencies or the advertising world. But these are useless for our purposes of macro-understanding and macro-policies formulation. We need a fresh environment, which is autonomous and scholastic in approach. For this new institution building is required.

Current research on development is criticized not so much because it is "Western research" as because it is "poor" research. This type of research still represents perspectives and evaluations of development which favour the dominant paradigm and top-down development decision-making.

This form of research imperialism *continues* to *distort* the nature of the communication process in social change as related to the historical and cultural aspects of the developing world. Obviously, this type of research is not intended to help the nations of the Third World, but to maintain the existing world-system. In an earlier publication, Halloran (1974, p. 13) asserted, "Research is a form of *social control*, although we often tend to rationalize our intentions in terms of clarification, increased knowledge, informed decision- making, better understanding, and so on."

Most researchers do not understand certain concepts as "self-reliance" or "popular participation." Because such concepts are difficult to implement and measure, they assume that they do not play salient roles in development. They have not quite come to the realization that "It is the task of social science to 'discover' the role and place of a variable, not to assume it" (Felstehausen

1971, p. 8). Sometimes, social scientists go into a research situation with a set of answers and try to find the problems which fit those answers. Rather than investigating problems, if any, then finding appropriate answers. In addition, misperceptions can take place. Some researchers may label a situation as a problem, even though the indigenous population may not consider it a problem or the reverse situation may occur.

This problem has it root in two areas. One is that communication research is not geared towards problem solving and the other is that there are not enough Third World- oriented researchers in the field of communication.

Evaluating the past twenty years of communication research, Lee Thayer (1983) commented that communication has not lived up to the promises of conducting brilliant research to solve major human and social problems. Seldom have communication experts pondered over the profound, idealistic research which would have greater and long-range effects on society. Thayer's criticisms are especially evident in the field of communication and international development. In this particular field, MacLean's (1966) observations are just as valid today. When he stated:

> I think that most of the research we have done has been done at too advance a stage of precision—as though we *presumed much more theory than we have .... As it is now, analysis of variance can take the place of exploration, thinking and theory.*

Many approaches in the field do not get at the heart of the problem (Mansell 1982). For example, it has long been realised that a problem with developing nations is not that they have low economic productivity and limited industrialization, but that they lack self-help programmes which allow them to attack problems which are pertinent to them. Yet, researchers continue to focus on economic indicators and refuse to look at any constructs such as "self-reliance." They will negatively evaluate a nation such as Cuba because it does not have large-scale industrialisation, while overlooking the fact that this nation has brillantly used self-development strategies of communication to almost eradicate illiteracy, a condition which was an enormous problem before the Cuban revolution. Many researchers are still unwilling to consider that there are many paths to developments. Instead, they see other ways as "revolutionary" rather than, what they really are alternative approaches to development.

There is a need for more Third World-oriented researchers in communications. Latin Americans social scientists were in the forefront of the criticism voiced against capitalist- oriented models. They were among the first to voice the notion of "dependency" and coined the concept of "underdevelopment" (Gunder Frank 1969) and call for social-equity in distribution of goods and services. Beltran recognized a new breed of researchers emerging in Latin America during the 1970s. He said that their new approaches stemmed from the understanding of communication as an integral and dynamic process and the conviction that this "process is inextricably interwoven with the structure of total society and, particularly, with the economic determinants of this structure. "He concluded," It is to be hoped that from the auspicious beginnings, such as those just reported there will emerge in the near future, ... a communicology of liberation which should help shape the new Latin America... (p. 35 and 37). Unfortunately, this new type of research did not take hold. There are no significant critical research methods flowing from the Third World in the areas where the "poorest of the poor" exist. These are the areas where socialist models are desperately needed to establish equity and provide basic services.

Traditionally, the problem has been with Western researchers who do not fully understand the *historical problems and needs of the* developing world. But on many occasions this also refers to native researchers. These Third World researchers tend to be more "anti-nationalist" than an outsider (Halloran 1890). Rogers et al. (1976), p. 17 reminds us that researchers are bounded by the particular training they receive.

A social scientist's perception of problems... is structured by the concepts and theories that he has been taught. *He sees status, ailenation, fatalism, as concepts. And, of course, he does not perceive phenomena for which he lacks concepts. So his scientific language structures limits his perceptions of the world and it affects his choice of concepts, theories and methods for investigation.*

There is a great need to improve the quality of research being conducted by Western and Third World researchers. Perhaps, the way to do this is *to stress historical and cultural studies in educational institutions.* So that researchers may understand the type of political and socio- economic systems, *which are natural for the people of a particular country.* In addition, new types of research methods can be developed. Hedebro (p. 120) gave examples of two ways of conducting research that communication scientists may use in developing countries. The first, "action cum research" means that the researcher is not a passive observer, "instead, he or she initiates and takes active part in the change process, while following and documenting all relevant events as accurately as possible." Another type is "participatory research." "The researcher participates in a local village or region, studying problems from the perspective of the weakest groups. The aim of these types of research is to allow the people in the developing areas to benefit from research projects and the researchers to fully understand the social systems in which societies progress the most.

11

BEYOND A ONE-SIDED NORTH-SOUTH DIALOGUE

So far in this book we have treated communication as an internal, national subject. But communication also connects us to the world at large and therefore, there is its international aspect. In particular, there is the great tussle for communication power between the developed North and the under-developed South.

Till recently the arena for this battle was UNESCO and in some notable cases the U.N. as will be evident from some U.N. debates and resolutions detailed in this chapter.

But the whole scenario has changed dramatically. The developed West have suddenly changed the label on Communication: from the "services" sector under which it always used to be categorised, and it is now coming in the domain of "goods" and therefore, the battle has now errupted of all the places, in GATT where Information is being regarded as a "commodity", subject to all the controversies which articles of foreign trade are subject to.

The reason for this is not far to see. Information has always meant "power". But under the new dispensation of an Information Society it also increasingly means "wealth".

Forty per cent of the G.N.P. of the U.S.A. for example derives from the Information sector. This by any reckoning is a collosal figure in money terms. Fifty per cent of U.S. work force is engaged in Information industry, and this figure is likely to go up to 70% in a decade. And 30% of U.S. exports come out of what is known as the Knowledge industry. For years the only growth sector in the U.S. economy has been the Information sector.

Information easily becomes a product of foreign trade in many ways. Countries like the U.S. increasingly want the manufacturing industries to be located offshore to capitalise on cheap labour of the Developing world, but control of this operation is effected through Information control. Again multi-nationals and other Developed countries' agencies exercise control on Developing countries markets through Transborder flow of information. How is this new genii of international Information economics to be tackled and coped with? We are presently doing it clumsily through the aegis of the External Affairs Ministry. But the subject is far too technical and complicated to be left to the drawing-room courtesies of diplomats.

We have already advocated all along in this book the dire necessity to develop the discipline of Information Economics in India. Along with this we will have to develop the discipline of International Information Economics & Foreign Trade. Only work on theory and conceptualisation can prepare us to stand up to the onslaughts of this new Information assault. This chapter purports to provide the background for such thinking.

And this chapter does this by analysing our role in North-South dialogue in international communication which has been the subject of long drawn controversy. The question is: have we cared to protect our long-term interests.

The media have long been noted for their ability to socialize groups of people; entertain, inform, and educate the populace; and persuade social members. In some countries, these attributes are packaged into media programmes for commercial consumption. For other countries, the media represent the best way to socially control their citizens. Still, for the bulk of the world's nations, utilization of media is their best hope to obtain development and a better quality of life for their people. This latter view is the essence of what has come to be known as the New World Information Order (NWIO).

The term "information" has continued to expand over the past decades. "Information no longer refers only to conventional bodies of statistics, facts, academic knowledge, scientific data, or daily news; it now includes electronic sensing and computer analysis of the human heartbeat, electrical impulses measuring physical phenomena in outer space or beneath the sea, and numeric digits holding passengers' airplane seats or transferring funds to and from bank accounts" (Eger, 1984, p.9). As a result, information, its many aspects, application, and implications have become hot topics in international discussions.

NWIO's proponents' (the non-aligned nations) basic aim is to utilize information-communication systems as means to achieve their potential for social enhancement, cultural autonomy, political stability, and economic independence. But some nations do not agree that there is a need for such an order. Representing extremist views are some in the Western world who insist *that information is a commodity* that should be dependent on the marketplace and employed only by those who have the technical and economic ability to develop and utilize it. Also, there are those of the Eastern bloc who advocate that communication should be used to preserve national sovereignty by means of governmental control. The non-aligned nations see neither approach as the solution to their primary problem which is underdevelopment. Instead, they view communication as a means to achieve true independence. "To the LDC's the current world communication system is an outgrowth of prior colonial patterns reflecting commercial imperatives of former times. Now LDC's (less developed countries) want to remove the last vestige of colonial control by promoting NWIO" (McPhail, 1981, pp.14-15).

Their policies hope to insure that the modernization process progresses within the natural order of the society. According to them, this can be accomplished by means of a "free and balanced" flow of information between the nations of the north and the nations of the south. McPhail states that:

> The NWIO is an evolutionary process seeking a more just and equitable balance in the flow and content of information, a right to national self-determination of domestic communication policies, and finally at the international level a two-way information flow reflecting more accurately the aspirations and activities of the less developed countries (p.14).

The continum of international debate shifted to discussions on transboder data flow (TDF). TDF deals mainly with the economic and technical aspects of international information flow. Currently, the emphasis is on how to regulate the flow of international data, thereby, establishing ground for a New World Information and Communication Order. This chapter is a survey of the evolutionary process of the international information debate. It culminates with a special focus on the need for international policy and on the International Telecommunications Union (ITU) and the Intergovernmental Bureau for

Informatics where policy deliberations are expected to be held until the end of the century.

The call for freedom in acquiring and disseminating information is not a new one in the international circle. The old familiar tune of "freedom of information" and "equal access" is a part of Western ideology. During world War II, American journalists complained that their ability to obtain information was being hindered by the news agencies of Europe. American media, especially the Associated Press (which was expanding its international markets), found on various occasions that the channels of access were often closed or revealed very little useful information. They advocated that the freedom of press philosophy of the United States be expanded internationally. The American Society of Newspaper Editors went as far as to suggest that the philosophy be included in the peace treaties. They recommended the inclusion of a pledge for nations not to censor news at the source and not to establish policies that allowed governmental control of the press. They referred to this as the "free flow" policy (Blanchard, 1983).

The principle was carried into the United Nations by the victorious Western allies as a mean of assuring world peace and stability. The United Nations' "Declaration on Freedom of Information" summed up the ideal by affirming that:

> All states should proclaim policies under which the free flow of information, within countries and across frontiers, will be protected. The right to seek and transmit information should be insured in order to enable the public to ascertain facts and appraise events. (As quoted in Gunther et al., 1979, p.17).

To counter Western support of the free flow of Information principle, the non-aligned nations ask:— Has "free flow" ever existed? Probably not. Initially, custom laws, tariffs, visas, telecommunications regulations, preferential rates, and availability of trans-atlantic cable had an impact on early international despatches. Reuter's tried to block competing wire services, particularly American ones, so also other competitive and commercial pressures have affected news flow from the beginning" (Mcphail, p. 33).

Over time it was realized that free flow of information, however, meant a "one-way" flow. For the newly emerging nations, free flow meant needed help in establishing telecommunication infrastructures, but at the price of cultural domination, economic dependency and, at times, political interference. Smith (1980) notes that the one-way flow of media products is not an accident. It was designed to work to the advantage of the exporting corporations. The one-way flow from the West has been manifested in several aspects. First, it perpetuated domination of Western languages and cultures through imported programmes (Smith). Next, despite Western denial, one-way flow is expressed in the policy of UNESCO. Nordenstreng (984) points out that "there are indeed obstacles to "sound management 'in UNESCO's Secretariat due to Western bias, as 44 per cent of the higher-and middle-ranking executives come from Western Europe and North America" (p. 141).

Third, one-way flow of information is evident due to heavy media investment in the developing areas. Beltran and de Cardona (1979) comment on the Latin American situation. They mention that the three U.S. national networks, NBC, ABC, and CBS, alongwith American industries have significant investments in most media in Latin America. According to their study, this has had adverse effects by distorting reality "in a direction that favours the economic and political dependency of Latin America on the United States" (p. 59). Finally, the Western transnational news agencies remain major gatekeepers of information in the developing countries. In a study of 29 press systems in 113 countries, the "big four" news agencies, Associated Press, United Press International, Reuters, and Agence France Presse, were the second most important set of sources of information on international news (Mohammadi, 1984). So, in practice, the policy of free flow benefitted the West.

Slowly, the non-aligned nations began to comprehend that there were some serious problems with the existing order. They noticed that:

> Global information flows are marked by serious inadequacy and imbalance, that the means of communicating information are concentrated in a few countries, and that the majority of countries are reduced to being passive recipients of information which is disseminated from a few centers.

> The situation perpetuated the colonial era of dependence and domination. It confines judgments and decisions on

what should be known and how it should be made known, into the hands of a few. In a situation where the means of information are dominated and monopolized by a few, freedom of the few to propagate information in the manner of their choosing and the virtual denial to the rest of the right to inform and be informed objectively and accurately (Legum, 1978, p. 32).

Beginning with these observations, the problem of information flow and its consequences have occupied international discussions for more than a decade.

Several events took place during the early 1970s which shifted media into international controversy. First, attention was being focused on the role and impact of the media. The developing countries became concerned because they realized that they had very little control ober these powerful instruments. Also, the relationship between information and economics was becomig apparent. The transnational corporations were able to make profits mainly because of their access to information provided by interactive communication systems. If the developing countries had access to such information, it would greatly aid them in the development process.

Next, debate on the New International Ecomonic order (NIEO) was being held in the United Nationas. According to the non-aligned nations, media should have been included in debate. They argued that one of the reasons why their countries were economically poor was because they were media weak. Citing such facts as low media development, Western and superpower domination of the electro-magnetic spectrum, and lagging access to satellite capabilities, they claimed that the principle of free flow of information should be at the forefront of international affairs.

The topic of information came under the auspices of the United Nations Educational, Scientific and Cultural Organization (UNESCO). An early 1970s *UNESCO Chronicle* summarized the initial arguments in three trends.

1. The developing countries and the rest of international community "have become conscious of the onesidedness of the flow of information."
2. The developing countries have begun to articulate their own demands "for a more equal access and participation in the world flow of news and media programmes

as part of the search for a New International Economic Order based upon a better distribution of resources and justice."

3. The least developed countries have become "alarmed" at the growing information gap between North and South and "that their image in the world at large is formed by media originating from, and influenced by, other cultural values and, sometimes, ideologies (Legum, pp. 44-45).

Continuing to insist that media and economics were linked, the non-aligned nations at their Fourth Summit, 1973, held in Algiers declared in Article XIII of the Action Programme for Economic Cooperation that "developing countries should take concerted action in the field of mass communications ... in order to promote a greater interchange of ideas among themselves." Likewise, Article XIV stated that "non-aligned countries should exchange and disseminate information concerning their mutual achievements in all fields through... the news media of their rspective countries." Specifically, they decided to enhance the exchanging of scientific and technical information via their media and universities or similar institutions. Also, they favoured reduced press-cable rates and collective ownership of satellites and a "code of conduct" for their use. Morever, they called for the "promotion of the study of non-alignment" (Samarajiwa, 1984, p. 110).

The Annoted Agenda of the conference recommended the consideration of:

Effective dissemination of information of importance to non-aligned countries to the international community through suitable information media... to counteract the often tendentious, incorrect, non-objective and inadequate coverage given in the international information media which are controlled by agencies of developed countries which at present practically monopoloze the dissemination of world information and news (Samarajiwa, p. 111).

This movement was the initiation of the New International Information Order (NIIO). Mustapha Masmoudi, speaking for the non-aligned nations, described an order in which there would be a "balanced" flow of information providing "equality in relations between sovereign states." He recognized the right of the individual and the community in the decisions of communication policy. Also, he spoke of a better future, liberty, justice, ending racism and eliminating cultural domination. He advocated preserving indigenous cultures as well as exchanging ideas with other cultures (McPhail, pp. 237-238).

Some rationalized the NIIO in terms of Western and Eastern ideologies. Nevertheless, NIIO represented a means to achieve cultural and economic parity in the media for the less developed countries. These nations cannot compete with the news agencies and corporations of the developed countries. They lack the resources to do so. Western agencies spend over a $100,000 a year for a single correspondent (Perry, 1980). In 1982, the total expenditure for United Press International was $110 million and $190 million for the Associated Press (Giffard, 1984). For the less developed nations, media must be a product of national policy. Many Western states see this use of media as restricting press freedom. However, media for development is a part of a new style of journalism which highlights the accomplishments of developing areas rather than the negative aspects of the governments. Yet, this notion referred to as "development journalism" does not overlook blatant injustices. Indian journalist Dilip Mukerjee speaking of this style of journalism commented:

> Our need is urgent and acute; we belong to societies which are in the process of restructuring and reshaping themselves. In our environment there is, and there will be for a long time to come, much that is ugly and distasteful. If we follow the Western norm, we will be playing up only those dark spots, and thus erode the faith and confidence without which growth and development are impossible ....(As quoted in Tharoor, 1977, p. 29).

In a newly emerging nation, "all national resources—including the resource of information-must be directed toward development" (Rosenblum, 1979, p. 206). However, development journalism is not limited to the Third World.

> From a theoretical point of view, the concept of "free press," or the "free flow of information" philosophy, reflects a situation where the "free press" is basically a development press in favour of free enterprise and a capitalistic social system. The ideological role of the mass

media in Western nations is to protect, perpetuate and enlarge the role and influence of the capitalistic system in all phases of decision-making (McPhil, pl. 24).

In *The Effects of Mass Communication*, Klapper (1960) pointed out that one of the functions of the media in the United States is to maintain the status quo. Noting that the Western press is an "ideological arm" of the capitalistic and free enterprise system, the non-aligned nations contend that they have the right to use their media to support their sociocultural, ecomomic, and political systems.

Although the 1974 U.N. General Assembly adopted a declaration regarding NIEO, it refused to link the document with NIIO. Despite assurance of its positive nature, some, still view a new order as having Marxist orientations. Most of the developing countries abhor the authoritarian principle of the Soviet model. At the 1976 Nairobi UNESCO General conference, they expressed their disgreement with this policy by refusing to support a Soviet-sponsored article. The "Declaration on Fundamental Principles Governing the Use of the Mass Media in Strengthening Peace and International Understanding and in Combatting War, Propaganda, Racism, and Apartheid" sparked much debate. Much of the controversy concerned the interpretation of Article XII which asserted that "states are responsible for the activities in the international sphere of all mass media under their jurisdiction" (Legum, p. 43). The article implied that since governments are responsible for their media, they must be allowed to exert direct control of them.

By rejecting such move, the non-aligned nations illustrated that they are as dissatisfied with the Soviet system as with the Western form of control. A Nigerian commentator on Radio Lagos, reflecting on the issue, depicted the action in this matter:

> Members of the UNESCO conference argued that government control of the Press was certainly not a cure for the ills of the mass media in the Third World countries nor would it help the free flow of information....Besides, the imposition of regulations as implied in the draft declaration, restricting the dissemination of domestic news abroad or to state-controlled news services, would amount to placing curbs on the free flow of information. The Soviet inspired draft declaration was obviously shelved because of

the view of the majority of the UNESCO conference that the correct solution to the problem of the developing countries lies in measures which will give people the greatest possible diversity of opinions and to allow them to communicate easily with one another (Legum, p. 43).

Over the next two years, the debate on international information flow intensified. To defuse the situation in 1976, the General Assembly of UNESCO organized the International Commission for the Study of Communication (MacBride Commission). The MacBride Commission sought to come to an understanding for UNESCO on four major topics regarding: (1) "free and balanced" flow of information; (2) NIIO and its relationship with NIEO; (3) international implications of the "right to communicate"; and (4) maintainence of "freedom of the press."

The Commission's interim report, in 1978, prompted the Western nations to admit that there were indeed problems with the conceptualization of "free flow." They agreed to substitute the phrase with "free and balanced flow." Also, they agreed to accept the term a "new, more just and more efficient world information and communication Order," or in short, a New World Information order (Asante and Kim, 1984).

When it was finally issued in 1980, the Commission's report represented a middle-of-the-road approach.

> The Commission could not totally meet all the demands of the less developed nations; to do so would have meant the absolute abdication of the concerns of the industrialized nations. On the other hand, the Commission could not satisfy the most conservative voices of the industrialized mations. In the sense that the Commission sought to serve the advantages of all nations, it was successful (Asante and Kim, p. 146).

Controversy over the issue continued to rage. The U.S. accused UNESCO of becoming political and urged reforms in the organization's budget and management. However, UNESCO non-aligned members believed that Information flow was the major reason of the criticism. They felt that the issues surrounding a NWIO were too crucial to suppress. Thus, on December 31, 1984, the U.S. withdrew from the organization claiming that it could better carry out its duties through other more favourable organizations. Likewise, the British followed suit. Their withdrawal from UNESCO was effective from the latter part of 1986.

It must be noted that the question of international information flow has not subsided: it has simply shifted forums of debate from UNESCO to ITU and IBI. The expanding information and communications situation has caught the attention of many countries. Most countries are just beginning to realize that there are political, socal cultural, and economic ramifications of the information society in reference to transborder data flow and informatics. Because the movement of information is not restricted to national boundaries, many of the issues are now under discussion in intergovernmental organizations- "International involvement and interdependence are necessary because of the enormous burdens and profits to be made from the international flow of information" (Pipe, 1984).

The transborder data flow (TDF) issue is an integral element of the concept of information. The information involved is essentially of an economic and technical nature. This expanded definition of TDF will once again place the issues of information order and economic order back on the front burner of international debate. TDF clearly encompasses both issues. Renaud (1984) points out that both orders address the same issue of allowing every nation an opportunity to participate in the decision-making process of determining how information will flow into their borders and out of it, protect their natural resources and sovereignty, and implement models which allows them to use information in the development process.

A survey published in the 1980 *Transnational Data Report* questioned businessmen, government officials, and academicians of 67 countries as to how developed countries differed from less-developed countries. The respondents said that the two differ on the issues of whether or not data banks are kept within their national boundaries, transborder data flow, and the constraints on data flow by national regulations (Lloyd, 1981). TDF is considered as one of the most significant issues in the latter part of the century.

McPhail notes that currently the supporters of "free flow" principle are governments responding to pressure from multinational corporations that wish to expand their corporate, and not necessarily national interests. "What is good for IBM World

Trade, for example, in selling computers to the U.S.S.R. is not
.... good for the national or indeed international, interests of the
United States" (p.33).

Recent technological advances, such as miniaturization of the
microcomputer, the increased volume of capabilities of computer systems; and enhanced speed of global transmission
through telecommunication systems relying on optic fibers and
satellites, have increased reliance on computer systems. The
focus of economics is shifting from the manufacturing of
products to the initiation, storage, retrieval, and transplant of
information. The flow of information via computer systems and
satellites affect the entire international community. The success
of transnational companies lie as much with their ability to acquire and decipher information as with their ability to produce
goods. Information handling capabilities already offer industrialized countries and corporations considerable economic
and political leverage in North-South interactions; and it enhan-
ces the capacity of decision-makers to profit from such
knowledge (O'Brien, 1984). *Hence, information has become a valuable resource.*

Many corporations are expanding into the information in-
dustry. Exxon, Xerox, Chase Manhattan, General Electric, Aetna
Insurance, Columbia Broadcasting Corporation, Inc., and other
Fortune 500 American-based companies. In addition, many
small entrepreneurial endeavors are entering the field such as
Asoen Systems Corporation, Calspan On-Line Information Service, Data Courier, Dataflow Systems, Inc., Information Access
Corporation and Micromedia Limited. Some computer companies have branched into telecommunications. For example,
IBM has Satellite Business Systems (SBS) and Control Data
which has CYBERNET. Publishing and broadcasting companies
are also venturing into data resources as auxiliary services such
as the New York Times Index. Micrographics and electronic information systems are thought to be the wave of the future.
Also, some media companies rely on digital communications to
transmit materials to various editorial centers and redistribution
points. In Europe there is a similar trend and the expansion of
the information industry is sometimes subsidized with government funds (Pipe).

TDF encompasses several issues of social, cultural, economic
and political consequences. Pipe points out that these issues are

"interrelated but lack a fully developed theoretical or conceptual framework." He predicts that *"the post-industrial period, indeed the opening decades of the twenty-first century, can be expected to be an era of information communications. Acknowledging its far-reaching impact on countries at all levels of development will require a considerable expenditure of human and financial resources by national governments, international bodies, academic institutions, and private organizations."* Lastly, he noted that "attempts to deal with early manifestations of data flows are mostly in evidence on a regional basis and in a few United Nations organizations." But, "there is a pressing need for a more rational treatment of information communication topics which cut across traditional institutional arrangements (Pipe p. 201).

Although there are many issues connected with TDF, the major issues are *the social issue of privacy; the economic issue of treating information as a commodity; and the political issue of national sovereignty and remote sensing.*

With the advent of computers and their capacities for storing and transferring large amounts of information, protecting the privacy of individuals has become a paramount concern. Governments have for years attempted to regulate banks, credit agencies, insurance companies, medical agencies, and other companies dealing with large amounts of private information. To protect personal data stored in data systems several countries such as Sweden, France, Austria, and Germany have passed privacy laws. Other countries like the United States have a range of privacy laws deriving from the Constitution, regulatory agencies, and common law (Leeson, 1984). Wigand, Shipley, and Shipley (1984) reported that 63 per cent of the respondents in a recent survey said that privacy of individuals should be preserved even if it means curtailing computer capabilities.

Recently, the move has been to devise international law covering the privacy of citizens who are on data files in another country. International standards have been set up in the "Guidelines Governing the Protection of Privacy and Transborder Flow of Personal Data." This is a voluntary agreement drawn up by the United States and adopted by the Organization for Economic Cooperation and Development (OECD) in September of 1980. The Guideline set minimum standards of privacy protection, including:

- limitations on the collection of personal data,
- requirements that what is obtained be relevant, up-to-date, accurate, and complete,
- limitations on disclosure without the subject's consent or by authority of law,
- safeguards against unauthorized access,
- openness about developments, practices, and policies with respect to personal data, and
- the right of subjects to see information about them and to challenge, correct, or amend it (Leeson, p.92).

In October, 1980 the Council of Europe adopted a "Convention for the Protection of Individuals with Regard to Automatic Processing of Personal Data." The United States and three other countries have refused to ratify the Convention. The U.S. particularly wants the Convention to be amended to include statements and requiring data bases to be registered with a central authority.

Another point for regulation is that information should be valuated and taxed. *Like any commodity, information can be packaged and sold.* The market value is determined by competition and technological conditions which affect the supply of the information and by what the buyers think the information in use will be worth. "The international aspect of the value of information comes into play when information...is transferred among the geographically dispersed subsidiaries of a multinational firm. Officials of a particular country may consider that something of value is crossing the border, and that it ought to be subject to the same tarriff procedures or customs duties as other objects of value crossing the border. (Leeson, p.95).

A second reason for placing a value on information and taxing it is because of the volume and importance of international law regulating remote sensing. The United Nations Legal Subcommittee of the Committee on the Peaceful Uses of Outer Space is in the process of developing guidelines on remote sensing.

The seriousness of the issues call for governments to impose some type of restrictions on the flow of data in and out of their borders. For example, a government that cannot protect the privacy of its citizens has lost its national sovereignty. But, the steps taken by a government to protect its privacy must be done in such a way as not to inflict upon itself any economic loss. If a nation bars itself from any venture in computer or communication network it will be locked out of advances in information technology. Hence, constraints that a nation place on data flow must be weighed carefully against the benefits (Pipe).

Tarriffs and other barriers imposed by a nation affect the flow of data. Japan was effective in locking American companies out of its national trade by placing tight government restrictions and high costs on obtaining domestic circuits. For instance, Control Data had to wait two years for a circuit, but government regulations made it almost impossible to operate. The Canadians sought to restrict the personal data of their citizens from being stored in data banks in the U.S. The Consultative Committee on the Implications of Telecommunications for Canadian Sovereignty (the Clyne Committee) in its 1979 report to the Minister of communications recommended that the government immediately place restrictions on transborder data flows to ensure that the country maintains its sovereignty. The Committee suggested that the government require that data processing relating to Canadian businesses be performed in Canada unless otherwise authorized (Dordick, 1984). Dordick points out that restrictions can be both ways. "Opportunities may be lost to import attractive information business that not only brings revenue but also enables the importer to learn new techniques and upgrade its own facilities or develop new facilities with which to achieve competitive advantages" (p.214). Samiee (1984) warns that economic protectionism could become so pervasive that no nation nor business will benefit from data systems.

Because monopolies, primarily Western multinational corporations, have increased their holdings in the information field, international organizations and regulatory agencies have been asked to create international policy. Earlier international policy dealt with the more traditional types of information and communication—telegraph, telephone, and mass media. Today, policy is needed in the expanded areas of telecommunications, satellites, distribution of the radio spectrum, and computer-to-computer link systems. Emphasis for the most part has been placed on the need for written laws and regulations of international and regional information flows. Several countries have

begun to devise strategies and development policy to assure
that they reap some benefits from the Information Revolution.
In the respect of this paper, policy "refers to a programme that
specifies both the objectives to be attained and the means of
achieving them" (Leeson p.90).

Although the need for policy and international agreements
are acute, it seems unlikely that they will be reached in the near
future. Multinational companies regard any type of protectionist
legislation as hindering their economic interests. To assure harmony in international law, it would be to the interest of all
countries to review their policies, laws, regulations and
proposals in order to eliminate inconsistencies. "In particular,
requirements of one nation should not make it impossible to
comply with those of another nation" (Eger, 1979, p.128). Also,
regulation should generally be kept to a minimum. Excessive
regulation can be expensive for governments and business alike.
Regulations should focus on the critical issues. International
communication will develop best through agreements that encourage the rapid development and adoption of new technology.

Eger suggests that minimum regulation is needed in the areas
of communication equipment and standards, communications
tarriffs, facilities planning and multilateral agreements in
privacy and security. Agreements should be made on com-
patible equipment, standards and reciprocal certification so that
interfacing of equipment, and systems of cooperating countries
can be effective and affordable. He recommends that tariffs be
cost-based and cooperative. In addition, a forum for underseas
cable planning and satellite regulation is needed. Unilateral
decisions should not affect the planning. For example, the actions of an agency like the Federal Communications Commission should not hinder rational international planning.

R.J. Rankine, IBM director of Standards, Product Safety, and
Data Security, speaking at an Intergovernmental Bureau for Informatics Conference in Rome stated that:

> In general, the first step toward *developing a national infor-
> matics policy* should be to examine closely the present and
> potential impact of information on the major processes of
> the national economic and societal structure. *Understanding*

> the role of informatics does not mean simply launching an ex-
> panded training programme in information technology. If any-
> thing, information technology has occupied too dominant a posi-
> tion in most discussions. Instead, interaction is required be-
> tween specialists in the subject area under examination
> and with the information technologist as well. (IBI, 1980,
> p.17).

Presently, the controversy concerning policy is deciding which international body will develop it. A United Nations' organization is the most obvious forum for discussions of international policy. But which organization would be responsible for the development of policy? UNESCO would be suited for taking on some of the task. But, it is unlikely that it will be allowed to do so because of recent controversy surrounding its actions relating to the New World Information Order and the U.S. and Britain's withdrawal. Since, the policy would deal with telecommunications and TDF, the two most likely organizations for the job are the International Telecommunications Union (ITU) and the Intergovernmental Bureau for Informatics (IBI). ITU is concerned with telecommunications. IBI is a facilitator on issues of informatics which encompasses the aspects of TDF. Neither organization has been successful in developing specific policy because of accusations that they are biased in favour of Third World concerns. ITU tried to be just in its policies, but IBI emphatically states that it operates in the interest of Third World nations. Despite their tendencies, an examination of each shows that they are the organizations best suited for the development of international information policy.

ITU dates back to 1865 when it was called the International Telegraph Union. It became a part of the U.N. in 1947. Initially, it was established to deal with technical aspects of transborder telegraphic communication; and in the early 1990s, it added broadcasting to its responsibilities. ITU sets standards for telecommunications interchange, regulates use of the radio spectrum and gives technical assistance to developing countries. ITU began with 20 members, today there are some 157 members, mostly Third World countries. Member nations agree to abide by the International Telecommunication Convention. The Convention or agreement is revised at plenipotentiary conferences held at five-to-ten year intervals.

ITU has divided the world into three regions. This helps the organization better deal with geographical differences and regional needs. Region I is composed of Africa, Europe and the U.S.S.R. Region III comprises the Americas and some of the Atlantic and Pacific Islands. Region II comprises Asia and the South Pacific. At times, ITU finds it easier to adopt regional rather that universal rules. For example, the various regions differ on their allotment of direct satellite frequencies.

ITU is instrumental in aiding developing countries who are weak in telecommunication infrastructures such as telegraph and telephone lines, broadcast facilities and broadcast relay stations. Technical assistance is given to the countries by means of funds allocated by the World Bank and the United Nations Development Programme Assistance includes sending experts to assist with telecommunication development, donating equipment, recruiting temporary specialized personnel, providing on-the-spot training of indigenous personnel, and supplying fellowships for study abroad.

ITU has always maintained that it deals with technological and not ideological concerns. With most of the organization's members composed of Third World nations, clashes between their ideologies and that of the West often occur.

> The ITU has received promptings from many quarters to generate some structural and administrative reforms designed to furnish mechanisms for absorbing and taking into account political inputs. Currently, the ITU has developed neither traditions for dealing with political or ideological concerns nor the necessary administrative circuitry through which such conflicts could be channelled without crippling the ITU in its technical activities (McPhail, p.157).

WARC 1979 had been predicted to be a very heated conference. However, this did not occur because many controversial subjects were postponed until later conferences. According to a U.S. delegation, "there was no rhetorical debate over the New World Information Order; and in general, very little political discussion that was not directly relevant to the technical, economic and operational tasks which had been assigned to the Conference. The political issues of direct- broadcast satellite and remote sensing currently being discussed in the U.N. Outer

Space Committee never came up during the WARC" (U.S. Department of State, 1979, pp.16- 17).

The U.S. did consider the 1982 Plenipotentiary Conference as very political. Among the issues that the U.S. deemed as political were Indonesia's complaint of spillover from satellite broadcasting systems of First and Second World countries; a proposal from developing countries to replace the class-unit system of ITU contributions with the U.N. assessment scale; and various proposals designed to benefit developing countries with respect to access the geostationary satellite orbital parking slots and radio frequency bands. Codding (1984) concludes that "no matter how much we may wish that it were not so, it will be necessary to prepare to discuss political issues in all of the ITU conferences scheduled for the next decade" (p.144).

IBI deals directly with the technical and economic aspects of TDF. IBI is not as controversial organization as ITU, simply because it was created to be biased in favour of developing nations. The U.N. and UNESCO created IBI in 1961 and placed its headquarters in Rome, Italy. IBI has become one of the most active U.N. organizations. According to IBI, informatics is the discipline which is concerned with all aspects of the processing of information including hardware and software. Its aim is to create efficient mechanisms for the management of information (Altschull, 1984). IBI primarily supports the side of developing countries, "seeking ways to help them modernize and to induce industrialization to correct imbalances as far as the capacity to use information" (Altschull, p. 271). IBI's scope is to "permanently assist people in the field of Informatics, to help them live in the context created by this discipline, to better understand its possibilities." (IBI, 1980). IBI has supported several conferences on information strategies (SPIN); but as of yet no concrete policies have come out of the organization's meetings.

Policy considerations outside of ITU and IBI have mainly been on a regional level. The Latin American Informatics Authorities (CALAI) held in Buenos Aires, Argentina during October 1979; and the conference on African Informatics Integration held in Abidjan, Ivory Coast during November 1979 made no regional agreements. The call for TDF to be governed by regional and international organizations. Both urged agreements to protect privacy, cultural autonomy, and national sovereignty. The African conference said that *"socioeconomic information" should be considered as a commodity;* and that scientific and technical information be freely circulated (Valerdi, 1984).

So far, no solidified piece of international legislation has emerged to deal with TDF. If no regulation emerges soon, and if laws are narrowly made in the self- interest of a few nations, then the enormous benefits to be reaped from the Information-Communication Revolution will be limited.

The nations of the world are earger to enter the Information Age, but many are uncertain of its implications. Information came to the forefront of international attention, when research revealed that communication can have an impact on development. By the 1970s, it was apparent that the role of communication in developing societies had had negative side effects. Media in conjunction with socio- economic and political factors had led to cultural domination, increased economic dependency, and socio- economic gaps between social groups. The Third World had remained media weak as far as owning, operating, and programming the systems were concerned. Alternative paths of development were implemented and communication was expected to play a positive role in the process. In order to accomplish this, a New World Information Order would have to be established. The Non-Aligned Movement characterized the Order as a "free and balanced" flow of information throughout the world. It advocated a development style of journalism which used the media to support national development planning.

The call for a new order sparked nearly a decade of controversy in UNESCO, the site of much of the debate. The Mac-Bride Commission report in 1980 attempted to settle the issue in a fashion that would satisfy Western nations and the Non-Aligned Movement. Despite these efforts, the U.S. and Britain officially withdrew from the organization.

At the same time, the notion of information was expanding to include computer-to-computer link systems, satellites, and personal, scientific, governmental, and financial data stored in data banks. Much of the information is controlled by Western-based multinational corporations. When valuable information moves across national boundaries, it becomes known as transborder data flow (TDF). International discussions began to shift to TDF's economic and technical aspects. Included in the discussions were TDF issues like privacy, economic value of information, and threats to national sovereignty posed by remote sensing.

With information covering a broad scope of topics, issues, implications, and equipment, there is an urgent need for international policy to settle controversy and establish rules for the future. The ITU and IBI are the two international organizations which are best suited to develop international policy, however, they have been unable to do so. The ITU has been accused of becoming too political to develop fair policy. IBI is organized mainly to ensure that Third World nations get a fair stake in any TDF policy. As of now, there is no significant and coherent international information policy. Thus, it appears as if it will be another decade before there can be universal cooperation on information flow. Moreover, any type of just information and communication order seems to be farther in the future.

It is this context that India's role can be supreme. Of all the Developing countries India stands head above shoulders of others in the potential to be leaders of the Information Revolution not only in the Developing world, but in the whole world.

India has the third largest technical and scientific manpower in the world, Indians have mastery over the English language, in computer software development they are the leading and most sought after brains in the world, and just as two decades back Indian doctors ran the National Health scheme of U.K., now Indian scientists and engineers, to all intents and purposes are running major R & D establishments in the U.S.A...this has certainly made the Indian community the highest paid ethnic community in the U.S.A.

But we do not realise our own strengths, our own potentials. As Dr. Coomaraswamy would remind us: intellectually and spiritually we are still slaves, still tied to the apron strings of a debilitating image of First Industrial Europe. And so we are still fixated to an archaic, out dated concept of Mass Communications subservient to equally outmoded mass production systems. The world has moved on—we have to go "Beyond Mass Communications" and we will discover through a strange route that is where our strength in international affairs resides.

12

BEYOND THE PUBLIC SECTOR

In recent years there have been two remarkable cases of successful deregulation brought about in the field of Telecommunications. Both have been highly spectacular international events and everybody knows about these in the Communications field.

The first case is of the deregulation of the monopoly of the AT & T Corporation in the U.S. in the field of Telecommunications. The monopoly which AT & T enjoyed was stifling growth in this sector in the U.S. The deregulation has thrown open the environment not only to other operators, but more importantly to newer technologies and more rapid modernization in this field.

The second case is of British Telecom. This case is the most spectacular in the annals of Telecommunications history, in asmuchas so many company shares have not changed hands in any one transaction in the world.

As a result, British Telecom has got transformed overnight in the U.K. from a decadent, loss-making, government enterprise, into a highly efficient, profitmaking service.

There is a strong case for deregulation of the Telecommunications sector in India. If we find the public sector can no longer generate electricity or make steel efficiently and economically and we are throwing these open to the private sector, why should we burden the government budget with Telecom, which can be an extremely productive and profitable area? Let the private sector now do this job. We do not eleborate on this here, but present a suggestion for a national public debate that there be total deregulation of the Telecom sector in India. The Bell case history is given at Annexure.

At the time of the launching of the Energy-intensive development model of Mahalnobis four decades back it was all right for Jawaharlal Nehru to usher in the public sector as the "commanding heights of the economy." This was totally justifiable because there was no capital formation nor infrastructure in the country and in keeping with Kenesyian principles Government had to be the main investor into the public sector.

There is no earthly reason now however, for that to be repeated four decades later, when we propose to launch the In- formation- intensive model. Far from being at the commanding heights, the public sector is in total shambles. And that too not just financially, where it is a drag on the national budget, but even functionally there is nothing but politics and internecine warfare with the parent Ministry and controlling bureaucrats.

In the interim, the private sector has come into its own and is virile, dynamic and bursting with funds from shareholders and equity. Also there are any number of professionals working in independent capacities.

There is no earthly reason therefore, why the whole future development of Telecommunications, Electronics, Computers, Data- banks and allied industries be assiduously kept out of the benumbing and deadly hands of the public establishment.

There is a prima facie strong case for *De-regulation* in this sector and this subject merits serious public debate, scholarly intervention and 180 degrees change in policy. There is urgent need for a national public debate on this issue, because the crip- pling of the communications sector could affect adversely not only our economy, but our identity as a nation.

ANNEXURE

THE BELL SYSTEM:
TECHNICAL COMPATIBILITY AND
CROSS-SUBSIDIZATION

The Bell System has been the dominant communications in the United States for almost a full century. That system is a vertically integrated monopoly that not only provides local telephone services, but also operates research laboratories, manufacturing facilities, and long-distance telephone services. The Bell System can be viewed as having five major operating units: the local telephone companies; Bell Long Lines, which provides long-distance service throughout the nation; the Bell Laboratories, a premier research organization; Western Electric, which manufactures telephone equipment; and the organization's central management. The Bell System has been accepted as a monopoly for most of the twentieth century for the simple reason that the best interests of the nation have been served by having a technologically compatiable telephone network.

The price exacted from the Bell System for the enjoyment of its monopoly status has been regulation. On the national level, first the Interstate Commerce Commission, and after 1934 the Federal Communications Commission have overseen the system's operations. In addition, the Antitrust Division of the Department of Justice has instituted three major lawsuits against the system over the course of this century. Throughout, the system has been regulated at the local level by commissions empowered to set local telephone rates.

The consensus of opinion accepting the Bell System's monopoly power has slowly eroded over the last decades. Two broad efforts competed with one another from 1977 to 1981 in an effort to achieve a reorganization of the nation's telephone provides. A legislative updating of the Communication Act of 1934 was debated in Congress, and at the same time, an antitrust suit brought against the Bell System by the Justice Department slowly proceeded through the judicial system.

The year 1982 will stand as a watershed in the market structure and operation of the national telephone system. On 8 January 1982, the parties involved in the case of United States *v.* Western Electric Co.. and American Telephone & Telegraph Co. reached settlement. This antitrust case had been initiated in November 1974 by the Department of Justice, and resulted in the breakup of AT&T into twenty-two separate local operating companies. AT&T was left as the provider of long-distance telephone services. With the settlement of the antitrust case, congressional efforts to rewrite the Communications Act of 1934 colllapsed.

The section examines the evolution of the regulatory framework of the Bell System, and traces recent efforts to alter that framework. The historical context of regulation is considered, followed by a description of the now-failed efforts to amend the Communications Act of 1934, and finally, the antitrust settlement of 1982 is described in detail.

The Historical Context

This massive antitrust settlement is the most recent act in a drama that has spanned most of this century. AT&T is a corporate behemoth; the beneficiary of a monopoly status earned by the dictates of the technical capability. The magnitude of the Bell System can be grasped by looking at its operations statistics for the twelve months ended 30 November 1981.

- Over 200 billion telephone conversations were carried, including 18.6 billion long distance calls.
- Over 142 million company owned telephone were in service
- The company had more than a million employees.
- Its revenues were in excess of $ 57 billion, and its profits totalled almost 7 billion.

The Bell System's dominance was not achieved without struggle. The last quarter of the nineteenth century was marked by the founding of many hurdles of small, independent telephone companies, typically operating in very limited geographical areas. In the early twentieth century, a process of consolidation began as more and more independents were acquired by the nascent Bell System. An antitrust settlement, reached in March 1914, resulted in AT&T's agreement to seek the prior clearance of the Department of Justice for future acquisition process, as it subsequently took over more than one hundred independents. Of more lasting significance, AT&T

agreed, as part of the same antitrust settlement, to allow other companies to interconnect over the Bell System long-distance lines. By 1934, the Bell System owned some 85 per cent of all telephones in place in the United States, and required some 270,000 employees to operate the system.

The framework for the present-day structure of telephone communications regulation in the United States was established by the enactment of Communications Act of 1934. On 26 February 1934, President Franklin D. Roosevelt proposed the establishment of a Federal Communications Commission, with jurisdiction over both the Bell System and the emerging radio broadcast industry. Roosevelt's statement, which appears as a part of the following reading, noted that "there is today no single Government agency charged with broad authority" to regulate the nation's communications "utilities." With a speed that seems astounding today, President Roosevelt's proposal was enacted within four months of his initial request.

A part of the legislative history that underlines the enactment of the Communications Act of 1934 is presented in the following pages. The first selection is a report of the House Committee on Interstate and Foreign Commerce dated 1 June 1934, describing the provisions of the proposed legislation (enacted later with amendments), which dealt with "common carriers," including the Bell System. As described in the report, the twenty-one sections of Title 2 vested the new commission with a variety of responsibilities pertaining to common carriers, previously in the domain of the Interstate Commerce Commission. Powers over interstate rates, over new construction, and over the accounting requirements for each business may be found in Title 2 of the Communications Act of 1934.

The second reading, presenting another element of the legilsative history of the Communications Act of 1934, is an excerpt from the statement of Walter S.Gifford, then president of AT&T, made on 13 March 1934 before the Senate Committee on Interstate Commerce, Gifford's statement concerning the proposed legislation suggests that AT&T was dragged into the jurisdiction of the Federal Communications Commission kicking and screaming. His testimony opposing the legislation was followed by court challenges to the constitutionality of the act, eventually settled by the Supreme Court in the Commission's favor.

The final prelude to the legislative and antitrust efforts of the 1970s to reorganize the Bell System was the Consent Decree of 1956, which settled an antitrust action brought against AT&T by the Department of Justice in 1949. In that suit, the government had sought to break up the Bell System, and to restrict its activities in unregulated markets. The Consent Decree left the structure of the Bell System, intact, but prohibited it from entering the market for provision of computer services or any other unregulated market.

13

BEYOND DECAYING INSTITUTIONS

This chapter is more in the form of an epilogue. It is merely indicative and not exhaustive. It summarily indicates work that needs to be done in the future.

The word "Decaying" however, is used advisedly. As has been pointed out again and again: at the end of the 40 year cycle everything in India associated with the Mahalnobis model is on the downswing, institutions in particular, are in advanced stages of decay, but of all those dealing with Media and Communication easily exhibit the worst form of decay.

The restoration or reincarnation of these institutions therefore, acquires the utmost urgency. A few cursory points are made here.

The artificial Ministrial separation of Information- Boradcasting, Telecommunications, Electronics etc. will not hold for future systems in this area. A meshing of technologies is going on and also much greater concern with usage. There is also the question of policy fomulation in this sector.

This requires something of an apex Information Ministry which would overseas the others as departments under the apex Ministry.

Secondly, there should not be the overwhelming preponderance of career administrators in this area. The manning should be totally by technical and creative people.

A completely new institutional framework is called for - to which we have given no thought at all.

14

EPILOGUE

This Epilogue is being written after the proofs have come from the press for my scrutiny and before the printing of the book has started. Since I submitted the manuscript to the Publisher and uptill now when the proofs have come in, a number of traumatic experiences have occured in India, which all go to vindicate the main thesis propounded in this book, namely: that on the long Kondratiev what we are now witnessing in India is the exhaustion of the Nehru Mahalnobis paradigm of Energy-intensity, centralization, heavy industry, incessant long-haul of materials through an ever expanding transport corridor; in a word the prototype of the First industrial revolution in Europe, which I constantly label as Mechanical Engineering of which the heroic symbol is *Mass Communication*.

Since the traumatic events have been so utterly shattering, it is altogether impossible to ignore them in a book devoted to the search for a new Developmental paradigm for India. Hence the necessity for this Epilogue.

Some of the recent traumatic experiences we have suffered are:

(1) First the Mandal experience. An altogether catastrophic, meglanomaniac and shattering experience which sought to reverse the history of Hindu reform of the past 150 years since Raja Rammohan Roy, sorcerrer-like and as witches hovering around a cauldron over fire created phantoms of 3500 castes and in one sweep endeavourd to take the country back to the 1st century instead of forward to the 21st century.

(2) Quick on the heals of this has been the Mandir backlash of HINDUATTVA- the Hindus' understandbly refusing to be silent spectators to the total disintegration and even annihilation of the Hindu religion, especially when a spate of Hindu Reformist movements over a period of 150 years have aimed at purifying

Hindu Society and creating Hindu "sangathan".

(3) Hardly had this trauma finished, when the Gulf war broke hell in the region and its reverbrations have been felt around the world. To this has been added U.S.A.'s threat that next on its hit list is India.

(4) Next came the shock of India's foreign exchange insolvency and our begging for IMF loans.

(5) Even more nefarious and traumatic have been political antics which led to the collapse the Chander Shekhar Government and with it the Parliament.

(6) This is turn has led to crisis in managing a vote on account, postponement of US $ 2 billion I.M.F. loan and it would appear the complete shattering of prospects of the Eighth Plan.

(7) The almost total collapse—economic & political of what was known as the greatest experiment in world Communism Soviet Russia.

(8) And finally, like the foreign exchange crisis, India is well on the way to an internal debt crisis.

As far as the Gulf war is concerned it is worth noting that the crux of the war thrust by the Americans is represented by three overriding technologies:

Electronics

Communications and

Media

Typically for example, the use of electronics was at its deadlist in weapons like laser-controlled bombing which were incredibly accurate in homing into targets.

Communications was the network dominating the whole show, but more particularly the method by which Patriot missiles targeted the Scud missiles in the air. Communication antennas uplinking from Australia on one side and Spain on the other, crated a zone in which the Scud missile became visible and the signal was received on a ground computer and translated into a trajectory for the Patriot missile fired from the ground.

Media again was overpowerly in control. The reporting of the war was managed as never earlier and what appeared on the TV screen in people's living rooms was not as a war with blood and deaths and corpses, but as a melodramatic, sentimental family drama.

Now there are any number of highly capable Indian Scientists working in the U.S. in NASA, BELL Labs., Silicon Valley, U.S. Defence Labs etc. It is not inconceiveable therefore that they played a considerable role in this mini-Star War programme.

There is no reason whatsoever, therefore why India cannot be at the forefront in these three areas: Electronics, Communications and Media - and these are what the 21st Century is all about.

But as things stand, we are about the worst in all these three. At the macro planning level, all these three have been totally ignored for atleast four decades with the result that all the thrust has been on classical Mechanical Engineering paradigm of Mahalnobis and practically none whatsoever, on the technologies which in fact, constitute the core of the 21st century scenario.

The average journalist about town who has as much obsession to write copy as he had innate incapacity to master theory, has seen phantoms and nightmares in the current Indian situation, and editorial pages are witness to not so exalted perorations of doom—financial & otherwise.

The real position in India is totally different once we understand the basic conceptual frame, which then puts into place all these apparently unrelated phenomenon.

And the conceptual frame is in fact, the frame of this book itself. The various socio-institutional collapses which we are witnessing with domino-effect in India are because of the basic techno-economic model: the Nehru-Mahalnobis model which sustains them no longer; in fact, it is archaic, anachronistic and totally irrelevant to the ground realities of the ninetees. And is this not apparent from a purely commonsense point of view? Nehru's model was with reference to the India of the fifties. Is the India of the fifties same as the India of the nineties? And yet we carry on rigidly sticking to the assumptions of the fifties. We therefore, urgently need a new techno-economic model, which *adapts* itself to the realities of the 1990's going on to 2001. *It is by this pathway of thought that we arrive at the need for an Information-intensity model for India.*

The significance of the Information parameter is certainly not any direct causal acceleration of economic development. Some technocrats put forward such data to espouse the Information cause. C-DOT for example, ridiculously purports to display revolutionary change in a village with a telephone being installed. Neither is this possible nor measureable in say a six months period.

Information as an independent variable is the beacon light in assessing the nation's macro-economic thinking. Let us take the beaming face of Mr. Mohan Dharia displayed in newspapers recently and examine the statements he has made. The not so revolutionary of these: "Eighth Plan document will be ready, aiming atleast six percent growth rate with public sector outlay of Rs. 335,000 crores and no extra tax burden. National Development Council meeting will be called as soon as the new government is formed."

Does this scenario reflect the reality? Word for word - it is totally irrelevant to the realities of India in the nineties:

(a) Six percent growth per se is not going to solve the highly skewed nature of the present Plan frame: 200 million highly upwardly mobile; the rest eating leaves.

(b) Public sector outlay is an extension and affirmation of the Nehru-Mahalnobis "Commanding heights of the Public Sector." Is this the need of the country now or on the contrary: privatisation of whatever remains of a totally insolvent & redundant public sector?

(c) No taxes - did you say Mr. Dharia? What of the annual deficit of Rs. 12,000 crores - is this not the worst tax of all - reducing the value of the rupee, increasing prices - causing runaway inflation?

(d) NDC again - is emphasis on the political aspect only - consensus among Chief Ministers.

Nehru did effectively build in the political linkages in the Planning process: the Deputy Chairman is of Cabinet rank; State Plans are finalized with Chief Ministers; the NDC aims to carry consensus of all Chief Ministers.

But surely the political and even the resource aspects of the plan are the very best part of the planning exercise of prime importance in the Plan Frame and indeed the macro- aggregate model itself, which Mahalnobis created with such loving care, courage and originality.

What we are witnessing today is the total politicisation of the Planning process. Adnauseium talk of resource mobilization, political requirements of States, etc. The professional aspects of the Planning process which have to do with innovation in model building so it reflects an entirely altered reality are nowhere in sight.

The essential thesis of this book is that if this country is to overcome and survive total catasstrophe, then the only one sure signal the Information parameter is providing us is that *the Plan Frame must now be changed 180 degrees. The entire concept of the Macro-aggregate model must change. In fact, the whole nature of the Planning process and indeed the role of the Planning Commission must change drastically. Yojana Bhavan however, slumbers sound asleep - a monument to unreality, disbelief, anachronism and irrelevance:-*

In this connection a point needs to be made regarding Soviet Russia. I stated in the beginning that this Epilogue had been necessitated by the fact that so many traumatic and catastrophic events have ocurred since I submitted my manuscript for printing.

The most catastrophic perhaps has been the virtual collapse and dismantling of what has been known as the U.S.S.R. The collapse is both political and economic. It is extremely pertinent to our present discussion because Jawahar Lal in his infatuation for Socialism, to a considerable extent based our Development strategy on the Russian model.

As is evident from what has been quoted verbatim from no less a personage than Mr. Dharia, our Yojana Bhavan Planners are in deep slumber totally oblivious of the fact that the world has completely changed since the 1950s of Jawaharlal. It has changed to the extent that what were Developmental strengths then, are our abject infirmities now. Witness of which is the fact that the Indian economy is in complete shambles and the political system complete in breakdown unable to cope with the altered environment.

There is not a trace of introspection, deep anxiety, heart searching in either the Planners or the political leaders or the bureaucracy for a new innovative way out despite the total collapse of the earlier model. We need close to a billion dollars (U.S.) per year to service our debts. Our exchange reserves are practically zero. A large number of Indian public sector companies are now facing acute liquidity crunches in meeting their payments in foreign exchange. Suddenly there is reduced profitability of India's nationalised banking system due to systematic criminal tampering with public funds for so-called development schemes. India's credit rating in the world is down to triple B minus, the lowest invertible level on the Standard and Poor chart.

Despite all this Mr. Dharia is able to give a disarming Colgate smile and with an air of marshalled confidence assure that God is in heaven and all is well in our great land. What sends shivers down the spine is not so much the state of the Union as the utter lack of awareness regarding the desparate nature of the fierce crisis which engulfs us.

These crises have all of a sudden precipitated since I completed the manuscript and quite independently vindicate the book's thesis that we are at the desperate end of the Nehruian forty year cycle and now need a complete paradigm shift in our Plan Frame and Macro-economic model. The main argument presented in the book is that this shift has to be towards an Information-intensity paradigm, which will enable large-scale decentralised manufacturing in batch production mode, dramatically increase employment, drastically cut down on long haulage transport, reduce energy consumption because of high electronic-communication management, curb urbanization and enrich local habitats and their ecology. Scenario building on these lines and the related Macro- economic modelling is what Messers Dharia and Company ought to be working on. Instead they are eager to call the next meeting of the NDC - a political gamborce - to flog dead ideas - leading to an assured path of death.

As readers will see the argument that has been repeated again and again in this book is that what our very strengths in the fifties - the upward swing of the Nehruvian model are now our weaknesses in the nineties - the downward swing of this model.

It is accepted world wide that India's development history of the past 40 years has been one of the most ideal development. For exampple:

    (a) The maximum foreign aid in the Plan budget never exceeded 7%.

(b)   The rest was all raised by internal resource mobilization.

(c)   Inflation throughout was very well controlled and certainly was never double-digit.

(d)   The Balance of Payment position was always under control; traditional exports and small scale industrial production chipped in to keep the country internationally solvent.

(e)   Finally, whatever, external loans we took, India had an envious reputation of being prompt in payment and never defaulting.

In a word, the reputation about India's planned Development effort was that here was one country, which for example, spectacularly unlike the Latin American countries did not show a pathetic state of deep "Debt trap"; on the contrary India had the very enviable record of total self-reliance.

What is the position now - simply unbelieveable - it is 180 degrees opposite showing India in abject misery, debt, impoverishment, and what is infinitely worse: economically lacking in will and direction, politically rudderless. The depth of the crisis is obvious from the following excerpts from Oxford Analytics, dated March 15, 1991. It is important to note in these excerpts that the very parameters which constituted our strength upto the seventies, now 20 years later in the nineties have shown a state of total collapse, disintegration and crisis:

"India" the report says, "is facing a Latin American style crisis." The postponement of a full budget for the fiscal year will greatly increase the difficulty in resolving the current macroeconomic crisis, which contains the following features :

(a)   The consolidated government budget deficit i.e. Union and State governments combined, is now running at more than 10 percent of GDP, twice as high as in the 70's.

(b)   The balance of payments current account which was surplus in the late 70's, changed to a deficit in 1981 after the oil price increases of 1979-81, and has worsened since.

(c)   The public internal debt is up from 40 percent of GDP in 1980 to 60 percent of GDP in 1990.

(d)   External debt is up from 125 percent of exports in 1980 to more than 250 percent of the exports in 1990.

(e) Inflation, moderate at 7 percent till recently, is now at 12 percent and might touch 20 percent.

The whole question however, is not so much the extent of the malaise, but as to whether and how far it is *reversible*. International agencies appear to think that reversibility is going to be very difficult, because of the erosion of political and bureaucratic austerity and the growth of populist politics.

This view is a lot of nonsense in terms of the thesis developed in this book. Because basically both the economy and polity are incredibly strong.

The first point has been very well elaborated recently by noted industrialist, Mr. Hari Shankar Singhania. He is on record recently as stating: "Despite political, social, temporary foreign exchange problems, *India's economy is basically sound*." He goes on to elucidate "Don't get a feeling that India is in a bankrupt situation. India is basically strong and will grow." Mr Singhania illustrated his point by stating: "India's middle class consists of about 200 million people. It has purchasing power and is larger than the population of most countries of the world." (In fact, larger than the population of the whole of Europe).

Expanding on India's inherent strengths, Mr. Singhania stated: "India has *tremendous resources*, next only to the U.S. *It has vast resources in manpower and materials.*"

Even India's polity is infinitely strong. What we are witnessing is the breakup of the 100 year old Congress party. Naturally and inevitably there has to be a period of political transition in which a new level of political stability will be achieved. In the interim the Indian political system; is showing amazing maturity, resilience and flexibility to cope with the pressures created by the sudden changes in power equilibrium. The uncertain situation has thrown up a person like Mr. Chandra Shekhar as Prime Minister, who across the political board, has been acknowledged for his statesmanlike qualities of head and heart.

No, neither India's politics is to blame, nor its economics. It is argued in this book that the malaise is merely a symtom of the fact that after the elapse of 40 years the techno-economic model needs a 180 degrees change - simply because India of the nineties is 180 degree different from India of the fifties. And in turn the socio-institutional framework is collapsing all round because of serious mis-match between techno-economic needs of the hour and the archaic and anachronistic social mechanisms purported to sustain it.

At this point, it is all right for persons like Dr. Raja Chelliah, former Member of the Planning Commission, to espouse Privatisation by recently stating: "the only solution is to divest the Central government of its vast economic powers through divestiture, partial privatisation, and 'marketisation' of the public sector." But correct as this view point is, it is not the core or the holistic solution of the problem; *it is only a small and peripheral part of it.*

It is argued in this book that *it is not merely privatisation, but in fact a full-scale restructuring of the entire Developmental model which is now urgently required.* And this restructuring has been defined in this book as a paradigm shift from the First industrial mode to the Second, from Energy-intensity growth model to Information-intensity allowing for decentralised manufacturing in batch production mode and finally integrating the whole economic system in an emerging recentralisation or rein-dustrialisation.

No thinking on these lies is forthcoming from our thinkers for the simple reason that our Economists are unaccustomed to think in terms of the centrality of Information. Information experts - mediamen and communication people - are totally innocent of the industrial, manufacturing and economic ramifications of Information. The third category: bureaucrats, politicians and policy makers do not see how any of this applies to a country like India, because in their *medieval incarnations* all they can conceive of is administration and polliticking.

The book forces an unceremonious intellectual challenge to all these primitive, antiquated, antedelluvian drags to thinking, by putting forth the idea that in the Developing world, India is absolutely unique, and just as forty years ago the Nehru-Mahalnobis model catapulted her into a mighty orbit of infrastructural, manpower and industrial development, a new incarnation of this model can now inject an innovation, which will catapult her to a new mode of Development based on the characteristics of the emerging Information paradigm.

The configuration of this paradigm has been presented in the earlier pages. But here pointed attention is drawn to some special characteristics of the Information paradigm which would encounter critical threats which have shown up as result of the crises enumerated above: the Gulf War, Mandal-Mandir issues, the critical external and internal debt positions, the galloping inflation.

The first characteristic Information-centred paradigm could provide to the economy is that, even more than "control" or "decentralisation" it could fecilitate high flexibility - which is the global need of the hour with rapidly changing technologies, processes and smaller turn-around time in innovations. The present static, out-dated mass-production, archaic systems just cannot compete in the world of emerging speciallizations, seg-mentations and constantly shifting market demands.

The second characteristic is that at present our industrial ef-fort, at best is "reactive", i.e. we react to certain perceived demands-but we are highly non-competitive globally, because by the time the production processes are installed, these are al-ready outdated. We have to shift therefore, from "reactive" to *"PROACTIVE"* approaches, and this is a supreme capability of Information inputs. By proactive we mean: more initiative, leadership role, origination of ideas, anticipating the environment and markets, simulating alternative scenarios, in a word: *setting world trends rather than following them.* At present we are setting no world trends except those of deprivation, negativity and confusion characterised by population growth, poverty and disarray.

Information-centring can lead to "just in time" philosophy, which the Japanese especially have mastered; with just about zero idling.

In our case, our Planners are all the time talking of problem of resource mobilization, but the biggest snag in the resources position is that practically the whole country is *"idling"* all the time-what is the use of mobilising resources when we are squandering them all the time in an utterly non-productive mode?

These are the highly critical issues. For the rest the book elaborates on

(a) Shifting the Development paradigm from Energy-in-tensity to Information-intensity

(b) Through Information systems, decentralisation of manufactureing in batch production mode

(c) New forms of industrial organizations which are non-heirarchical

(d) Economics of scope rather than of scale

(e) Shift from mass production to flexible specialization

(f) Optimal use of local materials

(g) Far less "transportation" - as the Information corridor would substitute many demands

(h) Far less "energy" use

(i) Massive increase in employment due to decentralised, local manufacturing resulting from Information centrality

(j) Drastic reduction of urbanization

(k) Ecology preservation

(l) Shift to "Commanding heights of the Private Sector"

(m) Privatization of the Planning process, inasmuch as a large number of independent, autonomous "think-tanks" be encouraged.

(n) Finally, integrating all the above through "Recentralization" and "Reindustrialization."

Quite stupidly some people have attributed ideological overtones to the Nehruvian-Mahalnobis model. There is in fact nothing ideological about it. Nehru was responding to the need of the hour, forty years back, when there was zero industrialization and zero agriculture. With a herculian mixture of will and vision the Nehruvian-Mahalnobis model took the aid of Mechanical engineering, energy-intensity, rapid "transport corridord," massive investments from government in Keynesian fashion, "Commanding heights of public sector," heavy industry publicly owned and finally heavy reliance on Mass Communication to propagate the implicit scenario.

Forty years later, in the nineties, each one of these parameters spells doom and disaster. Not only have we to rethink the Nehruvian model, we have to abandon it with the urgency of one who abandoms a sinking ship. And it is the emerging Information paradigm, which holds the key to this proposed change. It is argued in the book that this proposed Information paradigm is "Beyond Mass Communication" because now we have to go beyond mass rhetoric, mass propaganda, mass media, mass appeal, mass hysteria to new forms of manufacturing, organization, planning demography, reindustrialization - the key to these being the emerging Information technologies and their socioeconomic usage.

At this juncture I have thought it necessary to write the Epilogue because these traumatic events have merely borne testimony to the main thesis of this book, namely that the root of our national crisis is the highly skewed nature of our economic development. The Mandal and Mandir issues have very little to do with what these purport to be: namely great political expressions; on the contrary they are basically the traumatic expression of the economics of deprivation. The economic development these past forty years in India has been phenomenal—but it has been highly skewed-leading to polarisation. In these past forty years the Mahalnobis model has led to about 200 million persons in India become highly upwardly mobile and lower ranks going down even lower. Mandal and Mandir issues therefore, are not the disease, but merely the symptoms of the disease. The disease is the economic malaise due to skewed development.

Typically therefore, poverty haunts ever larger numbers in rural India, even as the upward mobile take more and more to crass consumerism and ostentatious lifestyles. Every Sociologist in the country, sees the ever growing violence as the result of unequal development.

The economy is in serious trouble not because the economy is weak; in fact thanks to the solid foundations of infrastructure, technical human resource, science and technology and a burgeoning private sector laid by the Nehru Mahalnobis model — the Indian economy is exceedingly strong; but the skewed development has created unmanageable economic disparities and therefore, unmanageable social and political tensions through the length and breadth of the country. No the country is not breaking up; the political economy is merely sending signals that the development model needs drastic change urgently—which in fact, is *the burden of this book*; and it is argued forcefully and consistently throughout the book that the model needs to be altered from *energy intensity to information- intensity*.

How else do you reach the poor of the poor the soonest possible? One of the great characteristics of Communications is that it compresses both time and space. Of course, we know how computers compress time. But to give another example from the Indian experience; just a few years ago we had practically no TV at all. If we had tried to wire up the country terrestrially it would have taken TV 100 years to reach the length and breadth of the country; in fact, we celebrated only recently the centenary of Radio Broadcasting. But thanks to the vision of scientists like Dr. Homi Bhabha and Dr. Vikram Sarabhai, since we had a national domestic satellite, we could, through about 200 Low Power transmitters cover almost the whole country by TV in just one year. Just imagine: 100 years being reduced to one year.

The same can be done with Backward Castes and Other Backward Classes and the disingeneous attempts of a perverse Mandal digging up another 3500 castes. If the political will is there, modern Communication interactive technologies could be the basis of decentralised industrialised production in batch production mode, changing the face of rural India almost instantaneously and thereby putting Mr. V.P. Singh and his gang of two out of the business.

This is what the thesis of this book is: the urgent need to build an infrastructure of a national Information corridor which through digital interactive technologies (Beyond Mass Communication) would decentralise the entire mode of industrial production and almost overnight change the skewed nature of our present economic development.

We must realise however, that the desired Information Society for India is not going to fall from the heavens. We are going to have to work desperately hard for it; and against expected opposition; and in fact, a tremendous amount of spade work in terms of conceptualisation, planning, modelling and policy enunciation has to be put in before we even begin to take steps in the direction of implementation.

In this context it is both sobering and educative to recall the obstacles Jawaharlal Nehru had to face when he decided to launch India on the course of planned development more than forty years ago. When Mahalnobis presented his model with emphasis on the public sector and heavy industry and large investments from Government in the Kenysian tradition there was tremendous opposition from the World Bank. It must be said to Nehru's credit however, that he did not pay any attention to this opposition, and went right ahead with the Mahalnobis model. It is because of this model that India has an indomitable infrastructure and heavy industry and scientific and technical manpower which has made it strong and invincible to all the ups and downs of political economy — not to speak of the world position it enjoys as a major scientific industrial and military power.

The public sector is widely criticised. We are told again and again that an investment of Rs. 80,000 crores is getting a return of only 1%. Be that as it may there are two facts in this regard which cannot be ignored and which again bring glory to Nehru's wisdom:

(a) The first is that long-gestation industries demanding large investments and no return for many years like Steel, Heavy Engineering etc. could not have taken off except in the mode Mahalnobis thought of.

(b) Secondly and even more importantly our Private sector (the second component of the mixed economy) really could not have blossomed as it has done unless it had a Public sector which provided the cushion for it. India then did not have the upward mobile 150 million middle-class which is the most unique phenomenon in terms of a captive market. Now the Private sector in India has come into its own, but we cannot forget the nurturing the Public sector did for so many years, apart from providing the infrastructure.

Nor did we have smooth sailing in other areas of development. The genius of Homi Bhabha encouraged by unflinching support from Nehru visualised the harnessing of Atomic Energy for the acute power shortage which Bhabha anticipated 40 years ago. But the West, particular U.S.A., put one obstacle after another. Like some other countries we did not attempt to build our Atomic capability surreptitiously, relying on espionage and smuggling. Bhabha went about it in an extraordinarily creative way by first establishing the theoretical disciplines: Mathematics and Nuclear Physics at the Tata Institute of Fundamental Research, where he gathered a galaxy of Indian scientists. The next step was the setting up of the Bhabha Atomic Research Centre across the bay at Bombay—one of the largest R&D centre in the world. Space technology had the same background under the able and creative leadership of the late Dr. Vikram Sarabhai.

First the Space-sciences-Cosmic Ray studies, Ionospheric studies, Radio Astronomy were established at the Physical Research Laboratory, Ahmedabad.

Even in the field of Agriculture the performance of the West apropos Indian effort must be regarded as pathetic. The British left behind the legend that India has a permanent history of famines, which is unalterable. But to cut a long story short we have proved that not only is it alterable, India now has the second largest manpower of highly trained Agricultural Scientists in the world (the first being U.S.S.R. and not U.S.A.) and India is well on the way to becoming totally self-sufficient in food and even a world exporter.

It is with this background that we have to now to devote ourselves to the Communication sector.

As in the case of Atomic Energy, Space and Agriculture etc. we must totally ignore the West, not care for their advice, not be prejudiced by their prejudices and not be deterred by fears real or imaginary they place before us. We should use our own genius and usher in the Information Revolution in our own unique way using our genius.

In that sense this book marks a sharp break with the era of about 30 years which was set in motion with the printing of Schramm's not so monumental book: "Mass Media & National Development." We no longer need Western professors to patronisingly tell us about the nature of Information, its role in Development, its effect on social change, its distribution in the world, and the efficacy of mass media campaigns.

That era of platitudnous gibberish, unresearched hunches, foggy ideas and a concept of development and modernisation equated with Westernisation is over—or at least for India it *has* to be over. Schramm, Lerner and others have played the same role in Mass Media and Development which Longmans and MacMillan played in publishing in the erstwhile empire: namely, one of overt, doctrinnaire imperialistic subjugation.

India in any case is no homeland of illiterate jungle tribes. India's has always been a civilizing role of world teacher in many many fields and in the Information sector Indians are particularly endowed. They are key leaders in many R&D establishments in the U.S.A., they are the Information Technology millionaires in Silicon Valley, California, they inundate Bell Labs and NASA and hold Professorial chairs all over the world. In computer software again Indians are sought after all over the world, Indian's scientific and technological capability in this field is stupendous but we have not capitalised on it.

It is for this reason that I have sounded the clarion call that India must immediately push forward to a state "Beyond Mass Communication." This slogan has implications for *technology, sociology, economics* and *policy*. In this sense this book hopes to mark for India not only the end of an era of Information ideas relying slavishly on the West, but the beginning of a new era in which Indians will develop creative and original ideas in Information which will contribute to world knowledge.

In this sense, definitions of the characteristics mentioned above assume significance. By the new technologies we mean those based on "microelectronics" particularly the marriage of computers and telecommunication in *digital* mode. By Sociology we mean that unlike Mass Communications, these new technologies have the characteristics of interactivity, demassification and asynchonicity. By Economics we mean the whole area of *Information Economics* which is totally untouched in India. And the analysis of these three parameters should contribute to Policy studies, especially in think-tanks outside the domain of Government so that fresh ideas may constantly be forthcoming, especially from outside the straight-jaket of bureaucracy.

There is therefore, only one overpowering thought to which this book is dedicated : how can India leapfrog the industrial revolution of Europe which we have so far copied, and instead catapult the country to an Information Society so as to correct the past skewed development, accelerate the path to new development effort, open up the private enterprise even more and make India one of the foremost nations in the world. As we have stated this is with the primary aim of urgently setting right the skewed economic development of the past 40 years, and thereby immediately bringing the most backward in India to the forefront. We earnestly believe that this is doable by immediately shifting the overall development model from energy-intensity to information intensity. We believe that microelectronics and the microchip are the key to future developmental success—just as mechanical engineering and oil—have contributed to our past success.

We further believe that this kind of change could lead to decentralised industrial growth in batch-production mode, to arrest of migration from rural to urban areas, to integrity not only of the political economy but also of ecology and lastly that this would ushere in a truly Gandhian economy albiet in a high technology mode.

Lastly, we believe that India is uniquely endowed with the wherewithal of thinkers, scientists, technologists, and administrators who can make all this realizeable.

This is the burden of this book. And therefore, it urges that we shift the application of energies from Mass Communication to the whole area which in the Information Technology spectrum is presently totally a void: the area "Beyond Mass Communication."

INDEX